THE
SEMANTICS/
PRAGMATICS
DISTINCTION

THE
SEMANTICS/
PRAGMATICS
DISTINCTION

edited by
CLAUDIA BIANCHI

CSLI
PUBLICATIONS
Center for the Study of
Language and Information
Stanford, California

Copyright © 2004
CSLI Publications
Center for the Study of Language and Information
Leland Stanford Junior University
Printed in the United States
08 07 06 05 04   1 2 3 4 5

Library of Congress Cataloging-in-Publication Data

The semantics/pragmatics distinction / edited by Claudia Bianchi.

p. cm. – (CSLI lecture notes ; no. 155)

Includes bibliographical references and index.

ISBN 1-57586-457-6 (alk. paper)
ISBN 1-57586-458-4 (pbk. : alk. paper)

1. Pragmatics. 2. Semantics. I. Bianchi, Claudia. II. Series.

P99.4.P72 S45   2003
306.44–dc22   2003020031
CIP

∞ The acid-free paper used in this book meets the minimum requirements
of the American National Standard for Information Sciences—Permanence
of Paper for Printed Library Materials, ANSI Z39.48-1984.

CSLI was founded in 1983 by researchers from Stanford University, SRI
International, and Xerox PARC to further the research and development of
integrated theories of language, information, and computation. CSLI headquarters
and CSLI Publications are located on the campus of Stanford University.

CSLI Publications reports new developments in the study of language,
information, and computation. Please visit our web site at
http://cslipublications.stanford.edu/
for comments on this and other titles, as well as for changes
and corrections by the author and publisher.

To Martine

Contents

Contributors

KENT BACH: Department of Philosophy, San Francisco State University, San Francisco, CA 94132, U.S.A.
kbach@sfsu.edu

ANNE BEZUIDENHOUT: Department of Philosophy, University of South Carolina, Columbia, SC 29208, U.S.A.
anne1@sc.edu

CLAUDIA BIANCHI: University Vita-Salute S. Raffaele, Milan & Department of Philosophy, University of Genoa, via Balbi 4, 16126 Genova, Italy.
claudia@nous.unige.it

ROBYN CARSTON: Department of Phonetics and Linguistics, University College London, London WC1E 6BT, UK.
robyn@ling.ucl.ac.uk

MANUEL GARCÍA-CARPINTERO: Department of Logic, History and Philosophy of Science, University of Barcelona, Baldiri Reixach, s/n, 08028 Barcelona, Spain.
m.garciacarpintero@ub.edu

STEFANO PREDELLI: Department of Philosophy, University of Nottingham, Nottingham NG7 2RD, UK.
stefano.predelli@nottingham.ac.uk

FRANÇOIS RECANATI: Institut Jean-Nicod (CNRS), 1bis, avenue de Lowendal, 75007 Paris, France.
recanati@ehess.fr

KENNETH A. TAYLOR: Department of Philosophy, Stanford University, Stanford, CA 94305, U.S.A..
taylor@csli.stanford.edu

Preface

The present volume brings together leading-edge work on the semantics/pragmatics debate, presenting research on a number of phenomena, including indexicals, proper names, conventional and conversational implicatures, force-markers, procedural meaning, and semantic underdetermination. The introductory chapter provides information on the historical and conceptual background for these papers and points out some of the links between them.

This book issues from the exchanges following the second workshop on contexts (WOC 2002) 'Semantics vs. Pragmatics', held in Genoa, Italy, in October 2002. The workshop brought together researchers from linguistics, philosophy of language, and psychology. Eight papers were presented at the workshop, along with commentaries prepared by eight discussants – sometimes leading to extensive debate both during and after the conference, and to intense mail exchanges between authors and commentators.

The workshop would not have been possible without the sponsorship of the University of Genoa, the Humanities Faculty, and the Philosophy Department. My thanks to all these organizations.

I would also like to thank the participants of the Genoa workshop, and especially the contributors (plus Steven Neale, whose paper is not included in the present volume) and commentators for their valuable work: Jonathan Berg, Emma Borg, Paolo Bouquet, Gennaro Chierchia, Eros Corazza, Diego Marconi, Carlo Penco, and Sandro Zucchi.

Many thanks also go to Claudia Caffi and Carlo Penco who co-organized the workshop with me, as well as to Massimiliano Vignolo and several Ph.D. and undergraduate students who helped the organizers during the conference.

I am especially grateful to Marcello Frixione, Carlo Penco and Nicla Vassallo, who encouraged me to publish the volume and supported me during all the phases of the editing process. Thanks also to Dikran Kara-gueuzian and Chris Sosa of CSLI Publications for their help and patience.

Claudia Bianchi

1

Semantics and Pragmatics: The Distinction Reloaded

CLAUDIA BIANCHI

Pragmatics is a young discipline with an ancient and eminent tradition – extending from Protagoras and Aristotle to present day research in cognitive science.[1] In addition, pragmatics is a discipline not easy to define[2] – for its often uncomfortable position on the boundaries of the philosophy of language, linguistics, sociology, psychology, rhetoric, and ethno-methodology. The Cinderella of syntax and semantics, long on the fringes of linguistics, pragmatics is nowadays enjoying an astonishing renaissance and intense development.

1 The Traditional View

Traditionally, semantics is the field of the study of language dealing with the conventional (or literal) meanings of words and sentences and the relations between those meanings, and between linguistic expressions and their denotations. Pragmatics, however, studies how speakers use context and shared information to convey information that is supplementary to the semantic content of what they say, and how hearers make inferences on the basis of this information.

---

[1] Prior to the twentieth century, we have only what has been called 'pragmatics without the name' or 'proto-pragmatics': for an 'archaeology' of pragmatics – limited to the nineteenth century – see the introductory chapter of Recanati 1981, Nerlich and Clarke 1994 and 1996.

[2] Cf. the fourteen definitions of pragmatics in Levinson 1983.

The Semantics/Pragmatics Distinction.
Claudia Bianchi (ed.).
Copyright © 2004, CSLI Publications.

In fact, the domain of pragmatics has long been defined in mostly negative terms: pragmatics was intended to deal with the facts for which an explication in syntactic or semantic terms (namely in terms of combinatory rules or linguistic conventions) was insufficient or defective. Hence, the distinction between syntax, semantics and pragmatics has been hiding an idea of pragmatics as the 'wastebasket' of semantics[3] – as a field of research dedicated to collecting semantic facts without explication, as well as puzzles, minor phenomena, and marginal problems. As a consequence, the linguistic facts contained in the field of pragmatics are extremely heterogeneous. Indeed, pragmatics has too often restricted itself to a mere description of fragmentary issues without proposing an unitary theoretical project. In a narrow interpretation, pragmatics has been identified with nothing more than the study of indexical expressions (pronouns, adverbs of time or space, etc.), i.e. expressions that depend for their semantic value on the context of utterance:[4] it resembles, in other words, a discipline that we would do better to call indexical semantics[5] or semantic pragmatics.[6] A more comprehensive interpretation of pragmatics includes not only indexicals, but also the study of ambiguity and ellipsis, on one hand, and of speech acts, conversational implicatures, loose talk, metaphor, figurative language and implicit meaning, on the other.

Hence, in the traditional philosophy of language, semantics and pragmatics are considered complementary research fields: semantics studies the conventional meaning of linguistic expressions, while pragmatics deals with how speakers use expressions in context. In other words, pragmatic processes play a role at the *semantic* level only in cases of indexicality – in helping to determine 'what is said' by an utterance. Otherwise, they are involved at the *pre-semantic* level, for picking up the appropriate syntactic construct in cases of ambiguity and ellipsis – in helping to determine 'what is uttered'; and finally at the *post-semantic* level, for the derivation of conversational implicatures – in helping to determine 'what is communicated' by a speaker making an utterance.[7]

2 Two Perspectives on Language

In the last thirty years, linguists and philosophers have started to rethink the distinction between semantics and pragmatics as it was traditionally conceived, and to reflect upon the nature of the facts and the fundamental theo-

---

[3]Bar-Hillel 1971: 401.
[4]The best-known example is Montague 1974.
[5]Cf. Bach 1999.
[6]See Cresswell 1973; cf. Lycan 2000.
[7]For the distinction between pre-semantic, semantic and post-semantic levels, see Perry 1998.

retical notions that a semantic theory is supposed to account for. It has become clear that many controversies in the philosophy of language arise from different ways of conceiving the semantics/pragmatics interface. As a consequence, many conflicting formulations of this interface have been proposed in recent years, and today any theory that purports to explain language and communication must draw a sharp line between semantics and pragmatics.

It is interesting to note that, when drawing this line, the two allegedly complementary fields of semantics and pragmatics have often found themselves in theoretical conflict. According to the traditional (semantic) view, if we abstract from ellipsis, ambiguity and indexicality strictly understood (i.e. concerning only a small number of expressions such as true indexicals and demonstratives), it is possible to attribute truth conditions to a sentence independently of its context, i.e. in virtue of its meaning alone. Hence, we must distinguish between the proposition literally expressed by an utterance ('what is said' by the utterance, its literal truth conditions) and the implicit meaning of the utterance ('what is communicated' by a speaker using the utterance): the former level is the object of semantics, the latter of pragmatics. When facing this same issue, scholars of pragmatics underline the phenomenon of *semantic underdeterminacy*: the encoded meaning of the linguistic expressions employed by a speaker underdetermines the proposition explicitly expressed by the utterance.

The divergence between these two perspectives stems directly from an opposition present at the very beginning of the contemporary philosophy of language – between philosophers interested mainly in formal languages, on one hand, and those interested mainly in natural languages, on the other. As it is well known, philosophers and logicians like Gottlob Frege, Bertrand Russell, the former Ludwig Wittgenstein, Alfred Tarski and Willard Quine wanted to built a perfect language for philosophical and scientific communication, an artificial language devoid of all the ambiguities and imperfections that characterize natural languages, while ordinary language philosophers (the later Wittgenstein, Friedrich Waismann, John Austin, Paul Grice, Peter Strawson) viewed natural languages (like English, French or Italian) as autonomous objects of analysis – and their imperfections as signs of richness and expressive power. Frege and Russell have inspired the traditional view in its thinking that truth conditions may be ascribed to a sentence (of an idealized language), independently of any contextual considerations; the ordinary language philosophers have founded the opposing pragmatic view that a sentence has complete truth conditions only in context.

Today, more and more theorists (including several contributors to this volume) put themselves on the pragmatic side. According to them, most sentences of a natural language do not express complete propositions, hence do not have fixed truth-conditions – even when unambiguous and devoid of indexicals. Every utterance expresses a proposition only when completed and enriched with pragmatic constituents that do not correspond to any syntactic element of the sentence (neither an explicit constituent, as in cases of syntactic ellipsis, nor a hidden indexical present at the level of the logical form of the sentence) and yet are part of the semantic interpretation of the utterance.

The cases motivating the underdeterminacy thesis are well known – although pragmatic scholars themselves do not agree on all the examples listed below:

(1) All the bottles [I just bought] are empty;

(2) Nobody [famous] goes there any more because it's too crowded;

(3) I have nothing [appropriate to the occasion] to wear tonight;

(4) Some [not all] children got stomach 'flu;

(5) Jill got married and [then] became pregnant;

(6) Mary has [exactly] three cars;

(7) Jack and Jill are engaged [to each other];

(8) John hasn't had breakfast [today];

(9) You're not going to die [from this cut];

(10) The conference starts at five [or some minutes later];

(11) France is hexagonal [roughly speaking];

(12) I need a Kleenex [or any paper handkerchief].

According to the pragmatic view, the *semantic* interpretation of utterances of (1) - (12) – in other words the propositions they express, their truth conditions – is the result of pragmatic processes of expansion and contextual enrichment (giving, as a result, the additional linguistic material in brackets). Those pragmatic processes are widespread in natural language, and generally unconscious; moreover the interpretation they generate is unproblematic. Nobody takes the speaker as if he were saying, with (8), that John has never had breakfast in his life; or the mother as if, uttering (9), she were saying to her child that he is immortal: the propositions expressed by (8) and (9) are enriched quite naturally and without any effort.

3 Drawing Distinctions

So far the consensus among those who favor the pragmatic perspective is more or less established. Far less agreement surrounds the analysis of the status of the pragmatically imbued level of truth-conditional content. We can distinguish at least five different accounts of this level, going from the indexicalist view held by Jason Stanley and Zoltan Szabò to radical contextualism, defended by François Recanati and, in a different version, by Relevance theorists. The papers included in the present volume not only offer a rich survey of some of the more interesting theories on the market – in their latest version – but also apply them to actual cases, showing how a pragmatic approach can solve some of the problems semantics has been confronting unsuccessfully.

As noted above, the traditional view holds that 'what is said' by an utterance (its truth-conditional content) is closely related to the conventional meaning of the linguistic expressions employed in it and departs from the conventional meaning only in cases of ambiguity or indexicality. Over the past thirty years, however, many philosophers have started to acknowledge the problem represented by examples like (1) - (12) above. What these examples seemed to show is that there is a significant distance between the level of the conventional meaning of a sentence and the proposition expressed by uttering that sentence – a distance not imputable only to ambiguity or indexicality. Pragmatic processes seemed required to bridge the gap between these two levels of meaning.

Semanticists such as Stanley and Szabò resist this interpretation and try to preserve the spirit (if not the letter) of the traditional view: every time that pragmatists postulate an alleged pragmatic contribution to the semantic interpretation of utterances like (1) - (12), they posit hidden indexical elements in the logical form of the sentence.[8] The only process affecting the truth conditions of an utterance is the mandatory semantic process of 'saturation', triggered by the presence of a syntactic element (explicit or hidden) occurring in the syntactic structure of the sentence. Stefano Predelli (Ch. 2 of this volume) offers an interesting alternative defense of the traditional view, pointing out a form of contextuality intervening 'at the post-

---

[8]See, for example, Stanley 2000: 391: 'all truth-conditional effects of extra-linguistic context can be traced to logical form'; cf. Stanley and Szabò 2000.

compositional level', i.e. not at the level of 'what is said' (the level of the truth conditions), but at the level of the evaluation of 'what is said' (the level of the truth values). Arguing in favor of traditional compositional modules, Predelli tries to provide a 'lean mean semantic machine', i.e. a semantic account of sentence-index pairs that avoids the semantic opulence of the indexicalist view and the pragmatic opulence of the pragmatists, who postulate pragmatic processes (such as free enrichment or strengthening) at the semantic level.

Many theorists today, however, opt for various forms of pragmatic opulence, and posit the existence of *pragmatic* processes affecting the truth conditions of almost any utterance – in other words the *semantic* level of 'what is said'. Among the defendants of the pragmatic perspective there is a wide variety of positions. Steven Levinson, for example, thinks that all the pragmatic effects at the semantic level must be construed as a kind of generalized implicature, acting locally and by default: these pragmatic processes are triggered by particular lexical expressions or constructions, as 'some', 'and' or 'if'.[9] Radical contextualists and Relevance theorists, in contrast, maintain a sharp distinction between enrichments and strengthenings at the semantic level, on one hand, and, on the other, conversational implicatures, that do not contribute to the truth-conditional content of the sentence, in accordance with the original Gricean proposal. Relevance theorists such as Robyn Carston (Ch. 5) disagree with Levinson's distinction between generalized and particularized implicatures: all implicatures are triggered as a matter of contextual relevance – neither by default nor by the presence of certain lexical items.[10]

In a similar vein, Recanati (Ch. 4) argues for the existence of pragmatic constituents in the proposition expressed by an utterance, i.e. for constituents that do not correspond to any syntactic nor semantic element of the utterance – called 'unarticulated constituents': 'No proposition could be expressed without some unarticulated constituent being contextually provided'.[11] 'What is said' is then identified with the proposition completed by primary pragmatic processes of enrichment and transfer.[12]

Kent Bach's position (Ch. 3) differs from the one held by radical contextualists and Relevance theorists. Relying on Austin's distinction between locutionary and illocutionary acts, Bach underlines the distinction between 'what is said' – strictly tied to the syntax of the sentence – and 'what is

---

[9] See Levinson 2000.
[10] Cf. Carston 1988, 1993, 1996 and 2002, Sperber and Wilson 1986/1995 and 1991, Wilson and Sperber 1993.
[11] Recanati 1993: 260; cf. Perry 1986, sect. 1 and 1998.
[12] Cf. Recanati 1989, 2001 and 2003.

stated', which includes components not present at the level of the logical form of the sentence. Among these components, we must begin with a 'communicative presumption', i.e. the presumption that the sentence is being used to communicate, which in itself is not part of the meaning of the sentence, but something the hearer presumes from the fact that the speaker is uttering the sentence.[13] The very distinction between 'what is said' and 'what is stated' thus amounts to postulating a fourth level of meaning between the purely semantic notion of 'what is said' and the uncontroversial pragmatic notion of 'what is (implicitly) communicated'.[14]

The last three papers in this volume are good examples of how diverse perspectives on the semantics/pragmatics distinction suggest innovative solutions to old semantic problems. Anne Bezuidenhout (Ch. 6) aims to show that parallels exist between the declarative/procedural divide, the semantics/pragmatics interface and the competence/performance distinction. In other words, a clear-cut distinction must be maintained between procedural knowledge, which belongs to the performance system and is pragmatic, on one hand, and lexical conceptual knowledge, which belongs to the competence system and is semantic, on the other. Manuel García-Carpintero's paper (Ch. 7) deals with another alleged oxymoron – the phrase 'semantics of force-indicators' – but this time with the intention of showing that a semantic account of assertion markers (traditionally analyzed in pragmatic theories of language use) is possible. In this manner, Carpintero argues against the widely accepted idea of semantics (underlying what I have called the traditional view) as a 'quasi-mathematical enterprise', having only to do with truth-conditional contents and their compositional determination and nothing to do with speakers' acts. In the final paper of the volume, Kenneth Taylor (Ch. 8) confronts a traditional battlefield in the contemporary philosophy of language, namely that of proper names, addressing the most classical problems that remain without a consensual solution: empty names, Frege's puzzle about statements of identity, substitutivity in propositional attitude contexts. Taylor's analysis is paradigmatic of the new perspective favored by pragmatists: instead of giving a semantic theory of proper names, he proposes an explanation in syntactic and pragmatic terms. He aims less to demonstrate that semantics is defective or inadequate than to show that pragmatics has a large battery of arguments at hand – and a rich collection of potentially elegant and efficacious solutions.

---

[13]Bach and Harnish 1979: 7.
[14]Cf. Bach 1994, 1999, 2000 and 2001.

4   To Be Continued (Revolutions)

In considering the debated distinction between semantics and pragmatics, we are faced with a continuum of different hypotheses. At one end, from the traditional perspective, the goal of semantics is to assign truth conditions to (unambiguous) sentences of natural language, relying on their conventional meaning and contextually fixing the reference of indexicals and demonstratives. At the other end of the continuum lies radical contextualism (the more radical pragmatic perspective), which claims that semantics can only give incomplete interpretations: in order to obtain a complete proposition (i.e. complete truth-conditions), it is *always* necessary to resort to pragmatic processes. From this perspective, semantics no longer has the task of giving truth-conditions: this task is now proper to pragmatics, or, even better, to 'truth-conditional pragmatics'.[15]

All the papers in this volume take a clear stand on the semantics/pragmatics distinction. This debate has the additional merit of submitting notions and concepts that are too often taken for granted – such as the very idea of semantics or truth conditions, or the controversial notion of 'what is said' – to conceptual analysis.[16] Several fundamental issues are still open, of course. Some clarification on the notion of semantic intuitions, for example, would surely be welcomed, together with more extensive reflection on the role that intuitions have – or must have – for semantic theory. As I said, in the traditional view, every contribution made by the context must be triggered by a constituent of the sentence – either explicit or implicit (tacit, not pronounced), but nevertheless present as a variable in the syntactic structure of the sentence: such a thesis complies with the extremely reasonable principle, that stipulates an isomorphism between syntactic structure and semantic interpretation.[17] By positing tacit or unarticulated constituents (such as those bracketed in examples (1) - (12)), radical contextualism objects to the principle of isomorphism between syntax and semantics – one of the benchmarks of the traditional view. Departure from this principle is usually justified in order to preserve the speakers' semantic intuitions on truth conditions. Radical contextualists, then, prefer to speak of 'intuitive truth conditions': the proposition expressed by a sentence doesn't correspond to the logical form of the sentence, but is the proposition individuated by the truth-conditional intuitions of the participants in the conversational ex-

---

[15]Recanati 1993.

[16]Quite unexpectedly, this debate still very often takes as its starting point (and yields as a consequence) a clarification of Grice's and Austin's theories.

[17]See, for example, Grice 1989: 87 and Fodor and Lepore 1991: 333.

change. If one understands an utterance, he knows which states of affairs make that utterance true, i.e. under which circumstances the utterance would be true. Underlying this idea is the Gricean thesis that 'saying' is a variety of non-natural meaning – and must be accessible to the addressee: non-natural meaning is a matter of intention recognition.[18] Of course, not everybody agrees on the fact that semantics should account for semantic intuitions, rather than semantic facts – nor that semantic intuitions could be relevant in determining what is said by an utterance, instead of, for example, what is communicated by a speaker. Moreover, intuitions on the propositional content of a sentence tend to be sensitive to extralinguistic information and are likely to reflect interpretations that are conveyed by typical, standard, utterances of that sentence – involving what Bach calls 'sentence nonliterality'.[19]

What interests me most, in closing, is to clear the field of a suspicion. For some, the debate concerning the semantic level, the level required for semantic evaluation (traditional truth conditions or intuitive truth conditions, minimal proposition or non-minimal proposition) has seemed purely a matter of definition or terminology. Yet, the controversy between semantic and pragmatic perspectives on this very point is far from being merely technical. The disagreement concerns something far more profound, i.e. what is implicit and what is explicit in what we say, the propositional content that we are responsible for, the *commitment* toward our interlocutors that we express by saying something – by choosing those particular words in those particular circumstances. An essential issue, not only in our philosophical thinking, but also in our everyday life.

References

Bach, K. 1994. Conversational Impliciture. *Mind and Language* 9: 124-62.

Bach, K. 1999. The Semantics-Pragmatics Distinction: What It Is and Why It Matters. *The Semantics-Pragmatics Interface from Different Points of View* (*Current Research in the Semantics/Pragmatics Interface, vol. 1*), ed. K. Turner, 65-84. Oxford: Elsevier.

Bach, K. 2000. Quantification, Qualification and Context. A Reply to Stanley and Szabò. *Mind and Language* 15: 262-83.

Bach, K. 2001. You Don't Say? *Synthèse* 128: 15-44.

Bach, K. 2002. Seemingly Semantic Intuitions. *Meaning and Truth,* eds. J. Keim Campbell, M. O'Rourke and D. Shier, 21-33. New York: Seven Bridges Press.

Bach, K. and R. M. Harnish 1979. *Linguistic Communications and Speech Acts.* Cambridge (MA): MIT Press.

---

[18]See Recanati 1995 and 2001; cf. Gibbs and Moise 1997.

[19]Bach 2002; cf. Bach 2001: 26 and Taylor 2001.

Bar-Hillel, Y. 1971. Out of the Pragmatic Wastebasket. *Linguistic Inquiry* 2: 401-407.

Carston, R. 1988. Implicature, Explicature and Truth-Theoretic Semantics. *Mental Representations. The interface between language and reality*, ed. R. Kempson, 155-81. Cambridge: Cambridge University Press.

Carston, R. 1993. Conjunction, Explanation and Relevance. *Lingua* 90: 27-48.

Carston, R. 1996. Enrichment and Loosening: Complementary Processes in Deriving the Proposition Expressed. *UCL Working Papers in Linguistics* 8: 61-88.

Carston, R. 2002. *Thoughts and Utterances: The Pragmatics of Explicit Communication*. Malden (MA): Blackwell.

Cresswell, M. J. 1973. *Logic and Language*. London: Methuen & Co.

Fodor, J. A. and E. Lepore 1991. *Holism: A Shopper's Guide*. Oxford: Blackwell.

Gibbs, R. and J. Moise 1997. Pragmatics in Understanding What is Said. *Cognition* 62: 51-74.

Grice, H. P. 1989. *Studies in the Way of Words*. Cambridge: Harvard University Press.

Levinson, S. 1983. *Pragmatics*. Cambridge: Cambridge University Press.

Levinson, S. 2000. *Presumptive Meanings: The Theory of Generalized Conversational Implicature*. Cambridge (MA): MIT Press.

Lycan, W. 2000. *Philosophy of Language. A Contemporary Introduction*. London: Routledge.

Montague, R. 1974. *Formal Semantics*. New Haven: Yale University Press.

Nerlich B. and D. Clarke 1994. Language, Action and Context: Linguistic Pragmatics in Europe and America (1800-1950). *Journal of Pragmatics* 22: 439-63.

Nerlich B. and D. Clarke 1996. *Language, Action and Context: The Early History of Pragmatics in Europe and America (1780-1930)*. Amsterdam: Benjamins.

Perry, J. 1986. Thought without Representation. *The Problem of the Essential Indexical and Other Essays*, ed. J. Perry, 205-18. New York: Oxford University Press.

Perry, J. 1998. Indexicals, Contexts and Unarticulated Constituents. *Computing Natural Language*, eds. Aliseda, van Gabeek and Westerstahl, 1-11. Stanford: CSLI Publications.

Recanati, F. 1981. *Les énoncés performatifs. Contribution à la pragmatique*. Paris: Les Editions de Minuit.

Recanati, F. 1989. The Pragmatics of What is Said. *Mind and Language* 4: 207-32.

Recanati, F. 1993. *Direct Reference: From Language to Thought*. Oxford: Blackwell.

Recanati, F. 1995. The Alleged Priority of Literal Interpretation. *Cognitive Science* 19: 207-32.

Recanati, F. 2001. What is Said. *Synthèse* 128: 75-91.

Sperber, D. and D. Wilson 1986/1995. *Relevance. Communication and Cognition.* Oxford: Blackwell.

Sperber, D. and D. Wilson 1991. Loose Talk. *Pragmatics. A Reader*, ed. S. Davis, 540-49. Oxford & New York: Oxford University Press.

Stanley, J. 2000. Context and Logical Form. *Linguistics and Philosophy* 23: 391-434.

Stanley, J. and Z. Szabò 2000. On Quantifier Domain Restriction. *Mind and Language* 15: 219-61.

Taylor, K. 2001. Sex, Breakfast, and Descriptus Interruptus. *Synthèse* 128: 45-61.

Wilson, D. and D. Sperber 1993. Linguistic Form and Relevance. *Lingua* 90: 1-25.

2

The Lean Mean Semantic Machine

STEFANO PREDELLI

1 Introduction

Suppose that on August 12, 2002 I say 'it rains' in rainy Prague. My utterance, hereinafter u, seems intuitively true. Imagine on the other hand that, on the very same day, I utter 'it rains' in sunny Palermo. My utterance, v, appears to be false. The meteorological state of the world on that day, let us call it m, has not changed. The utterances in question, so it seems, have different truth-values, given one and the same meteorological condition: with respect to m, u is true, but v is false. How may such a difference in their semantic profile be reflected within a theoretically adequate, systematic semantic account?[1]

2 Semantics and Intuitions

At the core of 'systematic semantic accounts' of the traditional kind lies what I shall call a *compositional module*. Compositional modules evaluate abstract items of a particular format: in particular, in the well-known compositional modules developed for the analysis of so-called indexical languages, pairs made up of a certain syntactic complex and of a collection of parameters, hereinafter referred to as an *index*. Simplifying considerably,

---

[1]The semantic community's sudden fascination with rain originates in Perry 1986. See also, among many others, Crimmins and Perry 1989, Crimmins 1992 and 1995, Recanati 1993 and 2002, Taylor 2001.

The Semantics/Pragmatics Distinction.
Claudia Bianchi (ed.).
Copyright © 2004, CSLI Publications.

but in a way not immediately relevant for my purpose here, the syntactic complex in question may be conceived of as a *sentence* of English, or at least as a construct mimicking the structure of such sentences in a straightforward manner. As for indexes, an index i may be presented as an n-tuple of co-ordinates, including the parameters eventually required by the meanings of the indexical expressions in the fragment under study — for the aim of this essay, an agent i_A, a time i_T, and a location i_L shall suffice. I refer to the pair consisting of a sentence (or a labeled tree or whatever type of syntactic complex one deems adequate), together with a suitable index, as a *sentence-index* pair.[2]

Given a particular sentence-index pair, the compositional module proceeds on the basis of certain hypotheses regarding the semantic behavior of the simple expressions occurring in the sentence in question. Such expressions are assigned a particular semantic profile, typically understood as a function from indexes to semantic constructs of an appropriate type. These constructs are in turn interpreted as functions taking as input what is sometimes called a *point* of evaluation, and yielding a particular *extension*. Given such results, the compositional module proceeds to the evaluation of the semantic properties of more complex expressions, and eventually maps the sentence-index pair under analysis to a function from points to truth-values, that is, it maps that pair to what is customarily called an *intension*.[3]

The concern of linguists and philosophers who earn their living as natural language semanticists is that of developing adequate compositional modules for certain presumably interesting fragments. Together with questions such as economy or elegance, a central criterion for the adequacy of a compositional module is that it bears a suitable relation to some (presumably semantically relevant) intuitions of competent speakers of the language. I now turn to a brief discussion of such intuitions, before addressing the question of their relationship to the results of the compositional module.

What is of particular interest for my purpose here is the assessment by competent speakers of the truth-values of certain *utterances* on particular situations. An utterance, at least as far as this essay goes, may be understood as the use of a declarative sentence within a particular setting. Among the features of such setting that may turn out to be of semantic relevance, it is

---

[2]What I call indexes are often labeled 'contexts'; though in itself unobjectionable, this terminology may invite the confusion between 'contexts' in the formal sense of the term, denoting the collection of parameters relevant for semantic interpretation, and 'contexts' understood as the situations in which an utterance takes place. The term 'context' shall here be employed only in the latter sense. My use of 'index' should not be confused with that in Lewis 1980, where it is roughly synonymous with what Kaplan 1977 calls 'circumstances', and with what I call 'points of evaluation'.

[3]For an apparatus of this type see for instance Kaplan 1977 or Lewis 1980.

customary to recognize the speaker's identity, the time and location of utterance, certain aspects of the surrounding discourse, the background information taken for granted by the conversants, and the aim and focus of the conversation. Following customary usage, I refer to the collection of information of this type as the *context* in which an utterance takes place.

Speakers competent in their understanding of English, and appropriately informed with respect to how things stand in the relevant portion of reality, tend to react with relatively firm intuitions regarding the *truth-value* of an utterance in a particular context. For instance, given that I am aware of Elvis' death, that I understand your employment of the name 'Elvis' and of the verb 'lives', and that I know when you are speaking, I unequivocally evaluate your utterance of 'Elvis lives' as false. As I mentioned above, it is a fundamental constraint for an adequate compositional module that it be compatible with pre-theoretic inclinations of this type, that is, that its results match in a suitable manner such intuitive verdicts of truth-value. However, the object for such inclinations are particular utterances in given contexts, such as your utterance of 'Elvis lives', that is, items importantly different from the type of entities suitable as input for the compositional module. For this reason, the assessment of the module's empirical adequacy presupposes the independent plausibility of a certain *representation*, whereby the utterance under analysis is represented within a suitable format, in particular, in a manner including an appropriate sentence-index pair. In the process of representation, the occasionally elliptical and ambiguous strings we ordinarily mumble are replaced by the sober syntactic constructs to which the module is attuned, and the multicolored, complex scenarios in which such mumbling takes place are regimented in terms of an austere sequence of parameters. For instance, as far as your utterance goes, a simple-minded syntactic structure such as

$$s: \quad [[[\text{Elvis}]_N]_{NP} \, [[\text{lives}]_V \, [\text{PRES}]_T]_{VP}]_S$$

may well do for the purpose at hand; as for the parameters the appropriate index is supposed to offer to the interpretation of the indexicals, the time of utterance seems appropriate as the only element requested by the lone indexical, $[\text{PRES}]_T$.[4]

Criteria of independent plausibility, such as consistency with an adequate syntactic apparatus, considerations of theoretical elegance, and a great deal of common sense, steer the process of representation to such an extent that the compositional module's conclusions may not always be salvaged by

---

[4] I have discussed the relationships between the parameters of utterance and the appropriate index's co-ordinates in Predelli 1997, 1998, and 2002.

tinkering at such a *pre-compositional* level.[5] On the other hand, relatively uncontroversially, the kind of regularities encoded *within* the compositional module do not suffice as justifications for the decisions made at the representational level. That your remark 'Elvis went to the bank' is to be represented in terms of a lexical item related to financial institutions is a conclusion that does not depend only on the conventional profile of the expressions you employed, and on the effects achieved by their arrangement in the uttered sentence. It also depends, among other things, on factors such as your obsession with cash, the fact that you were not holding a fishing rod, or our common belief that the king of rock n' roll would never approach the side of a river. If, for one reason or another, one decides to classify considerations of this kind as falling within the domain of *pragmatics*, it follows that questions of representation are, at least to a certain degree, pragmatic issues.[6] To the extent to which such decisions straightforwardly affect the outcome of the compositional module, pragmatic considerations do undoubtedly come into play in the process of the semantic interpretation of an utterance. Since I cannot recall a single noteworthy semanticist who ever expressed disagreement with such a commonplace, I shall not delve on questions related to this aspect of the semantics/pragmatics interface any further.

Suppose now that a sentence-index pair p, involving a particular syntactic construct and a certain index, appropriately represents an utterance u — assume for instance that your utterance of 'Elvis lives' is correctly evaluated by focusing on the construct displayed a couple of paragraphs ago, and by interpreting the verb's present tense on the basis of i_T, the time of utterance. What is required of an *empirically adequate* compositional module is that, when applied to p, it yields an outcome compatible with our intuitions regarding u, in this particular example, our semantic inclinations towards your utterance. The comparison between the compositional module's verdict and such inclinations is however not trivial. What the compositional module yields are results in terms of *intensions*, that is, truth-values across points of evaluation; what our intuitions involve, on the other hand, are decisions pertaining to the truth-value of an utterance on a certain occasion, *vis à vis* a particular way the world happens to be, such as the intuition that your utterance of 'Elvis lives' is false, given how things went with the founder of Graceland. For didactic purposes, issues pertaining to the interface between our intuitions of truth-value and the compositional module's output are typically ignored, or assumed to be of an inconsequential nature. The intuition that u has a truth-value t, given particular circumstances C, is thus typically (and tacitly) interpreted as the requirement that the pair representing u be

---

[5]See also John Perry's notion of pre-semantic uses of context in Perry 1997 and 2001.
[6]See Carston 1988 and Recanati 1993, 2001, and 2002.

mapped to an intension yielding *true* for any point 'corresponding to' *C*. For instance, if your utterance of 'Elvis lives' in 2002 strikes me as false, what I demand of the compositional module is that it accounts for falsity at any point 'corresponding to' the situation eliciting my verdict, one in which Elvis is dead in 2002. Leaving aside the *non-chalant* attitude towards what such 'correspondence' may involve, an assessment of this kind may well be unobjectionable. It is however often developed into a less unobjectionable methodological approach, pertaining to the employment of certain thought-experiments for the purpose of drawing conclusions regarding the intensional profile of two or more utterances. In these thought-experiments, one is invited to *fix* a particular course of history, for instance, the actual development of rock'n roll's golden age, and to take into consideration two (or more) utterances, say, an utterance *u* of 'Elvis lives' in 1975, and an utterance *v* of that sentence now, in 2002. Since *u* turns out to be intuitively true with respect to the actual circumstances, but *v* does not, so one typically concludes, *u* and *v* (or, more precisely, the pairs appropriately representing them) ought to be mapped to different *intensions* by any empirically adequate compositional module: given at least one point of evaluation, in particular any point corresponding to how things went with Elvis' life, one intension ought to yield a verdict of truth, the other a verdict of falsehood.

In this particular case, of course, a strategy along the foregoing lines yields the correct outcome: an utterance of 'Elvis lives' in 1975 and an utterance of that sentence in 2002 should indeed be assigned contrasting intensional profiles. It does however not follow that the aforementioned methodology, leading from our pre-theoretic assessment of certain utterances to the establishment of particular constraints on empirically adequate compositional modules, is *generally* sound. Indeed, as I explain in the next section, in only slightly less straightforward examples, things do not work out as smoothly.

3   Issues of Formality

At the entrance to my favorite restaurant a sign says 'formal attire required'. I show up in jacket and tie, they let me in. I remark, truly: 'my attire is formal'. On the invitation to the ambassador's party it is written 'formal attire required'. I show up in my restaurant outfit, they send me back home. I retort: 'my attire is formal', they rightly object: 'how false!'. My utterance *u* of 'my attire is formal' at the restaurant and my utterance *v* of that sentence at the embassy intuitively differ in truth-value. The former utterance is true, the latter is false, even though they both aim at describing one and the same attire, pertaining to the very same jacket and tie. What to do with examples such as these?

Here's how the issue is traditionally approached: since u and v differ in truth-value, notwithstanding the fact that one and the same portion of my sartorial biography is being assessed, it must be the case that any empirically adequate compositional module maps them to contrasting truth-values with respect to one and the same point of evaluation, i.e., that it maps them to distinct intensions. It may well be *prima facie* plausible to suppose (i) that the representation of either utterance includes one and the same syntactic construct, namely something along the lines of

s^*: $[[\text{my attire}]_{\text{NP}} [[\text{is formal}]_V [\text{PRES}]_T]_{\text{VP}}]_S$

and (ii) that since the only indexical expressions apparently occurring in s^* address the index's agent and temporal co-ordinates, and since the temporal lapse between my utterances may well be of no import, identical indexes are appropriate for either u or v. Yet, so common wisdom concurs, *prima facie* plausibility does not provide a reliable indication in this case: the result it yields, so it is concluded, is incompatible with the required outcome, since the choice of identical representations would inevitably render one and the same intension.

A variety of suggestions may then be entertained at this stage. Perhaps, and notwithstanding the contrary opinion of any sensible syntactician, my utterance at the embassy was elliptical for 'my attire is very, very formal', in virtue of a not so widely recognized rule of double emphasis deletion. Perhaps 'formal' is, surprisingly enough, an indexical expression, denoting alternative types of outfit with respect to different, contextually provided purposes of clothing. Perhaps, distinct degrees of formality are supplied by the appropriate indexes, and eventually partake in the intensional profile semantically associated with my utterances as unarticulated constituents, without being called for by any of the expressions I employed. A radical alternative looms at the other end of the spectrum: perhaps the naive proposal that both utterances be represented in terms of s^* and a certain index is on the right track, but our intuitive reactions should not be accepted without further ado as indications regarding those utterances' semantic profiles — my cry of 'my attire is formal' as they throw me out of the party may well have been strictly speaking true, though pragmatically imparting a false message. Perhaps. But nobody would reasonably engage in theoretical gymnastics such as these, unless she independently assumed that any semantic explanation of the cases under analysis burdens the compositional module with a requirement of intensional discrepancy. Yet, an assumption of this kind seems unjustified.

It is true that one and the same condition is being described by the utterances introduced above. My utterances at the restaurant and at the ambassador's party both aim at describing the very same outfit: it simply is not part of the story that, as I left the restaurant and headed towards the embassy, I cut my tie, ripped my shirt, and rolled in mud. But our intuitions regarding u and v are sensitive not only to the semantic profile of the uttered sentences, and to the state of the objects being assessed: knowledge of English and exhaustive information about how I was dressed that evening are insufficient for determining whether an utterance of 'my attire is formal' turns out as intuitively true or false. What is required, together with information of this type, is a certain degree of familiarity with the purposes for the classification of attires as formal or informal. The friend who assured me that I would be welcome at the embassy was well acquainted with my jacket and tie, and knew that 'formal' meant, roughly, 'conforming to accepted rules or customs': he just did not know enough about the rules and customs commonly accepted within the diplomatic community. Those who, unlike my friend, correctly understood the inadequacy of my remark at the embassy, did so not only in virtue of their familiarity with the English idiom, and on the basis of what I was wearing that evening: their semantic appraisal was shaped, together with these undeniably relevant factors, by their understanding that, for the purpose of the ambassador's party, nothing less than a tuxedo qualifies as conforming to the accepted customs.

If this much is at work in our intuitive evaluation of my utterances, it seems unfair to burden the compositional module with the task of rendering the pre-theoretically adequate verdicts, unless such module is suitably buffered, so as to take into account the contextual variations affecting our understanding of what counts as formal or not. Both my remark at the restaurant and my exclamation at the party aim at describing one and the same attire. Both, barring *ad hoc* maneuvers, put forth the same claim about that item, a claim to the effect that it is formal. But it is by no means one and the same point of evaluation which, within the scope of the compositional module, provides an adequate reflection of how things stand with my clothes and their formality. If it is the notion that my attire counts as formal which, among other things, motivates the intuition that u is true, it seems only fair that such truth-value be required as resulting from the intension assigned to u, with respect to points at which my jacket and tie belong in the extension of 'is formal'. And since it is an understanding of my attire as informal which shapes our pre-theoretic disagreement with v, a result of falsity ought to be rendered *vis à vis* any point at which that garment is not within that extension. Such a constraint for any empirically adequate compositional module is of course compatible with its assignment of identical intensions to the (sentence-index pairs representing) the utterances under analysis.

As I explain in section four, what motivates the aforementioned illicit assumption of contrasting intensions is an inadequate understanding of the roles context may play within the semantic analysis of particular utterances.

But before I expand on this remark, it is advisable that I return to the case with which I begun, 'it rains', and that I explain how semantic analyses of the traditional mold may render intuitively adequate results.

4   The Machine: Lean and Mean

Recall my utterances u and v of 'it rains' taking place (at a certain time t) respectively in Prague and Palermo. The former is true, but the latter is false, given one unique meteorological condition m, such that it rains in Prague but not in Palermo.[7] Since one utterance may be true and the other false without any intervening changes of the weather, so one may reason, it must be the case that their semantic analysis recognizes the possibility that (the pair representing) the former be true at a particular point, and (the pair representing) the latter be false at that very same point. Thus, so one may continue, if our intuitions are to be taken at face value, something must intervene in the process leading to the assignment of intensions to those pairs, appropriately discriminating between the two: that it rains, and that it does so at a certain time cannot exhaust that to which the intensional level is sensitive, since rain and one and the same time are apparently at issue in either case. Intensions, so the *opulent semanticist* concludes, are richer than it meets the eye.

How to explain such abundant intensional profiles? Perhaps, different hidden expressions lurk within the syntactic items appropriate in either case, so that u and v are to be presented in terms of pairs involving suitably different syntactic constructs. Perhaps, unexpected forms of indexicality end up generating equally unexpected discriminations, or more direct contextual contributions pop up at the right level, without being called for by the meaning of any expression in the uttered sentence. Moving to a very different kind of approach, a healthy semantic diet may be accompanied by a generous account of the information pragmatically conveyed by the speakers:

---

[7]That these states of affairs be regarded as one unique meteorological condition may well be the outcome of traditional philosophical semantics' obsession with possible *worlds*, that is, the result of its disdain for partial situations (thanks to Paolo Bouquet for pointing this out). I have no objection against the suggestion that what is relevant for the evaluation of, say, an utterance such as u is not the total meteorological state of the world, but rather how things are with the weather within certain locally relevant boundaries. Indeed, my considerations in the remainder of this section explain how this vague but intuitively correct suggestion may be incorporated within a systematic semantic account centered around the resources of traditional compositional modules. The insistence on partiality as an alternative to the unboundedness of worlds seems however idle with respect to cases such as those pertaining to 'is formal' (and the multitude of parallel examples left as an exercise to the reader). The apparatus developed in this essay aims at capturing a more general sense of contextuality, able to deal with the fundamental character of the phenomenon under study.

perhaps, u and v do share their truth-values (be it truth, falsehood, or neither of the above), but nevertheless impart claims regarding the meteorological conditions at different locations.[8]

As an alternative to opulent semantics (and to bony semantics accompanied by luxurious pragmatics), I propose the following *lean* analysis of u and v. When it comes to the pre-compositional issue pertaining to the correct representation of u and v, the appropriate pairs apparently include, in either case, the uttered sentence, that is, only slightly more precisely, a construct of the form

    s: $[[PRES]_T\,[[rains]_V]_{VP}]_S$.

As for the representation of the contextual parameters at least *prima facie* relevant here, only the time of utterance seems to have a bearing on the interpretation of the only apparently indexical item in s, $[PRES]_T$. Since both u and v may well be envisioned as taking place at the same time, we may thus settle for i_T as the co-ordinate appropriate in either case. Both u and v, in other words, are represented in terms of pairs including s, and indexes involving i_T, as one would reasonably expect.

Modulo a few non immediately relevant simplifications, the compositional module proceeds in the customary manner, i.e., it interprets 'rains' as a property of times, that is, it assigns to it, with respect to any index j, a function from points of evaluation to collections of temporal instants. PRES is in turn evaluated in the obvious manner, as denoting with respect to an index j the temporal co-ordinate in j. With respect to an index j and a point k, s is then evaluated as *true* iff the temporal co-ordinate of j is within the extension of 'rains' in k, that is, $[[s]]_{j,k} = true$ iff $j_T \in [['rains']]_{j,k}$.

How can an analysis along these lines be a *mean* one, in the complimentary sense of 'mean', that is, in this case, one compatible with the evidence provided by competent speakers' reactions? Those reactions consist in the intuitive assignment of contrasting truth-values to utterances of 'it rains' *vis à vis* one and the same meteorological condition, m. Uncontroversially, though rather vaguely, such reactions are in turn driven by certain differences in the *contexts* for those utterances. An utterance u of 'it rains' in Prague takes place as part of a conversation on the local weather: it is performed with the intention of commenting on the weather in Prague, it is addressed to an audience interested in the weather conditions in the Prague

---

[8]For accounts in terms of hidden forms of indexicality (or, more precisely, hidden variables), see Stanley and Szabò 2000. Note however that their stance is allegedly supported by considerations of binding relations, the so-called binding argument; for a critical discussion of the binding argument, see Recanati 2002 and Cappelen and Lepore 2002. For different appeals to unarticulated constituency, see Perry 1986, Crimmins 1992, Recanati 1993 and 2002; for solutions at the pragmatic level, see Bach 1994 and Borg forthcoming.

area, and it occurs within a conversation focused on the weather in the Czech capital. In a context of this type, neither Canadian snowstorms nor the Sicilian drought play a contextually relevant role as meteorological evidence of the type required: for these purposes, the actual meteorological condition is one in which it rains. An utterance v of 'it rains' in Palermo, on the other hand, typically qualifies as a meteorological remark taking place *vis à vis* a background in which Sicilian drizzles would be accepted as evidence that it rains, downpours in Seattle or Prague would not: for the purposes now salient, the way things happen to be in m are such that it does not rain.

What kind of constraint do intuitions of this type impose on empirically adequate compositional modules? If our intuition that u is true is shaped, among other things, by our understanding of the present time as a time of rain, what our pre-theoretic assessment of u prescribes is that a result of truth be obtained whenever (the sentence-index pair representing) u is evaluated at points where the contextually relevant time partakes in the extension of 'rains'. By the same token, since our appraisal of v as false depends on an interpretation of the weather as a condition in which, for all relevant purposes, it does not rain, an appropriate rendering of our intuitions within the compositional module should be committed to the assignment of falsehood to (the pair representing) v with respect to points at which the semantic value for PRES is not among the items within the extension of 'rains'. Of course, conclusions of this type are consistent with the 'lean' semantic analysis sketched above, and, more, generally, with any approach that does not assign distinct intensional profiles to u and v.

Slightly more precisely, what our pre-theoretic intuitions yield are verdicts pertaining to utterances, regarding their truth-values on particular occasions. Such intuitive assessments are shaped, among other things, by contextual considerations, in particular considerations pertaining to a location salient for the assessment of the weather conditions. At least according to the 'lean' analysis presented above, contextual factors of this type intervene neither at the pre-semantic level relevant for the choice of an appropriate syntactic construct, nor at the level appropriate for the interpretation of the indexical expressions occurring in the uttered sentence. Nevertheless, they play a determinant function in the *application* of the results yielded by the compositional module, and, consequently, in the assessment of its empirical adequacy.

5   Context and Semantics

What exactly went wrong in the reasoning for the requirement that u and v be mapped to distinct intensions? What went wrong was an illicit application of a methodology incorrectly assumed to have general validity: the recognition that u and v have different truth-values with respect to one, fixed meteorological condition does not in this case entail that an adequate treatment of u and v ought to include a compositional module in which their representations are mapped to distinct truth-values at some unique point of evaluation. In turn, a mistake of this kind is grounded on an incomplete understanding of the context's responsibilities with respect to the analysis of an utterance's semantic profile. According to this understanding, contextual factors, besides for playing a role at the post-semantic level relevant for the calculation of conversational effects, are involved at a level determinant for semantic results only in two respects: they provide the pre-semantic justification for the choice of an appropriate syntactic construct, as in cases of ellipsis or structural ambiguity, or they supply the kind of information required in cases of indexicality. In this paper, I highlighted a further form of contextuality, which intervenes at the *post-compositional* level, leading from an utterance's intensional profile to hypotheses pertaining to its truth-value and truth-conditions — in the customary sense of 'truth-condition' as truth-value across alternative situations. Both my utterances of 'my attire is formal', for instance, are associated by the compositional module to functions yielding truth at all and only those points in which my attire belongs in the extension of 'is formal'. Yet, only the former is true with respect to a scenario in which I wear my jacket and tie: it is only with respect to the criteria operative within a discussion of restaurant admission policies that such scenario may be represented by a point of evaluation at which 'my attire is formal' is evaluated as true.

It is the responsibility of an empirically adequate compositional module that it yields intuitively correct results of intension. The intuitive correctness of such results is assessed on the basis of our pre-theoretic evaluation of particular utterances, on particular occasions. When it comes to the comparison of such evaluation with the results yielded by the compositional module, what is required is an appropriate representation of the utterance under analysis. *How* such a representation is identified is a highly contextual matter, in a pre-semantically relevant sense of contextuality: the appropriate syntactic item and the additional parameters of semantic interest are selected on the basis of factors such as, very negotiably, the intentions of the speaker, the topic of the conversation, and the physical environment in which the utterance has taken place. *Some* of the parameters thus selected play a familiar role within the structure of the compositional module, and thereby affect the module's intensional outcome. These are the co-ordinates traditionally included within what I called an index, that is, the items required in virtue of the conventional meaning assigned to the indexical expressions within the language. If the proposal in this essay is on the right track, the index's parameters do not include all the contextual features relevant for the comparison of the compositional module with our intuitive assessment of an utterance—that is, equivalently, they do not exhaust the kind of contextually appropriate information relevant for the semantic evaluation of an utterance, understood as the identification of the situations in which it may be uttered truly. What a semantically appropriate representation of an utterance must include are also contextual indications that are idle with respect to the meaning of the expressions in the language, and hence with respect to the compositional module's assignment of intensions. Their relevance is rather related to the post-compositional task of interpreting such assignment in terms of the utterance's truth-conditions, that is, in terms of its truth-value across alternative occasions.[9]

6   Some Objections

'You repeatedly emphasize the role of contextual factors at a variety of levels, but you say nothing about the mechanisms responsible for the identification of such factors. Yet, the elements of importance for your project seem less automatic and straightforward than the regularities responsible for the contextual contributions to the interpretation of obvious indexicals.' Indeed they are, and this essay has no interesting contribution to offer pertaining to such an important question. But a solution to problems of this type is needed independently from the view I defended. Contextual elements of one kind or another must also come into play, for one reason or another, in accounts that appeal to pre-compositional tamperings at the syntactic level, to hidden indexicality or underarticulation, or to pragmatic mechanisms.

'Your approach embraces an intolerable form of metaphysical relativism. Things are one way or another independently of our desires and our intentions to categorize them one way or another: the weather does not shift with our conversational interests, and clothes do not change their form, style, or texture merely in virtue of our change of perspective.' Indeed they don't. It is a brute fact about my cheap suit and worn out tie that it may pass

---

[9]Traditional compositional modules are developed on the model of structures devised for the purposes of *logical* analysis, that is, for purposes in which one quantifies over the type of requirements suitable for the truth of certain items. This sort of concern, which well may be labeled a concern for 'truth-conditions', is obviously insufficient for an analysis of truth-conditions in the sense relevant for the present essay, that is, the establishment of the worldly conditions required for the truth of a particular utterance, on a particular occasion. The analysis of certain expressions' truth-values across alternative points of evaluation (with respect to alternative indexes) may be employed as an important component in the study of the semantic profile of an utterance (and, consequently, may be evaluated *vis à vis* our intuitions about its truth-value) only if accompanied by due attention to the post-compositional aspects of that utterance's context.

the test of formality for your average restaurant, while remaining well below the decorum requested to dine with the ambassador. What I need to do to be admitted at the party is to invest in a tuxedo, not to take a more down to earth perspective on diplomatic conventions.

'Your approach grants that context intervenes in the semantic process leading to the assignment of truth-value to an utterance — not only because it provides the elements required for the interpretation of the indexicals, and because it steers the pre-compositional processes of representation. Ignore issues of ambiguity resolution, reference assignment, and the like, and put aside matters of indexicality: you still need contextual features to end up with a result comparable with our semantic intuitions. How is this different from opulent semantics, and in particular from that most fashionable form of opulence, *truth-conditional pragmatics*?'[10] Of course I need what is needed to get the right answer. That utterances of 'it rains' in Prague and Palermo intuitively differ in truth-value, and that such a result depends on contextual factors such as the location of utterance or the topic of the conversation, are not controversial issues: they are what needs to be explained. The question is whether the correct explanation requires opulent forms of semantic analyses, in terms of so-called 'free enrichment' or 'underarticulation', and whether the only alternatives to such semantic opulence are luxuries at a syntactic or pragmatic level. More precisely, what is at issue (or, at least, one of the questions on the table) is whether compositional modules of the traditional mold, with their sympathy for full articulation and their 'packet of parameters' approach to contextuality, are indeed at odds with our semantic intuitions. As far as weather reports go, a positive answer seems premature.

References

Bach, K. 1994. Conversational Impliciture. *Mind and Language* 9: 124-62.

Borg, E. (forthcoming). Saying What You Mean: Unarticulated Constituents and Communication. *Ellipsis and Non-Sentential Speech*, ed. R. Elugardo and R. Stainton. Dordrecht: Kluwer Academic Press.

Cappelen, H. and E. Lepore 2002. Indexicality, Binding, Anaphora and A-Priori Truth. *Analysis* 62: 271-81.

Carston, R. 1988. Implicature, Explicature, and Truth-Theoretic Semantics. *Mental Representations*, ed. R. Kempson. Cambridge: Cambridge University Press.

Crimmins, M. 1992. *Talk About Beliefs*. Cambridge, MA: MIT Press.

---

[10]The label 'truth-conditional pragmatics' is borrowed from Recanati 1993; see also Recanati 2001 and 2002.

Crimmins, M. 1995. Contextuality, Reflexivity, Iteration, Logic. *Philosophical Perspectives 9, AI, Connectionism, and Philosophical Psychology*: 381-99.

Crimmins, M. and J. Perry 1989. The Prince and the Phone Booth: Reporting Puzzling Beliefs. *Journal of Philosophy* 86: 685-711.

Kaplan, D. 1977. Demonstratives. *Themes From Kaplan*, eds. J. Almog, J. Perry and H. Wettstein. Oxford: Oxford University Press.

Lewis, D. 1980. Index, Context, and Content. *Philosophy and Grammar*, eds. S. Kanger and S. Öhman. Dordrecht: Reidel Press. Reprinted in D. Lewis, *Papers in Philosophical Logic*, Cambridge: Cambridge University Press 1998.

Perry, J. 1986. Thought Without Representation. *Proceedings of the Aristotelian Society*, Supplementary Volume 60: 137-52.

Perry, J. 1997. Indexicals and Demonstratives. *A Companion to the Philosophy of Language*, eds. R. Hale and C. Wright. Oxford: Blackwell.

Perry, J. 2001. *Reference and Reflexivity*. Stanford: CSLI Publications.

Predelli, S. 1997. Talk About Fiction. *Erkenntnis* 46: 69-77.

Predelli, S. 1998. Utterance, Interpretation, and the Logic of Indexicals. *Mind and Language* 13.3: 400-14.

Predelli, S. 2002. Intentions, Indexicals, and Communication. *Analysis* 62.4: 310-16.

Recanati, F. 1993. *Direct Reference: From Language to Thought*. Oxford: Blackwell.

Recanati, F. 2001. What Is Said. *Synthèse* 128: 75-91.

Recanati, F. 2002. Unarticulated Constituents. *Linguistics and Philosophy* 25: 299-345.

Richard, M. 1982. Tense, Propositions, and Meanings. *Philosophical Studies* 41: 337-351.

Salmon, N. 1986. *Frege's Puzzle*. Cambridge, MA: MIT Press.

Sperber, D. and D. Wilson 1995. *Relevance. Communication and Cognition*. 2nd ed. Oxford: Blackwell.

Stanley, J. 2000. Context and Logical Form. *Linguistics and Philosophy* 23: 391-434.

Stanley, J. 2002. Making It Articulated. *Mind and Language* 17: 149-64.

Stanley, J. and Z. G. Szabò 2000. On Quantifier Domain Restriction. *Mind and Language* 15: 216-61.

Taylor, K. A. 2001. Sex. Breakfast, and Descriptus-Interruptus. *Synthèse* 128: 45-61.

Wilson, D. and D. Sperber 1981. On Grice's Theory of Conversation. *Conversation and Discourse. Structure and Interpretation*, ed. P. Werth. London: Croom Helm.

3

Minding the Gap

KENT BACH

1 The Semantics-Pragmatics Gap

I'm all for pragmatics. But I don't think it helps the cause to blur the boundary between semantics and pragmatics. The purpose of this chapter is to explain why.

The basic reason is this. Even though, as people have been pointing out for some years now, the linguistic meaning of a given sentence generally underdetermines what a speaker means in uttering it, it does not follow that linguistic meaning is infected or infested by what some of these same people call 'pragmatic meaning'. There is no such thing as pragmatic meaning, at least nothing that is commensurate with linguistic meaning. There is what the sentence means and what the speaker means in uttering it.

The semantic-pragmatic distinction is not fit to be blurred. What lies on either side of the distinction, the semantic and the pragmatic, may each be messy in various ways, but that doesn't blur the distinction itself. Taken as properties of sentences, semantic properties are on a par with syntactic and phonological properties: they are linguistic properties. Pragmatic properties, on the other hand, belong to acts of uttering sentences in the course of communicating. Sentences have the properties they have independently of anybody's act of uttering them. Speakers' intentions do not endow them with new semantic properties (here I mean sentence types, not tokens). Acts of uttering sentence types (producing sentence tokens) have pragmatic properties. The fact that a given sentence means what it does entails nothing about what a speaker means in uttering it. A speaker could mean precisely

The Semantics/Pragmatics Distinction.
Claudia Bianchi (ed.).
Copyright © 2004, CSLI Publications.

what it means, no more and no less, but nothing about its meaning guarantees this. The speaker might mean something else, something more, or nothing at all.

In what follows I will sketch a picture different aspects of which I have addressed in more detail in other places. In those places I have used illustrative examples and discussed alternative approaches to specific issues.[1] Here I will simply state my position and summarize the arguments for it. This will make the presentation more abstract (and dogmatic) but also more compact, so that the picture can be viewed more clearly as a whole.

2   Why There is a Gap

There are many phenomena that are thought to show that the semantic-pragmatic distinction is blurry, arbitrary, or even nonexistent. Here I will not review these phenomena or rebut these arguments but will instead suggest that such phenomena fit in with the distinction and that the distinction itself is immune to such arguments – at least if it is properly understood as the innocuous (but important) distinction that it is. As will be explained in subsequent sections, these arguments rest on blurring or disregarding certain other distinctions which, at least when pointed out, are too obvious even to need defending. Once we are clear on those other distinctions, we can stop worrying about the semantic-pragmatic distinction itself. This is not to say that there are not plenty of pertinent linguistic phenomena to worry about, but once the line between semantics and pragmatics is clear, there should generally be no question on which side of the line a given phenomenon falls. There may be some residual hard cases, linguistic phenomena that are not well-understood, and in some cases, there may be both a semantic and a pragmatic side to the phenomenon, but these facts do not create a problem with the semantic-pragmatic distinction itself.[2]

The reason there is a gap and a clear-cut one at that is that semantics and pragmatics have distinct subject matters, sentences and utterances, respectively. Semantics is the part of grammar that pairs forms with meanings. Presumably the meaning of a sentence is determined compositionally by the meanings of its constituents as a function of its syntactic structure. Pragmatics is concerned with what speakers do in uttering sentences. So if semantics concerns sentences, in particular their linguistic meanings, and pragmatics concerns uses that speakers make of sentences (and, correla-

---

[1]These other places will be cited in subsequent footnotes. The semantic-pragmatic distinction itself is discussed in Bach 1999a.

[2]For discussion of some seemingly problematic phenomena, see Bach 1999a: 75-80, and for discussion of some genuinely problematic phenomena see Bach 2001a: 31-40.

tively, hearers' understanding of speakers' uses), then, it would seem, the semantic-pragmatic distinction should hold up without incident.

Even so, there are certain linguistic phenomena that may seem to threaten the gap. Clefts, stress, and other devices for packaging or structuring information (see Lambrecht 1994), grammatical mood (imperative, interrogative, etc.), and utterance modifiers are examples of linguistic expressions and devices which, though they have no bearing on truth conditions, nonetheless semantically encode information that bears on use.[3] Is such information semantic or pragmatic? If such phenomena seem to threaten the gap, that is only because there is a certain ambiguity involving the term *semantic*. It can pertain specifically to linguistic information relevant to the truth conditions of a sentence, or it can be used more inclusively and concern any matter of linguistic meaning. The examples just mentioned have semantic content in the latter, more inclusive sense. Indeed, they pertain to use. Does that blur the semantic-pragmatic distinction? Not really. If a speaker uses the imperative form or a cleft construction, for example, there is still the distinction between the information encoded by the form or construction and the fact that the speaker uses it. Such semantic information is in a sense procedural, but that does not make it pragmatic in the sense of being a property of the speaker's act of utterance.

Even if what a speaker means consists precisely in the semantic content of the sentence he utters, this fact is not determined by that semantic content. The reason is very simple: no sentence has to be used in accordance with its semantic content. *Any* sentence can be used in a nonliteral or indirect way. That a speaker is attempting to communicate something, and what that is, is a matter of his communicative intention (if indeed he has one). If he is speaking literally and means precisely what his words mean, even that fact depends on his communicative intention. But what he utters, if a grammatical sentence, has the semantic content that it has whether the speaker is using it in a strictly literal way or not.

In any case, it is not the business of semantics to account for the contents of utterances that are not literal, since in those cases the speaker is trying to convey something that is not predictable from the meaning of the uttered sentence (or, if it is ambiguous, from its operative meaning).[4] Obviously not just anything a speaker means, no matter how far removed it is from what the sentence means, counts as semantic content, and the semantic

---

[3]Utterance modifiers, such as *by the way* and *frankly,* are discussed in Bach 1999b: 356-60.

[4] Disambiguation is a pragmatic matter, part of the process whereby the hearer figures out what the speaker means in uttering the sentence. The fact that a sentence is ambiguous and that someone who utters it intends it to be read in one way rather than another does not imply that in the context the sentence loses its other meaning(s).

content of the sentence is the same whether or not an utterance of it is literal. Semantic content is a property of the sentence, not the utterance.

The term *utterance* is often applied to sentence tokens, but there is no need to attribute semantic content to them (apart from that of the sentence types of which they are tokens). It is as an intentional act performed by a speaker that an utterance has a content distinct from that of the uttered sentence. But in this sense the content of an utterance is really the content of the speaker's communicative intention in making the utterance. So the only linguistic content relevant here is the semantic content of the sentence, and the only other relevant content is the content of the speaker's intention. Focusing on the normal case, where communication is successful (the listener succeeds in identifying the speaker's communicative intention), can make it seem as though an utterance has content in its own right, independently of the speaker's intention. But this is illusory, as is evident whenever communication fails. In that case, where the speaker means one thing and his audience thinks he means something else, there is what the speaker means and what his listener takes him to mean, but there is no independent utterance content.

In practice, we generally don't say what precisely we mean, because we leave much of what we mean to inference. Even when we are using words or phrases literally, we generally do not use the entire sentence literally. That is, what the sentence means, and what we thereby say in uttering it, comprises merely a skeletal version of what we mean. For example, if at a McDonald's you say, 'I want a hamburger with everything', presumably you mean that you want to be given, within a short time, a cooked, ready to eat, uncontaminated hamburger of normal size with all the trimmings. But you do not say most of this, and the sentence you use is not an elliptical version of some more elaborate sentence that spells these things out.[5]

This phenomenon of *sentence nonliterality* is so pervasive that we tend not to notice it, not just when engaged in ordinary conversation but even when theorizing about language and communication. We generally do not make fully explicit what we mean in uttering a sentence, even when we are using the individual words in them literally. Although for every sentence we do utter, there is a more elaborate, qualified version we could utter that would make what we mean more explicit, these are not the sentences we do utter. Indeed, they are not ones we even think to utter. We do not form a thought to express, think of a convoluted sentence that would express it fully explicitly, and then, in the interests of conversational efficiency, work out a stripped down version of the sentence to utter instead. Yet somehow

---

[5] For a variety of further examples and further discussion, see Bach 1994 and 2001b.

we often manage to make evident our relatively complex communicative intentions by uttering relatively simple sentences.

3 Communicative Intentions and Inferences

Austin (1962: 94-107) drew a fundamental distinction between *locutionary* and *illocutionary* acts. This distinction is easy to disregard, partly because the word 'say' plays a dual role as a locutionary and as an illocutionary verb, roughly synonymous with 'state' (or 'assert'). A locutionary act is the act of saying something in uttering a sentence. In this sense, one can say something without stating it. One might not be stating anything, or one might be speaking figuratively and be stating something else, though not expressly. The illocutionary act a speaker performs in saying something is a matter of his communicative intention.[6] What he means in saying what he says (if he means anything at all) may be just what he says, what he says and more, or something else entirely. What he says provides the linguistic contribution to the audience's inference to his communicative intention. Given what one intends to communicate, succeeding at communicating requires choosing a sentence whose utterance will make one's intention evident. One must utter a sentence which, given the mutually salient information that comprises the extralinguistic cognitive context of utterance, enables one's audience to recognize one's communicative intention. There is something distinctive here about a communicative intention. Unlike intentions of other sorts, its fulfillment consists in its recognition. Whereas you can't do a pirouette by way of anyone's recognizing your intention to do so, you can succeed in communicating something simply by enabling your listeners to recognize your intention to communicate it.

In uttering a sentence, a speaker normally expresses an attitude toward a proposition. For example, asserting is to express a belief, requesting is to express a desire, and promising is to express an intention. One does not just express a proposition. Here is a Gricean conception of what is it to express an attitude:

> *Expressing an attitude:* In making an utterance S expresses A(p) iff S intends H, partly by way of recognizing that this (entire) intention is to be recognized, to take the utterance as a reason to think S has A(p).

This definition, a slightly modified version of the formulation given by Bach and Harnish (1979: 15), allows for the possibility that the speaker

---

[6]Here I depart from Austin (1962), who assimilated all illocutionary acts to the regularized ones performed in special institutional or social settings. I follow Strawson (1964), who argued that most ordinary illocutionary acts are not conventional but communicative in character and succeed not by conformity to convention but, in Gricean fashion, by recognition of intention.

does not actually have the attitude he is expressing. After all, he could be lying (in the case of an assertion) or be otherwise insincere. This definition incorporates Grice's (1957) idea that the hearer is to rely partly on the fact that the speaker intends him to recognize the intention. This does not tell her what the intention is (that would introduce not just reflexivity but circularity into Grice's picture), but it does crucially constrain the inference involved in recognizing that intention.

Speakers and listeners rely on certain presumptions, speakers in order to make their communicative intentions evident and listeners to recognize those intentions. The listener presumes, and the speaker expects him to presume, that the speaker is being cooperative and is speaking truthfully, informatively, relevantly, perspicuously, and otherwise appropriately.[7] Because of their potential clashes, these presumptions should not be viewed as comprising a decision procedure. Rather, they provide different dimensions of considerations for the hearer to take into account in figuring out the speaker's communicative intention. They ground strategies for a speaker, on the basis of what he says and the fact that he says it, to make what he means evident to the hearer, and correlative strategies for the hearer to figure out what the speaker means. If an utterance superficially appears not to conform to these presumptions, the listener looks for a way to take the utterance so that it does conform. She does so partly on the supposition that she is intended to do so. However, contrary to the popular misconception that the maxims or presumptions play a role only in implicature (and in oblique and figurative speech generally), they are operative even when one means just what one says.

It is easy to exaggerate how well linguistic communication works. No doubt many failures of communication do not get noticed and, when they do, do not get mentioned. Still, in order for it to work as well as it does, we as speakers must be very good at selecting sentences whose utterance makes evident to our listeners what we mean, and as listeners we must be very good at figuring out what speakers mean in uttering them. To the extent that we leave much of what we mean to inference, we rely on our listener's ability to figure out what we mean on the basis of what we say, given the circumstances in which we say it, the fact that we said that rather than something else, and the presumption that we said it with a recognizable intention. How we manage to make ourselves understood and how we manage to understand others are very complex processes which, like most cognitive processes, are far beyond the reach of contemporary psychology to

---

[7]These presumptions correspond to Grice's maxims (1989: 26-7). Construing them as maxims treats them as guidelines for how to communicate successfully, but I think it is better to construe them as presumptions about speaker's intentions.

explain. As theorists, the best we can do is speculate on some of the features of these processes, most notably what it takes to implement Grice's discovery that communication involves a distinctively reflexive intention (and its recognition). Specifically, the intention includes, as part of its content, that the audience recognize this very intention by taking into account the fact that they are intended to recognize it.[8]

4   Muddling the Gap: Neglected Ambiguities

There are various key terms which, if not literally ambiguous, are at least used in two distinct ways. In each pair in the list below, the first use is semantic in character and the second is pragmatic. It is important to be cognizant of the two contrasting uses of each term.

meaning
- linguistic meaning: sense of an expression (word, phrase, or sentence)
- speaker's meaning: what a speaker means

speaker's meaning
- what a speaker means by a sentence (or phrase) when using it
- what a speaker means (tries to communicate) in uttering a sentence

reference
- by an expression to an object
- by a speaker with an expression to an object

utterance
- what is uttered
- act of uttering

utterance meaning
- meaning of an uttered sentence
- speaker's meaning in uttering a sentence

say
- perform a locutionary act
- state or assert, especially in using a declarative sentence without using any of its constituent expressions nonliterally

what is said
- the content of a locutionary act (or equivalently, the semantic content of sentence, relative to a context of utterance)

---

[8]The concepts in this section are explained much more fully in Bach forthcoming b. They were developed originally in Bach and Harnish 1979.

- the content of the assertion made in using an declarative sentence without using any of its constituent expressions nonliterally

context
- set of parameters whose values fix or delimit the semantic values of expressions with variable references
- set of salient mutual beliefs and presumptions among participants at a stage in a conversation

determine
- make the case (constitutive determination)
- ascertain (epistemic determination)

interpretation
- assignment of semantic values
- inference to speaker's communicative intention

demonstrative reference
- reference by a demonstrative
- speaker's reference by means by demonstrating

use (a term) to refer
- use a term that refers
- use a term and thereby refer

Most of these distinctions are self-explanatory, but a few require explanation and justification. As we will see in the next two sections, blurring these distinctions is essential to the various closely related doctrines that go by such names as *contextualism, truth-conditional pragmatics,* and *linguistic pragmatism.*

As mentioned above, Austin's distinction between locutionary and illocutionary acts, between saying something and doing something in saying it, is commonly neglected these days, perhaps because it is so easy to use 'say' interchangeably with 'state' or 'assert'. But stating or asserting is to perform an illocutionary act, of meaning and trying to communicate something, and that goes beyond mere saying (in the locutionary sense). Why is the locutionary notion of saying needed, along with the correlative, strictly semantic notion of what is said? It is needed to account for the each of the following cases, situations in which the speaker:

- says something but doesn't mean anything at all (by 'mean' here I mean 'intend to communicate')
- does not say what he intends to say, as in the misuse of a word or a slip of the tongue

- means what he says and something else as well (cases of implicature and of indirect speech acts in general)
- (intentionally) says one thing and means something else instead (non-literal utterances)

These are all cases in which what the speaker means, if indeed he means (intends to communicate) anything, is not identical to what he says, but cases in which he still says something.

What is loosely called 'context' is the conversational setting broadly construed. It is the mutual cognitive context, or salient common ground. It includes the current state of the conversation (what has just been said, what has just been referred to, etc.), the physical setting (if the conversants are face-to-face), salient mutual knowledge between the conversants, and relevant broader common knowledge. As I will explain more fully in the next section, context does not determine (in the sense of *constitute*), but merely enables the hearer to determine (in the sense of *ascertain*), what the speaker means. Because it can constrain what a hearer could reasonably take a speaker to mean in saying what he says, it can constrain what the speaker could *reasonably* mean in saying what he says. But it is incapable of determining what the speaker actually does mean. That is a matter of the speaker's communicative intention, however reasonable or unreasonable it may be.

The ambiguity of the phrase *utterance interpretation* is especially unfortunate. It already contains the ambiguous term *utterance,* which can mean what is uttered or the act of uttering it. Considered as the assignment of meanings to sentences, utterance interpretation is semantic interpretation, a mapping of sentence forms onto their linguistic meanings. In that sense, utterance interpretation is not a psychological process but something more abstract. However, this phrase is also used to mean the psychological process whereby listeners figure out what speakers are trying to communicate. This use would be unexceptionable but for the fact that this psychological process is often treated as if it were something more abstract, more akin to semantic interpretation. That is, some philosophers and linguistics treat utterance interpretation in this sense as if it were a mapping from syntactic structure to utterance contents, except that the mapping is sensitive to broadly contextual factors. In so doing, they seem to think that an utterance (as opposed to a sentence) can express things independently of what the speaker means in making it, just because of the context in which it is made. It is as if meanings could somehow be read off of utterances independently of inferring the speaker's intention, in a way analogous to semantic interpretations of sentences but without the constraint of being a projection of syntactic structure.

5   Putting Context in Context

It is often casually remarked that what a speaker says or means in uttering a given sentence 'depends on context', is 'determined' or 'provided' by context, or is otherwise a 'matter of context'. That is not literally true. Assume that by context we mean something like the mutually salient features of the conversational situation. Does context determine what a speaker says? Suppose a dinner host utters the ambiguous sentence *The chicken is ready to eat*. Presumably she is not saying that a certain chicken is hungry. Even so, given the ambiguity of the sentence, she could be saying that, however bizarrely. Context doesn't make it the case that she does not. Of course, she could not reasonably expect such a communicative intention to be recognized.[9]

Demonstratives and indexicals are often casually described as 'context-sensitive' or 'context-dependent'. These above point about context applies to these terms, although so-called pure or automatic indexicals, such as 'I' and 'today', are an exception. The reference of a pure indexical is determined by its linguistic meaning as a function of a contextual variable (call that the *semantic* context). However, the reference of other indexicals and of demonstratives is not so determined. They suffer from a *character deficiency*. For them the role of context is not to determine reference, in the sense of constituting it, but to enable the listener to determine it, in the sense of ascertaining it. But this is cognitive, not semantic context. Their reference is a matter of the speaker's communicative intention, which is not just another contextual variable. In fact, rather than describing them as referring, it would be better to describe speakers as using them to refer.[10]

It might be supposed that to the extent that the meaning of a sentence does not determine the content of an utterance of the sentence, the speaker's communicative intention does, and that this intention is part of the context. However, there is a problem with supposing that. If context were defined so broadly as to include anything other than linguistic meaning that is relevant to determining what a speaker means, then of course the speaker's intention would be part of the context. But if the context is to play the explanatory role claimed of it, it must be something that is the same for the speaker as it is for his audience, and obviously the role of the speaker's intention is not the same for both. Context can constrain what the speaker can succeed in communicating given what he says, but it cannot constrain what he intends to communicate in choosing what to say. Of course, in implementing his

---

[9]The uses and abuses of context are discussed more fully in Bach forthcoming a.

[10]Never mind that demonstratives and impure indexicals also have clearly non-referential uses, e.g., as something like bound variables.

intention (in order to get his communicative intention recognized), the speaker needs to select words whose utterance in the context will enable the hearer to figure out what he is trying to communicate.

6 Fudging the Gap: Semantic Incompleteness

Philosophers and linguists are coming to recognize that many if not most sentences do not express complete propositions, even when the sentence is devoid of ambiguity, vagueness, or indexicality. This is a very interesting fact, but it does not have the radical consequences some people think it has.

A sentence can fail to express a complete proposition either because it is missing an argument and is therefore *semantically incomplete* or because it is *semantically underdeterminate* and contains a word or phrase whose meaning needs to be tightened in one way or another.[11] Regardless of the reason that a given sentence fails to express a complete and determinate proposition, a speaker who utters such a sentence cannot mean merely what the sentence means. Presumably, what he means must be a complete proposition (something capable of being true or false).

This is an interesting fact, but it does not have radical consequences, either for semantics or pragmatics. Assume that the meaning of a sentence is determined compositionally, by the meanings of its constituents in a way that is predictable from how its constituents fit together syntactically. Even so, there is no guarantee that what is thus determined is a complete proposition. This may undermine the naive assumption that the output of a semantic theory for a language is a (recursive) specification of the truth conditions for all its (declarative) sentences, but it does not undermine semantic compositionality. It is just a brute fact about language that some syntactically complete sentences are not semantically complete.

Also, it might seem that if the semantics of sentences often fails to generate complete propositions, then pragmatics must intrude into semantics. The idea is that if a speaker utters a semantically incomplete or underdeterminate sentence and what he means must be a complete and determinate proposition, then the additional elements or tightening of meaning that is required to yield a proposition must automatically be incorporated in the semantic content of the utterance. This is the idea behind so-called truth-conditional pragmatics. It is also supposed that such sentences are in some sense context-sensitive or context-dependent. That leads to so-called contextualism in semantics, which not only supposes that semantics must deliver truth conditions but that context somehow comes to the rescue of semantics.

---

[11] So-called scope ambiguities may in some cases really be instances of underdetermination.

The trouble with these ideas is that they needlessly confuse the semantic contents of sentences with the intentional contents of utterances, that is, of the attitudes people express in making utterances. The fact that a sentence is semantically incomplete or underdeterminate does not mean that it is semantically defective. Yes, it does have a character deficiency, but still it has a definite content (or contents, if it is ambiguous), as given compositionally by the semantics. There is no empirical or theoretical reason why, at the level of *semantics,* the content of the sentence has to be supplemented or refined.[12] The fact that a speaker cannot mean merely what the sentence means comes into play when the speaker utters the sentence, insofar as the speaker has some communicative intention in uttering it. And the hearer, taking into account that he is to recognize that intention, must recognize that there is a gap between the semantic content of the sentence and the intentional content of the utterance. But there is no need for a truth-conditional pragmatics to fill out the semantic content of the sentence by treating it as a 'function' of 'context'. Pragmatic interpretation, as a cognitive process, cannot be understood as a abstract 'process', on the model of semantic interpretation. Rather, mutually evident facts enable the speaker, at least when communication goes well, to make his intention evident and enable the hearer to identify it.

Pragmatically speaking, when a speaker does mean merely what the sentence means, it makes little difference whether or not the sentence he utters expresses a complete and determinate proposition. Obviously, if the sentence is semantically incomplete or underdeterminate, the speaker *cannot* mean merely what it means, but it is generally as obvious that he *does* not mean what the sentence means even when the sentence does express a complete and determinate proposition. For it is generally true that the sentences we use do not make fully explicit what we mean. This is the norm, not the exception.

---

[12]I am not denying that with certain lexical items there may be syntactic or lexical reasons for supposing that they have an implicit argument position associated with them. However, such items are a source of hidden indexicality, not semantic incompleteness. The view that I am objecting to supposes that even in the absence of such an item, some sort of unarticulated constituent is present, mandated not by the grammar but by the need for a complete proposition to be expressed. In my view, this need is purely pragmatic. It cannot be assumed that since a sentence would not express a complete proposition unless it contained some hidden argument slot whose value is somehow provided contextually (or else the slot is quantified over), the sentence actually contains such an argument slot.

7 Missing the Gap: Faulty Intuitions

It is important to keep in mind that communication can fail and often does. We cannot just take a sample sentence and read off the likely communicative intention of someone who utters it, if only because they might be using it in some strange, perhaps even incomprehensible way. Displaying a sentence and putting a number in front of it does not make evident what a person means in uttering it. Moreover and more importantly, for a great many sentences it is not true that the most likely use of that sentence is a literal one. A great many sentences are very hard to use literally, even if one uses the individual words and phrases in them literally.[13]

In fact, there is nothing particularly normal about speaking literally. That is why it is naive to suppose that the semantic content of a declarative sentence (relative to a context) can be defined as what a speaker would normally assert in uttering the sentence. To suppose that for most sentences a likely use of it is a literal one can lead to erroneous semantic judgments. Relying on such 'intuitions' implicitly assumes that if a sentence would normally be used in a certain way, that use is a literal use. However, intuitions that purport to be about the semantic contents of sentences might in fact be responsive to what sentences are typically used to assert. Indeed, it is to be expected that these intuitions should be faulty, given our ability to say one thing and successfully convey something much richer and our correlative ability to recognize what others are doing when they are exercising that first ability. These abilities of ours are so fluent as to distort our reflective semantic judgments. What we think is expressed by a given sentence is colored by what we think a speaker is likely to mean in uttering it, especially if there is a typical sort of context which we tend to imagine it being used in. To keep one's semantic judgments from being pragmatically contaminated, it is always a good idea to imagine a variety of contexts of use, even wildly improbable ones.[14]

Intuitions are tainted by the fact that when a sentence is considered in isolation, certain default assumptions are made about the circumstances of utterance. We read things into the meaning of a sentence or into what a speaker says in uttering it that are really consequences of its being uttered under normal circumstances. These default assumptions depend on our knowledge of the world and of people's typical communicative purposes. So we tend not to discriminate between the semantic content of a sentence and the likely force of uttering a sentence with that content.

---

[13]As I have argued (Bach 2001b), even when one is using all the words in a sentence literally, one can still be speaking loosely, hence not strictly literally.

[14]For more on why seemingly semantic intuitions cannot be trusted, see Bach 2002.

Not only are these intuitions often responsive to nonsemantic information, they play no direct role in ordinary communication. In the course of speaking and listening to one another, we generally do not consciously reflect on the semantic content of the sentences we hear. We are focused on what we are communicating and on what is being communicated to us. Not only that, we do not have to be able to make accurate judgments about what information is semantic and what is not in order to be sensitive to semantic information.

Moreover, our seemingly semantic intuitions are responsive to *pragmatic regularities*. These include regularized uses of specific expressions and constructions that go beyond conventional meaning, as well as general patterns of efficient communication, which involve streamlining stratagems on the part of speakers and inferential heuristics on the parts of listeners. These regularities are pragmatic because it is the *use* of a given sentence, not the sentence itself, that carries the additional element of information. *That* a speaker says what he says rather than something else can contribute to what a speaker is likely to be taken to mean. Indeed, that he says it one way, by using certain words rather than certain others, can also contribute to what he is likely to be taken to mean in using those words.

Also, it is statistically unsound to focus on sentences representative of those we use or might use. That would be to commit a massive sampling error. English (or any other language) is just as capable of generating unusable sentences as usable ones. Even unusable sentences have perfectly good meanings, no matter how hard to parse or how absurd it would be to assert their semantic contents. Imagine that most of the (English) sentences that philosophers and linguists use as examples are representative of the vast variety of sentences that (English) speakers have used or might use. Even so, sentences actually used or even potentially usable are not representative of (English) sentences in general. That is not just because most sentences are far too long to be used in real life. Most sentences, even ones of fairly modest length, express things that are too bizarre ever to say, much less mean (the really long ones express things that are just too complex to understand).

This sampling error compounds the mistake of supposing that intuitive contents are semantic contents. Recognizing this error leads to a simple argument that encapsulates the disconnect between seemingly semantic intuitions and the semantics of sentences:

1. Most of the syntactically well-formed sentences of a natural language, even those of a reasonable length, do not express things we are ever likely to mean.

2. A natural language is not so designed that most of its sentences, even among those of utterable length, are sentences anyone would ever have occasion to use.
3. But if the semantic content of a sentence is its 'intuitive content', then if it doesn't have an intuitive content, it doesn't have a semantic content.
4. The contents of most sentences are just too weird to be their intuitive semantic contents.
5. So, either most sentences either don't have semantic contents or their semantic contents are not their intuitive contents.
6. All well-formed sentences, even useless ones, have semantic contents.
∴ The semantic contents of most sentences are not their intuitive contents.

8   Semantic Illusions

I have suggested that seemingly semantic intuitions are often illusory be-cause they tend to be insensitive to the difference between semantic facts and pragmatic regularities. So we cannot rely on such intuitions too heavily and should not draw hasty conclusions about the semantic content of a given sentence just because we have imagined the likely import of a typical utterance of it. Also, seemingly semantic intuitions can combine with sim-plistic theoretical assumptions about semantics to yield a variety of seman-tic illusions:

The conventionalization illusion: that a regularized use of an expression or construction can only be a matter of meaning (or semantic convention). This illusion assumes that there cannot be pragmatic regularities, cases of standardization without conventionalization of use.

The assertion illusion: that the semantic content of a declarative sentence is what a speaker would be asserting (the content of the belief he would be expressing) if he sincerely uttered it and used all of its constituent expres-sions literally. This illusion conflates minimal assertions with locutionary acts.

The processing illusion: that a proposition does not qualify as what is said in the utterance of a sentence if it is not represented in the process of under-standing the utterance. This illusion conflates information which is repre-sented in a cognitive process with information which is accessible to the process and to which the process is sensitive.

The illusion of utterance (or token) semantics: that because sentences (gen-erally) are neither true nor false independently of contexts of utterances, the proper subject of semantics is utterances, not sentences. This illusion trades on the ambiguity of 'utterance', which can mean either an uttered sentence or the act of uttering it. The problem is that the semantics of utterances in the first sense is sentence semantics and that the study of contents of acts of utterance belongs to pragmatics. So there is no role for utterance semantics.

The said-if-not-implicated illusion: that if a speaker means something that he doesn't merely implicate, he must be saying it. This illusion treats saying and implicating as an exclusive dichotomy. It overlooks the fact that part of what a speaker means can be implicit in what he says or, rather, in his saying it. This illusion is aided and abetted by the rampant use in certain circles of the neologism *explicature,* which is a cognate of *explicate* but is nevertheless used as if it meant explicit content. An explicature spells out something that is not explicit in what is said. It makes explicit what isn't. A better term is *impliciture*.[15]

The illusion of context dependence: that when content varies from one context to another, the variation in content depends on features of the context. This illusion conflates contextual variability with context dependence.

The one sentence, one proposition illusion: that a declarative sentence always expresses (modulo ambiguity and indexicality) one and only one proposition. In fact, many sentences fail to express a complete proposition, and many sentences express more than one proposition.[16]

9 Bridging the Gap

The semantic-pragmatic distinction is a well-defined and theoretically warranted distinction. Maintaining it requires recognizing the limitations of semantics and the reach of pragmatics. Semantics concerns the meanings of sentences, but these often fail to determine complete propositions, even modulo ambiguity, vagueness, and indexicality. As long as it is not assumed that the job of semantics is to give truth conditions of (declarative) sentences, there is no reason to suppose that pragmatics needs to intrude on semantics. This is to be expected, since pragmatics is concerned with utterances of sentences, not with sentences themselves. The fact that a speaker utters a sentence plays a key role in what he can reasonably expect to communicate in uttering it and in what the listener can reasonably take him to be communicating. When a sentence is uttered, it does not encode the fact that it is uttered. This is essentially a pragmatic fact.

References

Austin, J. L. 1962. *How to do Things with Words*. Oxford: Oxford University Press.

---

[15]The notion of conversational impliciture was introduced and explained in Bach 1994.
[16]For a detailed diagnosis and discussion of the second part of this illusion, see Bach 1999b: 343-55.

Bach, K. 1994. Conversational Impliciture. *Mind & Language* 9: 124-62.

Bach, K. 1999a. The Semantics-Pragmatics Distinction: What It Is and Why It Matters. *The Semantics-Pragmatics Interface from Different Points of View*, ed. K. Turner, 65-84. Oxford: Elsevier.

Bach, K. 1999b. The Myth of Conventional Implicature. *Linguistics and Philosophy* 22: 327-66.

Bach, K. 2001a. You Don't Say? *Synthèse* 128: 15-44.

Bach, K. 2001b. Speaking loosely: Sentence Nonliterality. *Midwest Studies in Philosophy*, vol. 25: *Figurative Language*, ed. P. French and H. Wettstein, 249-63. Oxford: Blackwell.

Bach, K. 2002. Seemingly Semantic Intuitions. *Meaning and Truth*, ed. J. K. Campbell, M. O'Rourke, and D. Shier, 21-33. New York: Seven Bridges Press.

Bach, K. forthcoming a. Context ex Machina. *Semantics vs. Pragmatics,* ed. Z. Szabò. Oxford: Oxford University Press.

Bach, K. forthcoming b. Speech Acts and Pragmatics. *The Blackwell Guide to the Philosophy of Language,* ed. M. Devitt and R. Hanley. Oxford: Blackwell.

Bach, K. and R. M. Harnish 1979. *Linguistic Communication and Speech Acts.* Cambridge, MA: MIT Press.

Grice, H. P. 1957. Meaning. *Philosophical Review* 66: 377-88.

Grice, H. P. 1989. *Studies in the Way of Words*, Cambridge, MA: Harvard University Press.

Lambrecht, K. 1994. *Information Structure and Sentence Form.* Cambridge: Cambridge University Press.

Strawson, P. F. 1964. Intention and Convention in Speech Acts. *Philosophical Review* 73: 439-60.

4

'What is Said' and the Semantics/Pragmatics Distinction

FRANÇOIS RECANATI

1

It is customary in pragmatics to ascribe to an utterance literal truth-conditions at variance with the intuitive truth-conditions which the conversational participants themselves would ascribe to that utterance. For example, the proposition literally expressed by

(1)   I have three children

is standardly taken to be the proposition that the speaker has at least three children, i.e., no less than three but possibly more. In certain contexts this corresponds to what the speaker actually means (as when I say, 'If I have three children I can benefit from lower rates on public transport') but in other contexts what the speaker means is quite different. Suppose for example that I am asked how many children I have and that I reply by uttering (1). Clearly, in this context, I mean that I have (exactly) three children – no more and no less. This is standardly accounted for by saying that the proposition literally expressed, to the effect that I have at least three children, combines with the 'implicature' that I have no more than three children (a generalized implicature that is accounted for in terms of the maxim of quan-

The Semantics/Pragmatics Distinction.
Claudia Bianchi (ed.).
Copyright © 2004, CSLI Publications.

tity);[1] as a result of this combination, what is globally communicated – and what I actually mean – is the proposition that I have exactly three children. Now *this is the only proposition I am conscious of expressing by my utterance*; in particular, I am unaware of having expressed the 'minimal' proposition that I have at least three children. To account for this obvious fact, the theorist claims that we are aware only of what is globally conveyed or 'communicated' by the utterance. Analyzing this into 'what is literally said' and 'what is implied' is the linguist's task, not something that is incumbent upon the normal language user. Figure 1 illustrates this widespread conception.

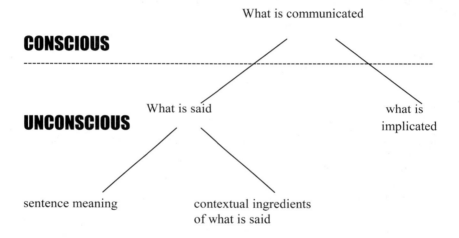

What is communicated

CONSCIOUS

UNCONSCIOUS

What is said

what is implicated

sentence meaning

contextual ingredients of what is said

Figure 1: The standard approach

One problem with this conception is that it lacks generality. It turns out that there are two sorts of case. On the one hand there are prototypical cases of implied meaning, in which the participants in the speech situation are aware both of what is said and of what is implied, and also of the inferential connection between them. On the other hand, there are the cases illustrated by (1). Given his willingness to treat certain aspects of the intuitive meaning of (1) as conversational implicatures external to what is literally said, the theorist must explain why those implicatures, unlike the prototypical cases, do not have the property of conscious 'availability'.

---

[1] As Grice puts it in one if his early papers, 'one should not make a weaker statement rather than a stronger one unless there is a good reason for so doing' (Grice 1961: 132).

The only explanation I have come across in the literature makes use of Grice's distinction between 'generalized' and 'particularized' conversational implicatures, i.e., between implicatures which arise 'by default', without any particular context or special scenario being necessary, and those which require such specific contexts. In contrast to the latter, the former are 'hard to distinguish from the *semantic* content of linguistic expressions, because such implicatures [are] routinely associated with linguistic expressions in all ordinary contexts' (Levinson 1983: 127). Generalized implicatures are unconsciously and automatically generated and interpreted. They belong to the 'micropragmatic' rather than to the 'macropragmatic' level, in Robin Campbell's typology:

> A macropragmatic process is one constituted by a sequence of explicit inferences governed by principles of rational cooperation. A micropragmatic process develops as a cryptic [= unconscious] and heuristic procedure which partially replaces some macropragmatic process and which defaults to it in the event of breakdown (Campbell 1981: 101).

But there are problems with this explanation. According to Horn (1992), the generalized nature of an implicature does not entail its conscious unavailability – its 'cryptic' character. In other words, it is possible for an implicature to be both 'generalized' and intuitively accessible as an implicature distinct from what is said. Thus Horn insists that the generalized scalar implicature from 'some' to 'not all' *is* consciously available (in contrast to that from 'three' to 'exactly three'). A speaker saying 'Some students came to the meeting' normally implies that not all students came, and when this is so there is (Horn claims) no tendency on the part of the interpreter to conflate the implicature with what is said. This is actually debatable, for the 'implicature' at issue can arise at the sub-sentential level (e.g., 'He believes some students came'), and in such cases there are reasons to doubt that the availability condition is satisfied. Be that as it may, the 'generalization' of an implicature does not seem to be necessary for its unconscious character. Many particularized 'bridging' inferences are automatic and unconscious. To take an example from Robyn Carston (1988), 'He went to the cliff and jumped' is readily interpreted as saying that the person referred to jumped *over the cliff*, even though this is only contextually suggested.

2

In earlier writings (Recanati 1989, 1993, 2001) I put forward a conception diametrically opposed to that illustrated by Figure 1 above. 'What is said', I held, *is* consciously available to the participants in the speech situation (Figure 2).

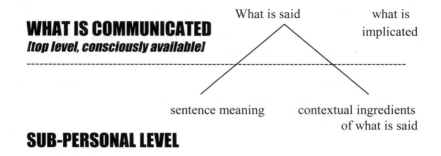

WHAT IS COMMUNICATED
[top level, consciously available]

What is said   what is
                                 implicated

sentence meaning   contextual ingredients
                        of what is said

SUB-PERSONAL LEVEL

Figure 2: The availability based approach

In this framework 'what is communicated' is not a distinct level where 'what is said' and 'what is implied' have been merged and integrated into a unified whole; it is merely a name for the level at which we find both what is said and what is implied, which level is characterized by conscious accessibility. On this picture, there are only two basic levels: the bottom level at which we find both the abstract meaning of the sentence and the contextual factors which combine with it to yield what is said; and the top level at which we find both what is said and what is implied, both being consciously accessible (and accessible as distinct).

The availability of what is said follows from Grice's idea that saying itself is a variety of nonnatural meaning (Grice 1989). One of the distinguishing characteristics of nonnatural meaning, on Grice's analysis, is its essential overtness. Nonnatural meaning works by openly letting the addressee recognize one's primary intention (e.g., the intention to impart a certain piece of information, or the intention to have the addressee behave in a certain way), that is, by (openly) expressing that intention so as to make it graspable. This can be done in all sorts of ways, verbal or nonverbal. Even if we restrict ourselves to verbal communication, there are many ways in which we can mean things by uttering words. *Saying* is one way; *implying* is another one.

The view that 'saying' is a variety of nonnatural meaning entails that what is said (like what is meant in general, including what is implied) *must* be available – it must be open to public view. That is so because nonnatural meaning is essentially a matter of intention-recognition. On this view what is said by uttering a sentence depends upon, and can hardly be severed from, the speaker's publicly recognizable intentions. Hence my 'Availability Principle' (Recanati 1993: 248), according to which 'what is said' must be analyzed in conformity to the intuitions shared by those who fully understand the utterance – typically the speaker and the hearer, in a normal conversational setting.

I take the conversational participants' intuitions concerning what is said to be revealed by their views concerning the utterance's truth-conditions. I assume that whoever fully understands a declarative utterance knows which state of affairs would possibly constitute a truth-maker for that utterance, i.e., knows in what sort of circumstance it would be true. The ability to pair an utterance with a type of situation in this way is more basic than, and in any case does not presuppose, the ability to *report* what is said by using indirect speech; it does not even presuppose mastery of the notion of 'saying'. Thus the proper way to elicit such intuitions is not to ask the subjects 'What do you think is said (as opposed to implied or whatever) by this sentence as uttered in that situation'? I therefore agree with Bach's criticism of the experiments through which Gibbs and Moise (1997) attempted to support my availability based approach:

> [They] thought they could get their data about what is said, and thereby test the validity of Recanati's Availability Principle, by asking people what is said by a given utterance, or by asking them whether something that is conveyed by a given utterance is implicated or merely said. Evidently they assume that what people *say* about what is said is strongly indicative of what *is* said. In fact, what it is indicative of is how people apply the phrase 'what is said'... It tells us little about what is said, much less about the cognitive processes whereby people understand utterances (Bach 2002: 27).

However, Bach himself uses what he calls the 'IQ test' to determine what is said, that is, *he ties what is said to indirect speech reports of what is said* (Bach 1994a: 278, 1999, 2001). I find this procedure most objectionable, and that is *not* what I mean when I claim that what is said should be individuated according to the intuitions of normal interpreters. Thus I strongly disagree with Cappelen and Lepore's surprising statement:

> We ourselves don't see how to elicit intuitions about what-is-said by an utterance of a sentence without appealing to intuitions about the accuracy of indirect reports of the form 'He said that...' or 'What he said is that...' or even 'What was said is that...' (Cappelen and Lepore 1997: 280).

I find this statement surprising, because there obviously *is* another way of eliciting truth-conditional intuitions. One has simply to provide subjects with scenarios describing situations, or, even better, with – possibly animated – pictures of situations, and to ask them to evaluate the target utterance as true or false with respect to the situations in question. That procedure has been used by several researchers to test speaker's intuitions about e.g. the truth-conditions of donkey sentences. Thus Bart Geurts describes his experimental set-up (inspired from earlier work by Yoon) as follows:

> Twenty native speakers of Dutch were asked to judge whether or not donkey sentences correctly described pictured situations. Instructions urged subjects to answer either true or false, but they were also given the option of leaving the matter open in case they couldn't make up their minds (Geurts 2002: 135).

This procedure presupposes that normal interpreters have intuitions concerning the truth-conditional content of utterances. On my view, those intuitions correspond to a certain 'level' in the comprehension process – a level that a proper theory of language understanding must capture. That is the level of 'what is said'.

3

From a psychological point of view, we can draw a helpful parallel between understanding what one is told and understanding what one sees. In vision, the retinal stimuli undergo a complex (multistage) train of processing which ultimately outputs a conscious perception, with the dual character noted by Brentano: the subject is aware both of what he sees, and of the fact that he is seeing it. Although more complex in certain respects, the situation with language is similar. The auditory signal undergoes a multistage train of processing which ultimately outputs a conceptual experience: the subject understands what is said. This is very much like (high-level) perception. If I am told that it is four o'clock, I hear that it is four o'clock, just as, when I look at my watch, I see that it is four o'clock. Like the visual experience, the locutionary experience possesses a dual character: we are aware both of what is said, and of the fact that the speaker is saying it.

In calling understanding an *experience*, like perception, I want to stress its conscious character. Understanding an utterance involves entertaining a mental representation of what it says that is both determinate enough (truth-evaluable) *and* consciously available to the subject. Thus we may equate 'what is said' with (the semantic content of) the conscious output of the complex train of processing which underlies comprehension. As Ian Rumfitt once put it, 'what is said in the course of an utterance is nothing other than what somebody who understands the utterance understands to be said' (Rumfitt 1993: 439).

To be sure, that output itself is subject to further processing through e.g. inferential exploitation. Consider, once again, vision. Seeing John's car, I can infer that he is around. Similarly, hearing John say that it is late, I can infer that he wants me to leave. Just as what is seen corresponds to the primary conscious output of visual processing, not to what can be secondarily derived from it, 'what is said' corresponds to the primary truth-evaluable representation made available to the subject (at the personal level) as a result of processing the sentence.

Accordingly, I distinguish between two sorts of pragmatic process. The contextual processes which are (subpersonally) involved in the determination of what is said I call *primary* pragmatic processes. In contrast, *secondary* pragmatic processes are ordinary inferential processes taking us from what is said, or rather from the speaker's saying of what is said, to something that (under standard assumptions of rationality and cooperativeness) follows from the fact that the speaker has said what she has said. To the extent that the speaker overtly intends the hearer to recognize such consequences as following from her speech act, they form an integral part of what the speaker means by her utterance. That is, roughly, Grice's theory of 'conversational implicature' (Grice 1989). An essential aspect of that theory is that the hearer must be able to recognize what is said and to work out the inferential connection between what is said and what is implied by saying it. Again, it follows that what is said must be consciously available to the interpreter. It must satisfy what I call the Availability constraint.

4

The psychological notion of 'what is said' we end up with by following this route is different from the standard notion used in semantics: it is not as close to the linguistic meaning of the sentence. To get what is said in the standard, semantic sense, we must assign semantic values to indexicals and free variables in logical form. That process, which I call 'saturation', is (besides disambiguation) the only pragmatic process that is allowed to affect what is said in the standard semantic sense. However, there are other pragmatic processes which contribute to shaping what is said in the *psychological* sense. In contrast to saturation, which is linguistically mandated (bottom up), the other pragmatic processes are optional and context-driven (top-down), so they are construed as semantically irrelevant. The paradigm case is free enrichment, illustrated by example (2):

(2)   Mary took out her key and opened the door

In virtue of a 'bridging inference', we naturally understand the second con-junct as meaning that Mary opened the door with the key mentioned in the first conjunct; yet this is not explicitly articulated in the sentence.

In typical cases free enrichment consists in making the interpretation of some expression in the sentence contextually more specific. This process has sometimes been described in the literature as 'specifization'. For exam-ple the mass term 'rabbit' will be preferentially interpreted as meaning *rab-bit fur* in the context of 'He wears rabbit' and as meaning *rabbit meat* in the context of 'He eats rabbit' (Nunberg and Zaenen 1992). This not a matter of selecting a particular value in a finite set; with a little imagination, one can think of dozens of possible interpretations for 'rabbit' by manipulating the stipulated context of utterance; and there is no limit to the number of inter-pretations one can imagine in such a way. Nor can the process of specifiza-tion be construed as linguistically mandated, that is, as involving a hidden variable. Were it linguistically mandated (bottom up), it would be manda-tory, but it is not: In some contexts the mass term 'rabbit' means nothing more than RABBIT STUFF ('after the accident, there was rabbit all over the highway').

The converse of enrichment is loosening (Sperber and Wilson 1986, Carston 1996).[2] There is loosening whenever a condition of application packed into the concept literally expressed by a predicate is contextually dropped so that the application of the predicate is widened. An example is 'The ATM swallowed my credit card'. There can be no real swallowing on the part of an ATM, since ATMs are not living organisms with the right bodily equipment for swallowing. By relaxing the conditions of application for 'swallow', we construct an *ad hoc* concept with wider application.

A third type of primary pragmatic process that is not linguistically man-dated (bottom up) but contextually driven is semantic transfer (Nunberg 1979, 1995). In transfer the output is neither an enriched nor an impover-ished version of the concept literally expressed by the input expression. It is a different concept altogether, bearing a systematic relation to it. Thus 'parked out back' denotes either the property a car has when it is parked out back, or a different property, namely the property a car-owner has whenever his or her car has the former property ('I am parked out back'). Arguably, 'parked out back' literally denotes the former property, and comes to denote the latter property as a result of transfer (Nunberg 1995). Similarly, the ex-

---

[2]Similar notions include 'feature cancellation' (Cohen 1971, Franks 1995) and 'pragmatic generalization' as opposed to 'pragmatic specialization' (Ruhl 1989). Paul Ziff speaks of 'augmenting' and 'diminishing' senses (Ziff 1972: 719).

pression 'ham sandwich' in 'The ham sandwich left without paying' arguably denotes, through transfer, the derived property HAM_SANDWICH_ORDERER rather than the linguistically encoded property HAM_SANDWICH.

Despite their optional character, pragmatic processes such as enrichment, loosening and transfer affect the intuitive truth-conditions of utterances. If we use the availability criterion to demarcate what is said, as I suggest, then such processes must be treated as primary rather than secondary. And the same consideration applies to the so-called generalized conversational implicature which is responsible for the 'exactly' reading of the numeral in example (1). In this way, we solve the difficulty raised in Section 1. We no longer have two sorts of case of implicature – the prototypical cases where the interlocutors are aware of what is said, aware of what is implied, and aware of the inferential connection between them, and the cases in which there is no such awareness. Conscious awareness is now a built-in feature of both what is said and the implicatures. That is so because what is said is the conscious output of linguistic-*cum*-pragmatic processing, and the implicatures correspond to further conscious representations inferentially derived, at the personal rather than sub-personal level, from what is said (or, rather, from the speaker's saying what is said). The alleged cases in which the speech participants themselves are not distinctly aware of what is said and of what is implied are reclassified: they are no longer treated as cases of 'implicature', strictly speaking, but as cases in which a primary pragmatic process operates in the (sub-personal) determination of what is said.

5

So far I have followed Grice, who construes saying as a variety of meaning. But this pragmatic approach to 'saying' is controversial. Most philosophers use the notion of 'what is said' (or 'the proposition expressed') in such a way that it is *not* a 'pragmatic' notion – having to do with what the speaker means or with what the hearer understands. What is said is supposed to be a property of the *sentence* (with respect to the context at hand) – a property which it has in virtue of the rules of the language.

I will discuss the nonpragmatic construal of what is said in the next section. For the time being, I am interested in the pragmatic construal, based on Grice's idea, and the alleged objections it raises.

The first objection is this. If, following Grice, we construe saying as a variety of meaning, we will be prevented from acknowledging an important class of cases in which the speaker does not mean what he says. Irony is a good example of that class of cases. If I say 'John is a fine friend' ironically, in a context in which it is obvious to everybody that I think just the opposite, it is clear that I do not mean what I say: I mean the opposite. Still, I *say* that John is a fine friend. Grice's construal of saying as a variety of meaning prevents him from acknowledging that fact. According to Grice, when I say 'John is a fine friend' in the mentioned situation, I do not *really* say that John is a fine friend – I *pretend* to be saying it. The pragmatic construal of saying forces Grice to draw a distinction between 'saying' and 'making as if to say'.

As far as I am concerned, I find Grice's distinction (between genuine saying and making as if to say) perfectly legitimate, but I can understand the worries of those who feel that the notion of 'saying' he uses is too much on the pragmatic side. We certainly need a notion of 'what is said' which captures *the objective content of an utterance irrespective of its pragmatic force as a serious assertion or as an ironical utterance*. Still, I find the objection superficial, for it is quite easy actually to construct the desired notion within Grice's own framework. Grice uses 'say' in a strict sense. In that sense whatever is said must be meant. But we can easily define a broader sense for 'say':

> S says that p, in the broad sense, iff he either says that p (in the strict sense) or makes as if to say that p (again, in the strict sense of 'say').

I will henceforth use 'say' in that broad sense, which remains within the confines of the pragmatic construal.

Another objection to the pragmatic construal focuses on the loss of objectivity that allegedly goes with it. What is said is objective in the sense that it is possible both for the speaker to make a mistake and say something other than what he means, and for the hearer to misunderstand what the speaker is saying. Those mistakes are possible, the objector will argue, because what is said is an objective property of the sentence (in context). But on the pragmatic construal, it is not clear that this objectivity can be captured. Imagine the following situation: the speaker wants to say that Paul is tall, and, mistaking Tim for Paul, says 'He is tall' while pointing to Tim. The speaker thus inadvertently says that Tim is tall. Now imagine that the hearer also mistakes Tim for Paul. Thanks to this lucky mistake, he grasps what the speaker means, thinking that this is what he has said. The speaker and the hearer therefore converge on a certain interpretation, which is not objectively what was said, but which they both (mistakenly) think is what was said. How, in the framework I have sketched, will it be possible to dissociate what is actually said from the protagonists' mistaken apprehension of what is said? Have we not equated what is said with their understanding of what is said?

We have not. We have equated what is said with what a *normal interpreter* would understand as being said, in the context at hand. A normal interpreter knows which sentence was uttered, knows the meaning of that sentence, knows the relevant contextual facts (who is being pointed to, etc.).[3] Ordinary users of the language *are* normal interpreters, in most situations. They know the relevant facts and have the relevant abilities. But there are situations (as in the above example) where the actual users make mistakes and are not normal interpreters. In such situations their interpretations do not fix what is said. To determine what is said, we need to look at the interpretation that a normal interpreter would give. This is objective enough, yet remains within the confines of the pragmatic construal.

6

I have presented the availability based approach as an alternative to the standard view. But why not combine them? Many authors hold that *there are two equally legitimate notions of what is said*: a purely semantic notion, corresponding to the 'minimal' proposition resulting from saturation, and a pragmatic or psychological notion corresponding to the content of the speech act actually performed by uttering the sentence ('what is stated', as Bach puts it). Only what is said in the pragmatic sense needs to satisfy the Availability constraint. So one can maintain that (1) expresses the proposition that the speaker has at least three children, while conceding that what the speaker states is that he has exactly three children. On this picture saturation maps the linguistic meaning of a sentence to the minimal proposition literally expressed, while primary pragmatic processes of the optional variety map that proposition to that which is actually asserted (Figure 3).

This view – which I call the Syncretic View – has been argued for by many authors, such as Kent Bach, Nathan Salmon, and Jonathan Berg. A recent statement can be found in Scott Soames' book *Beyond Rigidity*. He writes:

> When speaking of the information carried by an assertive utterance of a sentence in a context, one must distinguish (i) the semantic content of the sentence uttered in the context; (ii) what the speaker says (asserts) by uttering the sentence; (iii) what the speaker implies, implicates, or suggests... (i) is standardly included in (ii), but... in the case of many utterances, (ii) is not exhausted by (i) (Soames 2002: 86).

---

[3]This is all tacit knowledge, not the sort of 'conscious awareness' I talk about in connection with the Availability Principle.

What we have at level (i) is already a truth-evaluable proposition: a Kaplanian 'content' (as opposed to a Kaplanian 'character'). But it is, or may be, distinct from the (typically more specific) proposition that is the content of the speech act. This proposition, which we find at level (ii), heavily depends upon speaker's intentions, background assumptions, etc., yet it does not include what the speaker 'implies' by saying what he says (in the pragmatic sense).

In Recanati 2001 I have criticized the Syncretic View, on the following grounds. What is said, in the purely semantic sense, is generally taken to be what *the sentence* says as opposed to what *the speaker* says. As such, it is supposed to be determined by the rules of the language (with respect to the context) independently of speaker's meaning. As Bach points out, what is said, in the semantic sense, 'excludes anything that is determined by [the speaker's] communicative intention (if it included that, then what is said would be partly a pragmatic matter)' (Bach 2001: 21). Precisely for that reason, I claim that there is no such thing: no such thing as a complete proposition autonomously determined by the rules of the language with

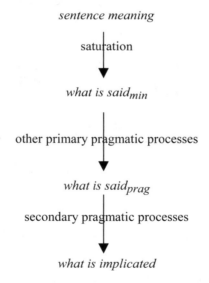

Figure 3: The Syncretic View

respect to the context but independent of speaker's meaning. In order to reach a complete proposition through saturation, we *must* appeal to speaker's meaning. That is the lesson of semantic underdeterminacy. Thus the demonstrative pronoun 'he' refers to the male person whom the speaker who utters the demonstrative refers to in uttering it. No semantic reference without speaker's reference, in such a case. Because of the well-documented phenomenon of semantic underdeterminacy, there is no such thing as 'what the sentence says' (thus understood).

There is another possible interpretation for the semantic notion of 'what is said', however. Instead of construing what is said as a nonpragmatic property of the sentence, independent of speaker's meaning, we can start with the pragmatic notion of what is said, and define the semantic notion in terms of it. What is said in the minimal sense can thus be defined as what is said in the full-fledged, pragmatic sense *minus* the contextual ingredients that are optional and whose provision is context-driven. To filter out the optional ingredients, while retaining the contextual ingredients that are necessary for propositionality (reference of indexicals, etc.), one may follow Soames and define the semantic content of a sentence s relative to a context C as

> that which would be asserted and conveyed by an assertive utterance of s in any normal context in which the reference of all indexicals in s is the same as their reference in C (Soames 2002: 106).

Soames' strategy therefore consists in *abstracting* what is said in the semantic sense *from* what is said in the pragmatic sense. That is possible because, according to Soames, the semantic content of the sentence is *included in* the content of the assertion. To get to the semantic content, one only has to filter out those aspects of assertion content that go beyond semantic content and are tied to specific contexts of utterance. What remains, i.e. the 'common denominator', is the minimal proposition expressed by the sentence itself:

> The semantic content of a sentence relative to a context is information that a competent speaker/hearer can confidently take to be asserted and conveyed by an utterance of the sentence in the context, no matter what else may be asserted, conveyed, or imparted. It is a sort of minimal common denominator determined by the linguistic knowledge shared by all competent speakers, together with contextually relevant facts such as the time, place, and agent of the context; the identity of individuals demonstrated by the speaker; and the referents of the names, as used in the context. As such, the semantic content of a sentence functions as a sort of minimal core around which speaker/hearers can structure the totality of information the sentence is used to communicate in a given context (Soames 2002: 109).

This alternative strategy is also a failure, however. What is said in the minimal, semantic sense cannot be abstracted from what is said in the pragmatic sense simply because *it need not be part of it*. Soames' claim that semantic content is included in assertion content seems plausible because his examples are all cases in which the asserted content is richer than the alleged semantic content. He gives the following sort of example:

> A man goes into a coffee shop and sits at the counter. The waitress asks him what he wants. He says, 'I would like coffee, please.' The sentence uttered is unspecific in several respects – its semantic content does not indicate whether the coffee is to be in form of beans, grounds, or liquid, nor does it indicate whether the amount in question is a drop, a cup, a gallon, a sack, or a barrel. Nevertheless, it is obvious from the situation what the man has in mind, and the waitress is in no doubt about what to do. She brings him a cup of freshly brewed coffee. If asked to describe the transaction, she might well say, 'He ordered a cup of coffee' or 'He said he wanted a cup of coffee', meaning, of course, the brewed, drinkable kind. In so doing, she would, quite correctly, be reporting the content of the man's order, or assertion, as going beyond the semantic content of the sentence he uttered (Soames 2002: 78).

Now Soames thinks that in such cases several propositions are asserted, including (i) the unspecific proposition literally expressed (to the effect that the man wants coffee in some form or other) and (ii) more specific propositions recoverable from the literal proposition and the context. Those more specific propositions resulting from enrichment are tied to the particular context in which they are generated, hence they can be filtered out by considering other contexts in which that sentence would be uttered and the indexicals would be given the same semantic values. Soames equates the minimal proposition expressed by the sentence with the proposition which would be asserted in *all* such contexts.

The problem is that enrichment is only one pragmatic process among others. Beside enrichment, there are other primary pragmatic processes, like loosening or semantic transfer, which are optional and take us away from the 'minimal' proposition allegedly expressed by the sentence. Only in the case of enrichment, however, is it plausible to suggest that the minimal proposition itself is part of what is asserted.

Soames glosses assertion in terms of commitment: 'assertively uttering a sentence with the intention to assert or convey p involves doing so with the intention of committing oneself to p' (Soames 2002: 73). Since one cannot commit oneself to the truth of a specific proposition p without committing oneself to the truth of a less specific proposition q which it entails, it makes sense to say that the minimal proposition q is asserted when one (intuitively) asserts an enriched proposition p. But the principle that the minimal proposition is part of what is asserted (hence can be abstracted from it) does not hold when the primary processes at issue are instances of loosening or transfer. The speaker who assertively utters 'The ham sandwich left without paying', thereby referring to the ham sandwich orderer, does not assert the minimal proposition that the sandwich itself left without paying! Hence the minimal proposition cannot be defined as the common denominator – what is asserted in all contexts in which the sentence is uttered and the indexicals are given the same semantic values as in the current context.

To be sure, the counterexamples involving loosening or semantic transfer are taken care of, in Soame's framework, by the notion of a 'normal' context, that is, of a context in which the sentence 'is used with its literal meaning', i.e. 'is not used metaphorically, ironically, or sarcastically'. However this qualification cannot be invoked in the context of the present debate without begging the question. We are supposed to start with the intuitive (pragmatic) notion of what is said, which sometimes *is* affected by loosening or transfer. If, following Soames, we want to build the notion of the minimal proposition out of what is said in that sense, we cannot arbitrarily set aside the cases that potentially threaten the enterprise.

7

The minimal proposition which the Syncretic View posits as the semantic content of the utterance, and which results from saturating the (disambiguated) meaning of the sentence, is not autonomously determined by the rules of the language independently of speaker's meaning. At the same time, the minimal proposition does not necessarily correspond to an aspect of what the speaker asserts. The minimal proposition is a hybrid which goes beyond what is determined by the rules of the language yet has no psychological reality and need not be entertained or represented at any point in the process of understanding the utterance (Recanati 1995, 2001).

Do we need such a notion in theorizing about language and communication? Many philosophers and linguists claim that we do, but I can hardly understand why. In a recent paper ('Semantics, Pragmatics, and the Role of Semantic Content'), King and Stanley argue against semantic theories which ascribe (functional) characters to sentences on the basis of the characters of their parts, on the grounds that 'the job of character is to give us content, and we can assign contents to complex expressions in contexts using only the characters of the parts, and combining the contents they determine in those contexts.' They conclude that

Both a semantics that assigns characters to simple expressions and recursively assigns characters to complex expressions *and* a semantics that assigns characters to only simple expressions allow for an assignment of the same contents in contexts to simple and complex expressions. So unless the functional characters of complex expressions have some *additional* job to do, they are unnecessary. But there seems to be no such additional job.

The same sort of argument seems to me to rule out the minimal proposition as unnecessary. What must ultimately be accounted for is what speakers say in the pragmatic sense. The job of characters, contents etc. is to contribute to the overall explanation. But it is sufficient to assign semantic contents (in context) to simple expressions. Pragmatic processes will operate on those contents, and the composition rules will compose the resulting pragmatic values, thereby yielding the content of the speaker's assertion. Of course it is possible to let the composition rules compose the semantic contents of the constituent expressions, thereby yielding the minimal proposition expressed by the sentence. (An absurd proposition, in many cases.) However, the content of the speaker's assertion will still be determined by composing the pragmatic values resulting from the operation of pragmatic processes on the contents of the constituent expressions; so it is unclear what additional job the minimal proposition is supposed to be doing.

If one insists in using a purely semantic notion of 'what is said', i.e. a notion of what is said which is propositional (truth-evaluable) yet 'excludes anything that is determined by the speaker's communicative intention', there is a much better candidate than the alleged minimal proposition. For every utterance, there arguably is a proposition which it expresses in virtue solely of the rules of the language, independent of speaker's meaning: that is the 'reflexive' proposition in the sense of John Perry (a variant of Stalnaker's diagonal proposition).[4] The main difference between the minimal proposition and the reflexive proposition is that the reflexive proposition is determined *before* the process of saturation takes place. The reflexive proposition cannot be determined unless the sentence is tokened, but no substantial knowledge of the context of utterance is required to determine it. Thus an utterance u of the sentence 'I am French' expresses the reflexive proposition that *the utterer of u is French*.[5] That it does not presuppose saturation is precisely what makes the reflexive proposition useful, since in most cases saturation proceeds by appeal to speaker's meaning. If one wants a proposi-

---

[4]See Stalnaker 1999; Perry 2001.

[5]This is distinct from, and additional to, the singular proposition which the speaker asserts, to the effect that he or she is French. Perry distinguishes several levels of content for a single utterance. The (minimal) singular proposition is the 'official content', but the reflexive proposition plays a crucial role from a cognitive point of view.

tion that is determined on purely semantic grounds, one had better not have it depend upon the process of saturation.

Soames considers the possibility of equating 'what the sentence says' with the reflexive proposition or something close to it, but he rejects that option with the following argument:

> Consider... the first-person singular pronoun as it occurs in a sentence *I am F*. There is no such thing as 'what this sentence says' independent of the context of utterance in which it is used. The competence conditions associated with the first-person singular pronoun guarantee that when I assertively utter the sentence, I use it to say something about me, whereas when you assertively utter it, you use it to say something about you. One might be tempted to suppose that there is some more general thing that the sentence 'says' in every context – namely, the proposition expressed by *the speaker is F* (or some such thing). But this will not do. Our notion of 'what a sentence says' is tied to what speakers who assertively utter the sentence say. Typically, when I assertively utter *I am F*, I don't assert that I am speaking or using language at all. Further, the proposition that I assert when I assertively utter such a sentence may be true in a possible circumstance in which no one is using language, and someone may believe this proposition without believing anything about me being a speaker (Soames 2002: 104).

Soames' main objection is that the alleged reflexive proposition is not (part of) what the speaker asserts. As we have seen, however, the same thing often holds for the minimal proposition posited by the syncretists. The advantage of the reflexive proposition over the minimal proposition is that it (the reflexive proposition) is determined solely by the rules of the language, independently of speaker's meaning, in such a way that there *is* a path to the reflexive proposition that does not go through the speaker's meaning; hence it does not matter much if that proposition cannot be reached by abstraction from what the speaker asserts.

The reflexive proposition is admittedly distinct from that which the speaker asserts – they have different possible worlds truth-conditions, as Soames points out – but why is this an objection? In the 'syncretic' framework advocated by Soames, are we not supposed to draw a distinction between *the proposition expressed by the sentence* and *the proposition asserted by the speaker who utters that sentence*? Note that we can, if we wish, incorporate into the reflexive proposition something to the effect that the linguistic mode of presentation associated with the first person pronoun will not be part of the proposition asserted, while the reference it contextually determines will be. Thus we might take the reflexive proposition expressed by an utterance *u* of 'I am French' to be the proposition that *there is an x such that x utters u and u is true iff x is French*. This comes as close as one can get to capturing, in propositional format, the information provided by the utterance in virtue solely of the linguistic meaning of the sentence 'I am French'. (See Recanati 1993 for an analysis along those lines.) Such a reflexive proposition determines that the proposition contextually asserted by 'I am French' will consist of the reference of 'I' and the property of being French. The reflexive proposition is therefore 'tied to what speakers who assertively utter the sentence say', even if it is not (part of) what they say.

I conclude that there may be a way of preserving the notion of 'what the sentence says', in the purely semantic sense, if one wants to; but it does not support the Syncretic View with its four levels (sentence meaning, what is said in the semantic sense, what is said in the pragmatic sense, and what is implied). What characterizes the reflexive proposition is that, although fully propositional, it does not incorporate those contextual ingredients whose provision is linguistically mandated; it is much closer to the linguistic meaning of the sentence – indeed it is directly and immediately determined by the linguistic meaning of the sentence. Appealing to the reflexive proposition instead of the minimal proposition takes us back to the availability based approach with its three basic levels: the linguistic meaning of the sentence (and the reflexive proposition it directly and immediately determines); what is said in the pragmatic sense; and what is implied or otherwise conveyed by the utterance.[6]

References

Bach, K. 1994. Semantic Slack. *Foundations of Speech Act Theory*, ed. S. Tsohatzidis, 267-91. London: Routledge.

Bach, K. 1999. The Myth of Conventional Implicature. *Linguistics and Philosophy* 22: 327-66.

Bach, K. 2001. You Don't Say? *Synthèse* 128: 15-44.

Bach, K. 2002. Seemingly Semantic Intuitions. *Meaning and Truth*, ed. J. K. Campbell, M. O'Rourke and D. Schier, 21-33. New York: Seven Bridges Press.

Berg, J. 1998. In Defense of Direct Belief: Substitutivity, Availability, and Iterability. *Lingua e Stile* 33: 461-70.

Campbell, R. 1981. Language Acquisition, Psychological Dualism and the Definition of Pragmatics. *Possibilities and Limitations of Pragmatics*, ed. H. Parret, M. Sbisà and J. Vershueren, 93-103. Amsterdam: Benjamins.

Cappelen, H. and E. Lepore 1997. On an Alleged Connection Between Indirect Speech and the Theory of Meaning. *Mind and Language* 12: 278-96.

---

[6] I am indebted to Jonathan Berg for his comments, suggestions and objections, both during the Genoa workshop and after.

Carston, R. 1988. Implicature, Explicature, and Truth-Theoretic Semantics. *Mental Representations: the Interface between Language and Reality*, ed. R. Kempson, 155-81. Cambridge: Cambridge University Press.

Carston, R. 1997. Enrichment and Loosening: Complementary Processes in Deriving the Proposition Expressed? *Linguistische Berichte* 8: 103-27.

Cohen, J. 1971. Some Remarks on Grice's Views About the Logical Particles of Natural Language. *Pragmatics of Natural Languages*, ed. Y. Bar-Hillel, 50-68. Dordrecht: Reidel.

Franks, B. 1995. Sense Generation: A "Quasi-Classical" Approach to Concepts and Concept Combination. *Cognitive Science* 19: 441-505.

Geurts, B. 2002. Donkey Business. *Linguistics and Philosophy* 25: 129-56.

Gibbs, R. and J. Moise 1997. Pragmatics in Understanding What is Said. *Cognition* 62: 51-74.

Grice, P. 1961. The Causal Theory of Perception. *Proceedings of the Aristotelian Society*, Supplementary Volume 35: 121-52.

Grice, P. 1989. *Studies in the Way of Words*. Cambridge MA: Harvard University Press.

Horn, L. 1992. The Said and the Unsaid. *SALT 2: Proceedings of the Second Conference on Semantics and Linguistic Theory,* ed. C. Barker and D. Dowty, 163-92. Colombus: Ohio State University.

Kaplan, D. 1989. Demonstratives. *Themes from Kaplan*, ed. J. Almog, H. Wettstein and J. Perry, 481-563. New York: Oxford University Press.

King, J. and J. Stanley forthcoming. Semantics, Pragmatics, and the Role of Semantic Content.

Levinson, S. 1983. *Pragmatics*. Cambridge: Cambridge University Press.

Nunberg, G. 1979. The Non-Uniqueness of Semantic Solutions: Polysemy. *Linguistics and Philosophy* 3: 143-84.

Nunberg, G. 1995. Transfers of Meaning. *Journal of Semantics* 12: 109-32.

Nunberg, G. and A. Zaenen 1992. Systematic Polysemy in Lexicology and Lexicography. *Proceedings of Euralex 2*, ed. H. Tommola, K. Varantola and J. Schopp, Part II, 387-98. Tampere: The University of Tampere.

Perry, J. 2001. *Reference and Reflexivity*. Stanford: CSLI Publications.

Recanati, F. 1989. The Pragmatics of What is Said. *Mind and Language* 4: 295-329.

Recanati, F. 1993. *Direct Reference: From Language to Thought*. Oxford: Blackwell.

Recanati, F. 1995. The Alleged Priority of Literal Interpretation. *Cognitive Science* 19: 207-32.

Recanati, F. 2001. What is Said. *Synthèse* 128: 75-91.

Ruhl, C. 1989. *On Monosemy: A Study in Linguistic Semantics*. Albany: State University of New York Press.

Rumfitt, I. 1993. Content and Context: the Paratactic Theory Revisited and Revised. *Mind* 102: 429-53.

Salmon, N. 1991. The Pragmatic Fallacy. *Philosophical Studies* 63: 83-97.

Soames, S. 2002. *Beyond Rigidity: The Unfinished Semantic Agenda of* Naming and Necessity. New York: Oxford University Press.

Sperber, D. and D. Wilson 1986. Loose Talk. *Proceedings of the Aristotelian Society* 86: 153-71.

Stalnaker, R. 1999. *Context and Content.* New York: Oxford University Press.

Ziff, P. 1972. What is Said. *Semantics of Natural Language*, ed. D. Davidson and G. Harman, 709-21. Dordrecht: Reidel.

5

Truth-Conditional Content and Conversational Implicature[*]

ROBYN CARSTON

1   Background and Overview

1.1   Grice on Implicature

Grice made a distinction between what is said by a speaker of a verbal utterance and what is implicated. What is implicated might be either *conventional* (that is, largely generated by the standing meaning of certain linguistic expressions, such as 'but' and 'moreover') or *conversational* (that is, dependent on the assumption that the speaker is following certain rational principles of conversational exchange). What appears to have bound these rather disparate aspects of utterance meaning together, and so motivated the common label of *implicature*, was that they did not contribute to the truth-conditional content of the utterance, that is, the proposition it expressed, or what the speaker of the utterance *said*.

This truth-conditional/non-truth-conditional distinction was essential to Grice in his concern to defeat the 'illegitimate use' arguments of a certain group of ordinary language philosophers (Grice 1967: lecture 1). I will not

---

[*]Many thanks to Alessandro Zucchi for his lucid challenge to my main argument, and to Richard Breheny and Deirdre Wilson for very helpful discussion of the issues.

The Semantics/Pragmatics Distinction.
Claudia Bianchi (ed.).
Copyright © 2004, CSLI Publications.

review those arguments here, but the utility of the distinction and the line of argument it enabled can be demonstrated with the following example. It is odd to produce an utterance of the sentence 'This looks red to me', referring with 'this' to a patently red pillar-box directly in front of one and in good lighting conditions. However, this oddness need not militate against the use of such statements in a theory or analysis (in this case, of perception), as some philosophers had argued, because the statement made (the proposition expressed/said) by the utterance is perfectly true and that is all that matters for the theory or analysis. The oddness or infelicity lies outside the truth-conditional content of the utterance; it is due (merely) to the conversational implicature that such an utterance would be likely to convey: that there is some doubt about the redness of the pillar-box, an implication which, in the given circumstances, is false. A similar story can be run for a case of conventional implicature which gives rise to some conversational infelicity (e.g. 'This looks red to me but it is red'). The general situation is summarized as follows:

(1) what is said   vs.   what is implicated
     truth-conditional   non-truth-conditional
     if false, utterance is false   *if false, utterance is*
                                          merely odd

According to the standard interpretation of the Gricean account, what is said (the truth-conditional content of the utterance) is very closely related to the conventional meaning of the linguistic expression employed. Of course, that linguistic expression may include ambiguous or indexical elements, so that contextual considerations have to be brought to bear for a full determination of 'what is said' (Grice 1975: 44–45). However, it seems that Grice conceived of the role of his Cooperative Principle and system of conversational maxims (quality, quantity, relevance and manner) as confined to the determination of conversational implicatures; that is, these maxims come into play in resolving the issue of why a speaker, who is assumed to be a rational agent, has said what she has said, or, in other words, what she means (intends to communicate) by having uttered a particular linguistic expression. This then leaves open the questions of *how* it is that the referent of a use of 'she' or 'that' is determined and *how* the intended sense of an ambiguous form like 'coach', 'bank' or 'bug' is determined. On this matter, Grice was essentially silent, mentioning just a vague criterion of best contextual fit.[1]

---

[1]However, Neale (1992) suggests that Grice may have envisaged some kind of relevance maxim as playing a role in disambiguation and reference resolution; this hinges on the inter-

1.2   Semantic Underdeterminacy and Grice's circle

The issue of how context-sensitive aspects of truth-conditional content are determined by an addressee/interpreter has become more pressing in recent years, as more and more pragmatists have come to accept the 'semantic underdeterminacy' view of verbal utterances. According to this view, the discrepancy between the explicit content (what is said) of an utterance and the conventional (or 'encoded') meaning of the linguistic expression employed is far greater than that presented by ambiguous words and overtly indexical expressions, and pragmatic inference (that is, maxim-guided inference) is required to make up the shortfall. Some of the cases discussed in the literature as instances involving this underdeterminacy are listed in (2)-(6):

(2)   a. I slept well. How about you?
      b. I haven't eaten yet.

(3)   a. It'll take time for your knee to heal.
      b. Your application requires some processing.

(4)   a. Everyone left early.
      b. There's nothing on.

(5)   a. You're not going to die.
         [uttered by mother to small child wailing over a scratched
         elbow]
      b. She gave him the key and he opened the door.
      c. The road layout had changed and she lost her way.

(6)   a. Only 22,000 miles. Like new.
         [uttered by a used car salesman]
      b. Ann: Mary is refusing to answer my emails.
         Bob: Typical.

Let me briefly indicate some of the elements of the propositional content of these utterances which seem not to be linguistically specified: in (2), the relevant temporal spans of the sleeping and the not eating are considerably narrower than that encoded in either the simple past or the past perfect (*I slept well last night, I haven't eaten dinner yet this evening*); similarly in (3), the 'taking time' and the 'some processing' are not understood as in-

pretation of a passage in Grice's early paper on meaning, reprinted in Grice (1989b, 222). For discussion, see Neale (1992: 530) and Carston (2002: 105-6).

volving just any quantity but as an amount relevant to mention in that context (perhaps more time/processing than the addressee appears to expect in each case); in (4), the domain of the quantifiers, 'everyone' and 'nothing' has to be determined (perhaps: *everyone at such and such a party, nothing worth watching on television*); in (5a) (example due to Bach 1994) and (5b), meaning expressible using prepositional phrases seems to be recovered: *from that scratch* and *with that key*; (5b) is further enriched with a temporal ordering relation so the event in the first conjunct is understood as preceding that in the second, and in (5c), as well as the temporal order, a cause-consequence relation is understood as holding between the first and second conjuncts, though there is no linguistic element encoding either of these relations; finally, the (nonelliptical) subsentential utterances in (6) require substantial recovery of contextually available material in determining the proposition expressed.

Among those who support the underdeterminacy view are relevance theorists, such as Sperber and Wilson (1986/95) and Carston (1988, 2002), and philosophers and linguists, who follow Grice to varying degrees, including Recanati (1989, 1993, forthcoming/2003), Bach (1994, 2000), Stainton (1994), Levinson (1988, 2000) and Neale (forthcoming), though some of them might not agree that all the examples given in (2)-(6) are pertinent cases. There is a fair amount of variation in the proposals that different theorists make for a semantic/pragmatic account of the underdeterminacy phenomena and in their analyses of particular cases. In this paper, I shall start by looking at some of Stephen Levinson's recent observations about the problem underdeterminacy poses for the classical Gricean account and go on to consider the direction in which he looks for a solution, comparing it with the approach pursued within relevance theory.

According to Levinson, this situation gives rise to a kind of circularity, an untenable interdependence, between saying and implicating (as Grice conceived of them):

> Grice's account makes implicature dependent on a prior determination of 'the said'. The said in turn depends [on implicature: it depends] on disambiguation, indexical resolution, reference fixing, not to mention ellipsis unpacking and generality narrowing. But each of these processes, which are prerequisites to determining the proposition expressed, [may] themselves depend crucially on [processes that look indistinguishable from] implicatures. Thus what is said seems both to determine and to be determined by implicature. Let us call this *Grice's circle*.
>
> ... Then truth-conditional content depends on most, perhaps all, of the known species of pragmatic inference; or the theory of linguistic meaning is dependent on, not independent of, the theory of communication. (Levin-

son 1988: 17-18; 2000: 186-87). [Square brackets in the quote indicate disparities between the 1988 and 2000 versions.]

As given here, there seem to be two distinct charges of circularity: (a) that between saying and implicating; (b) that between semantics and pragmatics. Of course, for those who equate linguistic meaning with what is said, as Levinson seems to do here, there is no such distinction to be made. However, there is a perfectly respectable sort of theory of linguistic meaning for which this equation does not hold and which does not depend on a theory of communication, at least not synchronically. This is the account of the meaning or information encoded in linguistic expression *types*, which provides the scaffolding on which processes geared to the recovery of communicated meaning (speaker meaning) build. The linguistic meaning of a phrase or lexical item is obviously not propositional, and the linguistic meaning of a sentence is also not generally, if ever, fully propositional. What it provides is a template or schema, that is, clues to, or constraints on, the process of recovering the proposition the speaker intended to express. It is, plausibly, the output of an encapsulated language processor, hence free from the modifications that come with access to extra-linguistic context and speaker intentions. This kind of semantics is, by definition, independent of the account of communication; thus there is no circularity between semantics so construed and pragmatics.

Be that as it may, I shall concentrate here on the alleged saying/implicating circle, leaving aside for now the issue of whether that distinction is to be usefully equated with a semantics/pragmatics distinction. This interdependence is, I think, an inescapable issue once one accepts that the proposition expressed (what is said) is heavily dependent on pragmatics (the underdeterminacy thesis) and puts this together with the standard Gricean assumptions given in (7a) and (7b):

(7)   a. All pragmatically-derived (maxim-dependent) meaning constitutes conversational implicature.
       b. Conversational implicatures arise from the application of conversational maxims to 'the saying of what is said' and so require the *prior* determination of what is said.

The point is that these Gricean assumptions are not compatible with there being pragmatic (maxim-driven) input to what is said, and as the truth of the latter seems indisputable (anyway, it is not disputed by any of the theorists I am discussing here), something has to give in the Gricean account.

1.3 Outline of Some Possible Solutions

The solution favored by semanticists such as Jason Stanley, Zoltan Szabò and Jeffrey King involves a revision of (7a): 'broadly Gricean mechanisms' do play a crucial role in determining what is said (Stanley and Szabò 2000: 236). However, this role is kept clearly distinct from their role in determining implicatures. The maxims have only a 'weak' pragmatic effect on 'what is said', that is, they merely supply values to indexicals that occur in the linguistic form of the utterance (a process known as 'saturation'). Implicature derivation is a 'strong' pragmatic effect in that it is 'free' from linguistic mandate or control. The Gricean assumption in (7b) can be maintained on this view; the maxims can first perform their role of determining the semantic content of the utterance (what is said), which is then input to the next phase, that of implicature derivation.

Among the various solutions to the problem at hand, this one is the most 'semantic' and the most preservatory of the original Gricean story. As Stanley (2000: 391) puts it: 'all truth-conditional effects of extra-linguistic context can be traced to logical form'. The cost of the approach, however, is the positing of a great many covert indexical elements in linguistic form, one for every instance of a pragmatically derived contribution to explicit utterance content, each of which requires independent justification. I will not address this account in any detail in the rest of the chapter, though certain details of King and Stanley's (forthcoming) work along these lines will be mentioned when they bear on the analyses I do want to discuss; see Breheny (forthcoming) for an assessment of their account.[2]

Levinson, on the other hand, accepts that there are 'strong' (as well as 'weak') pragmatic effects on truth-conditional content. He does not offer any sort of overall solution to the circularity problem that he has emphasized as arising from this, but suggests that his independently motivated theory of default (or generalized) conversational implicature can make substantial inroads on it, reducing its dimensions.

He draws a theoretical and empirical distinction between two kinds of conversational implicature: generalized (GCI) and particularized (PCI). The following exchange exemplifies the two kinds of implicature, each of which,

---

[2]On the face of it, indexical saturation accounts seem more plausible for certain cases of pragmatic effects on propositional content than for others, for instance, the case of quantifier domain restriction as opposed to, say, the case of causal connections between the conjuncts in cases of 'and'-coordination. However, on the one hand, both Bach (2000) and Neale (2000) argue against Stanley and Szabò's (2000) indexical account of quantifier domains, and, on the other, King and Stanley (forthcoming) argue for an indexical saturation account of the pragmatic contribution to 'and'-conjunctions in particular linguistic contexts (see section 3 below). For more general arguments against the indexicalist approach and in favor of 'strong' pragmatic effects on propositional content, see Carston (2000) and Recanati (2002).

in his view, is derived by a distinct kind of inferential process, governed by distinct pragmatic maxims or heuristics:

(8)   A: Did the children's summer camp go well?
        B: Some of them got stomach 'flu.
           GCI: Not all the children got stomach 'flu.
           PCI: The summer camp didn't go as well as hoped.

While the PCI of B's utterance depends on the context provided by A's question and would not arise in a different context (e.g., a context in which the issue is whether all the children were able to sit their exams), the GCI arises quite generally across contexts and only drops out if it encounters a context with which it is inconsistent.

The claim, then, is that this sort of generalized pragmatic inference can contribute to the propositional content of certain kinds of utterance, such as that in (9). The second part of the utterance, the comparative, makes a perfectly coherent statement, but this is only possible if we interpret 'some' (of your exams) as *some but not all* (of your exams).

(9) You shouldn't be too upset about failing some of your exams; it's much better than failing the whole lot.

On this approach to the phenomenon of pragmatic contributions to the proposition expressed by an utterance, the Gricean assumption in (7a) appears to be preserved, though, in fact, only by virtue of an extreme loosening of the sense of the term 'implicature' (this point will be pursued later), while (7b) is modified so that a restricted kind of pragmatic inference (local, default) can apply without the prior determination of 'what is said'. This sort of inference is generated by a system of default rules which are attached to particular lexical items and constructions, the word 'some' in the case of (8) and (9). These rules are implemented in parallel with the process of linguistic decoding, so in (8), for instance, the inference to *not all the children* will have been made before the predicate 'got stomach 'flu' is processed.

However, as Levinson acknowledges (2000: 236-39) some PCIs also seem to affect truth-conditional content and, as I'll claim later, a substantial subset of cases that fall in his class of GCIs do not, so in fact this approach makes quite limited headway with the task of accounting for the underdeterminacy phenomena and the issue of Grice's circle.

A third approach also recognizes strong (as well as weak) pragmatic effects on truth-conditional content, that is, pragmatic contributions which are not triggered by the requirement of indexical saturation but are entirely pragmatically motivated, but it does not construe these as a kind of implicature. Rather, it makes a distinction between these 'free' pragmatic contributions to content, on the one hand, and conversational implicatures, on the other, which as Grice maintained, lie outside truth-conditional content. This position, which is known as 'truth-conditional pragmatics', is held by pragmatists across a range of otherwise different frameworks, including Francois Recanati (1989, 1993, 2003), Kent Bach (1994, 2000), Anne Bezuidenhout (1997, 2002b), and Stephen Neale (2000, forthcoming). It has also been central to the relevance-theoretic framework since its inception (Sperber and Wilson (1986/95), Carston (1988, 2002)), and it is this particular manifestation of the truth-conditional pragmatic position that I'll call on in the rest of the paper. The relevance-theoretic term for the pragmatically imbued level of truth-conditional content is 'explicature', while Recanati, Levinson, King and Stanley and others continue to use the term 'what is said'; in what follows I shall use the terms interchangeably depending on whose work I am discussing, but it is worth bearing in mind that this conception of 'what is said' is quite different from Grice's original conception (which was independent of considerations of speaker intentions, hence of maxim-driven inference).

Relevance theorists make no distinction of any theoretical import between generalized and particularized implicatures. Of course, implicatures vary in their generality, some being very general, others less so, and some being essentially one-off (nonce), but this is a continuum situation. No implicatures are a matter of default inference; rather, all must be warranted by contextual relevance. The Gricean assumption in (7a) is dropped, since one and the same pragmatic principle (based on the concept of 'optimal relevance') is responsible for both all cases of conversational implicature and all pragmatic contributions to truth-conditional content. The assumption in (7b), that 'what is said' is determined prior to the derivation of conversational implicatures, is also relaxed and the two levels of communicated content are taken to be derived in parallel via a mechanism of 'mutual adjustment', so that, for instance, an interpretive hypothesis about an implicature might lead, through a step of backwards inference, to a particular adjustment of explicit content. For detailed justification and exemplification of this account, see Wilson and Sperber (2002) and Carston (2002: section 2.3.4).

By way of brief illustration, omitting all technical detail, let us consider B's utterance in each of the following exchanges:

(10)   A: Will John get any support from accident compensation?
       B: Someone left a manhole cover off and John broke his leg.
       Implicature: John will get accident compensation payments.

(11)   A: I was planning to climb Mt Snowdon next week.
       B: Your knee needs time to heal properly.
       Implicature: A should not go mountain-climbing next week.

In (10), the answer to A's question is indirect; B conversationally implicates that John will get financial compensation. We know that such financial compensation depends on the cause of the incapacity to work being negligence in the workplace, hence the statement here is not just that the two events expressed by the conjuncts took place, nor just that they took place in the given order, but the richer proposition that there is a cause-consequence relation between them. Given that A's question narrowly circumscribes the expected relevance of B's response (essentially to a 'yes' or 'no'), it is fairly easy to see that this expectation warrants the derivation of the implicature, for which the explicature (what is said) has to be appropriately enriched, thereby ensuring an inferentially sound interpretation. A similar explanation can be given for B's utterance in (11); the quantity of time involved must be understood as extending some way into the next few weeks if the proposition expressed is to provide a proper inferential basis for the implicature. Note that, in both cases, the contextual contribution to the explicature (what is said) has been motivated by pragmatic considerations alone.

My main concern in this paper is to consider the relative merits of the second and third approaches to the underdeterminacy issue (Levinson's and relevance theory's). In particular, I will take a close and critical look at Levinson's account of what he describes as the 'pragmatic intrusion' of generalized implicatures into certain complex constructions, including conditionals, comparatives, negations and disjunctions. Before that, though, I will consider a question that arises for the 'truth-conditional pragmatics' approach, including relevance theory, and a response to it which involves this same set of complex constructions.

2   Truth-Conditional Pragmatics and the Scope Criterion

Suppose we have an element of utterance meaning which is clearly pragmatically derived (i.e., we can show that it is not encoded in the linguistic expression used but depends on pragmatic principles/maxims geared to the recovery of the speaker's communicative intention). This raises the following question(s): is it an implicature or does it, rather, contribute to what is said (explicature)? How do we know? What distinguishes the two?

Various criteria for distinguishing the two kinds of pragmatic meaning have been proposed in the literature. In the end, they all rest, I think, on speaker/hearer intuitions. However, there is one that has been used to sharpen up intuitions and which has a bearing on the assessment of positions in the following sections, so I want to spend a little time looking at it. Within relevance theory, this is known as the 'embedding test' and was introduced by Deirdre Wilson as a useful tool for deciding whether some element of utterance meaning is or is not a component of the truth-conditional content of an utterance; Recanati (1989, 1993) called it the Scope Principle (or Scope Criterion), and formulated it explicitly as follows:

> A pragmatically determined aspect of meaning is part of what is said (and, therefore, not a conversational implicature) if – and, perhaps, only if – it falls within the scope of logical operators such as negation and conditionals.

The general idea seems to have begun with Cohen's (1971) use of an embedding procedure in order to demonstrate that Grice could not simultaneously maintain the truth-functionality of 'and' and of 'if'. On a Gricean account, the meaning of 'and' is identical to its truth-functional logical counterpart '&', so that the two conjunctive utterances in (12) have the same truth-conditional content (they 'say' the same thing). The difference in what they communicate, concerning the order in which the events described took place, arises at the level of conversational implicature (based on the manner maxim of 'orderliness'):

(12) a. The old king has died of a heart attack and a republic has been declared.
b. A republic has been declared and the old king has died of a heart attack.

The problem with this analysis that Cohen pointed out becomes apparent when the conjunctions are embedded in the antecedent of a conditional as in the following:

(13) a. If the old king has died of a heart attack and a republic has been declared, then Tom will be quite content.
b. If a republic has been declared and the old king has died of a heart attack, then Tom will be quite content.

Given the alleged truth-functionality of 'and', the antecedents of the two conditionals must be truth-conditionally equivalent, and given the alleged truth-functionality of 'if', to which Grice was equally committed, it follows that the two conditionals in (13) must be truth-conditionally equivalent.

However, this does not seem to be so: the temporal relation understood to hold between the conjuncts seems to be an integral part of the antecedents, so that the two conditionals are truth-conditionally distinct and could well differ in truth-value, Tom being happy with one sequence of events but unhappy with the other. The same result can be achieved by embedding the sentences, or similar ones, in the scope of other operators, including negation, disjunction, and comparatives:

(14) They didn't steal the money and go to the bank; they went to the bank and stole the money.
(15) Max and Mary have a terrible relationship: either he gets drunk and she screams at him or she screams at him and he gets drunk.

If the only options in accounting for the non-truth-functional connections were a Gricean implicature or a richer sense for 'and', there would be good reason to favor the latter, as Cohen did. Relevance theorists, however, have used the results of this embedding test, together with a pragmatic account of how the temporal ordering and cause-consequence meanings arise, to support an account on which they are seen as pragmatic contributions to the proposition expressed (explicature, 'what is said'); see Carston (1988; 2002: chapter 3).

However, Manuel García-Carpintero (2001) swiftly dismisses this scope embedding procedure as providing any sort of useful test or criterion for distinguishing between pragmatic contributions to the proposition expressed, on the one hand, and distinct implicated propositions, on the other. His claim is that there are clear cases of conversational implicature for which the criterion makes the wrong prediction. He takes Grice's well-known 'gas station' example, where B's utterance, in the situation laid out in (16), is claimed to conversationally implicate that the garage is open and selling petrol:

(16) A is standing by an obviously immobilized car and is approached by B; the following exchange takes place:
A: I am out of petrol.
B: There is a garage round the corner.
(Gloss: B would be infringing the maxim 'Be relevant' unless he thinks, or thinks it possible, that the garage is open, and has petrol to sell; so he implicates that the garage is, or may be, open, etc.)

García-Carpintero then presents examples in which the sentence uttered by B in (16) is placed in the antecedent of a conditional, as in (17a), or in the scope of a negation, as in (17b), and claims that the implicated content of

B's utterance is, as he puts it, also 'inherited' here; that is, it contributes to the truth-conditional content of these more complex utterances.

> (17) a. If there is a gas station around the corner, I do not need to worry any more.
>   b. There is no gas station nearby.

He says that (17b) 'can be regarded as not falsified by the existence of a closed gas station around the corner' (García-Carpintero 2000: 113). Let us suppose that he is right about this, and that we are strongly disposed to take it that the truth-conditional content of (17a) is something like 'If there is a currently operative gas station around the corner, then I do not need to worry any more', and of (17b) is 'There is no currently operative gas station around the corner'. Then, according to the Scope Criterion, what this indicates is that, contrary to the standard Gricean analysis, the pragmatic inference here is not one that eventuates in an implicated proposition but rather one that contributes to the explicit content of the utterance (the explicature or 'what is said'). García-Carpintero takes this to be an 'uncontroversial case of an implicature', as is also another Gricean example, given in (18), on which he runs the same argument:

> (18) I saw John with a woman.
>   *Implicature*: I saw John with a woman different from his wife, sister or mother.

But once one embraces the view that there is an appreciable pragmatic input to the truth-conditional content of an utterance, whether or not this pragmatic content is a function of the same maxims/principles as those responsible for implicature derivation, then it is not obvious that these are uncontroversial cases of conversational implicature. The status of these elements of pragmatic inference is exactly what is brought into question by the semantic underdeterminacy thesis. In his recent work, Recanati (forthcoming/2003) reconsiders the gas station example and denies that it is a case of conversational implicature. He claims that the content of B's utterance in (16) is enriched into a proposition which could be made more linguistically explicit by an utterance of the sentence in (19):

> (19) There is a garage around the corner which sells petrol and is open now.

He goes on to point out that this is entirely at one with the current idea within relevance theory that there are pragmatic processes of *ad hoc* concept construction which fine-tune encoded linguistic meaning and contribute to the explicit content of utterances. Possible examples involving this process are given in (20a) and (20b):

(20) a. Bill opened the curtains.
   BILL OPENED* THE CURTAINS
   b. France is hexagonal.
   FRANCE IS HEXAGONAL*
   c. THERE IS A GARAGE* ROUND THE CORNER.
   d. I SAW JOHN WITH A WOMAN*

[Small caps are used for communicated propositions/thoughts, as distinct from the linguistic expressions (sentences, etc) employed in the utterance; an asterisk attached to a conceptual constituent of the proposition expressed indicates that it has been pragmatically constructed from a linguistically encoded concept.]

In (20a), the pragmatically inferred concept OPEN* has a narrower denotation than the general concept encoded by the word 'open' and is quite distinct from other concepts that might be expressed by the word 'open' in different linguistic and extra-linguistic contexts (the dentist who says 'Open wide', the concept of opening a conference, etc.) In (20b), the denotation of the concept HEXAGONAL* is broader in some respects than that of the concept encoded by the word 'hexagonal'. Similarly, the use of the word 'garage' in (16) can be taken to contextually express the *ad hoc* concept GARAGE*, roughly paraphrased as 'a garage that is currently open and has petrol to sell', a concept whose denotation is rather narrower than that of the encoded concept GARAGE. It is this narrower GARAGE* concept that, arguably, is a constituent of the proposition expressed by B's utterance, as shown in (20c).

Of course, the scope embedding test is useless if it leads to the prediction that all and any elements of pragmatically derived meaning are constituents of the truth-conditional content of an utterance, but it does not. Consider the following cases:

---

[3] In fact, this treatment of the example is not very secure. First, not everyone shares García-Carpintero's intuitions about the embedded cases in (17), which I accepted for the sake of the argument. Second, as Grice presented it, this is an epistemically qualified implicature (*as far as the speaker knows* the garage is open and selling petrol, etc) and it seems unlikely that this kind of pragmatic meaning can or should be seen as part of the proposition expressed. For discussion of such 'speaker's grounds' aspects of utterance meaning, see Breheny (forthcoming).

(21) a. Ann: Does Bill have a girlfriend these days?
      Bob: He flies to New York every weekend.
      Implicature: Bill (probably) has a girlfriend in New York.
      b. He doesn't fly to New York every weekend.
      c. If he flies to New York every weekend he must spend a lot of money.

From Bob's answer to her question, Ann can infer that Bill probably does have a girlfriend (who lives in New York). But this pragmatic inference does not affect the propositional content in the scope of the corresponding negation in (21b), nor does it fall in the scope of the conditional in (21c); the consequent (that Bill must spend a lot of money) depends just on the proposition that Bill flies to New York every weekend and not also on his having a girlfriend there.

Similarly, a typical utterance of (22a) communicates that the speaker does not know where in the south of France Chris lives, but, as Green (1998: 73) points out, that is not understood as contributing to the proposition expressed by the more complex (22b) in which the original sentence is embedded. If it did, an utterance of (22b) should be found tautologous (or, as he puts it, '*prima facie* plausible'), which is not the case:

(22) a. Ann: Where does Chris live?
      Bob: Somewhere in the south of France.
      Implicature: Bob doesn't know where in the south of France Chris lives.
      b. If Chris lives somewhere in the south of France, then I do not now where.

So, by the embedding test, the pragmatically inferred elements of meaning in (21) and (22) are non-truth-conditional aspects of utterance meaning, i.e. implicatures (conversational ones).

To conclude this section, the view is that pragmatic inference can contribute constituents to the explicature of an utterance or make adjustments to constituents of linguistically encoded meaning, and that this may be undertaken on purely pragmatic grounds, without any indication in the linguistic form, such as an indexical, that it is required. The embedding tests (and perhaps other criteria not discussed here) provide us with a useful means of checking intuitions on when this is happening.[4]

---

[4]I do not mean to suggest that this is a definitive test. I doubt that there is any foolproof test or criterion that can be applied in this mechanical manner. Levinson (2000: 195-98, 238) is highly critical of relevance theory in this regard, since it provides no way, he says, of distin-

3 'Intrusive' Constructions and the 'Embedded Implicature' Hypothesis

Let us take a closer look at Levinson's account of generalized implicatures, which are the primary focus of his work; he says very little about particularized implicatures, or 'nonce' pragmatic inferences, which, in his view, are the domain of a distinct kind of pragmatic theory.

The idea is that generalized implicatures contribute to 'utterance-type' meaning, a species of meaning which is distinct from both linguistic-type (sentence) meaning and speaker meaning. It is pragmatic in that it involves an element of meaning which is ultimately communicatively based, that is, dependent on certain principles of appropriate communicative behaviour. However, it has become established as the preferred or default interpretation of a linguistic expression so that it bypasses familiar Gricean processes of pragmatic reasoning, and considerations of the speaker's intended meaning, and arises through the automatic activation of default inference rules which are attached to particular expression types. These are, of course, defeasible rules, so that if their results are inconsistent with an entailment of the expression or with some particular salient contextual assumption, then they are defeated/cancelled. So, for each of the examples in (23)-(27) below, the meaning designated a generalized implicature is generated in this default sort of way by a rule associated with a particular expression in the utterance: 'some' in (23), 'three' in (24), 'and' in (25), 'drink' in (26), 'bring to a standstill' (and the other variants) in (27):

> (23) Some of the students passed the exam.
> *Generalized implicature*: Not all of the students passed the exam.

---

guishing pragmatic aspects of explicature from 'other' conversational implicatures. There are two lines of response: (a) as briefly indicated in section 1.3 above, at the heart of the RT approach is a concrete proposal for a cognitive system (a module) that does the pragmatic work of utterance interpretation and which, through its mechanism of pragmatic mutual adjustment, delivers the two distinct communicated assumptions; (b) Levinson himself faces this problem in an acute form, as we shall see, since even if there is a delineated set of GCIs, distinct from other implicatures, this set is neither necessary nor sufficient (it both overgenerates and undergenerates) to account for the phenomenon at issue (that is, pragmatic contributions to truth-conditional content).

(24) The home team scored three goals.
Generalized implicature: The home team scored at most three goals.

(25) Tim turned the key and the engine started.
Generalized implicature: Tim turned the key thereby causing the engine to start.

(26) I'd love a drink
Generalized implicature: U would love an alcoholic drink.

(27) Sue caused the car to stop.
Sue brought the car to a standstill.
Sue was instrumental in stopping the car.
Generalized implicature: Sue stopped the car in an unorthodox manner.

Three pragmatic heuristics are taken to underlie the generation of these implicatures: *the Q-heuristic* (what is not said is not the case) is responsible for the scalar inferences in (23)-(24); *the I-heuristic* (what is said in a simple (unmarked) way represents a stereotypical situation) is responsible for (25)-(26); *the M-heuristic* (what is said in an abnormal (marked) way represents an abnormal situation) is responsible for (27). Detailed discussion of these heuristics would take me too far away from the main issues of this paper; for critical assessments of the overall GCI program, see Bezuidenhout (2002a) and Carston (1998, forthcoming).

My concern here is with just one characteristic of Levinson's account, which is the way in which the content of generalized implicatures can, according to him, enter into what is said. This is probably best approached by comparing some of the examples just given with the more complex cases in (28)-(30), all taken from Levinson (2000):

(28) a. If each side in the soccer game got three goals, then the game was a draw.
b. IF EACH SIDE IN THE SOCCER GAME GOT *EXACTLY* THREE GOALS, THEN THE GAME WAS A DRAW

(29) a. Because the police have recovered some of the gold, they will no doubt recover the lot.
b. BECAUSE THE POLICE HAVE RECOVERED SOME *BUT NOT ALL* OF THE GOLD, THEY WILL NO DOUBT RECOVER THE LOT.

(30)   a. Driving home and drinking three beers is better than drinking three beers and driving home.
b. DRIVING HOME AND *THEN* DRINKING THREE BEERS IS BETTER THAN DRINKING THREE BEERS AND *THEN* DRIVING HOME.

In each case, an utterance of the sentence in (a) expresses the proposition (has the truth-conditional content) given in (b), where the italicized element of meaning has been pragmatically derived. Now, according to the Scope Criterion discussed in the previous section, what these examples show is that the element of pragmatic meaning contributes to truth conditions – not just to the truth conditions of these complex utterances but also to those of utterances of the unembedded sentences: 'Each side in the soccer game got three goals', 'He drove home and drank three beers', etc. So these elements of pragmatic meaning are not usefully (or, indeed, coherently) to be thought of as conversational implicatures.

However, Levinson's take on the situation seems to be a bit different. For him, each of the examples in (28)-(30) involves what he calls an 'intrusive' construction (this class of constructions includes negations, conditionals, disjunctions, comparatives, etc). He calls them intrusive because they have the property that '*the truth conditions of the whole expression depend on the implicatures of some of its constituent parts*' (Levinson 2000: 198, 213-14).[5] The idea here seems to be that, while the unembedded sentences containing a scalar term ('some', 'three') in (23) and (24), and the unembedded conjunction in (25), each conversationally implicates the pragmatically inferred meaning, when they are embedded in one of the 'intrusive constructions' that implicated meaning gets composed into the semantics (the truth-conditional content, the 'what is said') of the larger structure and so is an implicature no longer. This point is made several times over and seems to imply that these implicated elements of meaning are NOT composed into the truth conditions of utterances of the simple unembedded sentences.[6]

---

[5]The label 'intrusive construction' seems an odd usage to me, since the point surely is, not that these constructions are themselves intrusive, but rather are 'intruded upon' by pragmatically inferred meaning, that is, they are 'pragmatically penetrable'. However, I'll continue to use the label when alluding to Levinson's views.

[6]Here's another quote that points in the same direction: 'Thus the default properties of GCIs account for their intrusive abilities: such inferences can and will be made on the fly and, if not canceled ..., will *end up within the propositional content of complex sentences* whose parts are semantically evaluated with respect to each other (as in comparatives and conditionals, and in the case of denials, evaluated with respect to the corresponding affirmative.)' (Levinson 2000: 259; my emphasis)

I am hedging a bit, since whether this is really what Levinson intends is not perfectly clear to me. He talks briefly of generalized implicatures also playing a role in 'ellipsis unpacking' and 'generality narrowing', giving examples of simple (non-intrusive) constructions, and saying that without these processes 'the proposition expressed by many sentences will be general to the point of vacuity' (Levinson 2000: 183-86). But whether the implicatures he has in mind here merely play some role in these processes, comparable perhaps to the role of bridging implicatures in determining reference, or their content is actually composed into the truth-conditional content of the utterance, is not elucidated.

Anyhow, a large chunk of Levinson's book is taken up with the 'intrusive' constructions and he clearly takes them to be the key data in establishing as fact that pragmatics plays an essential role in determining truth-conditional content. So, in setting out to convince 'the obstinate theorist' (that is, the semanticist who resists the idea of pragmatics playing any role in semantic interpretation), he concentrates on these constructions, along with the role of pragmatics in reference fixing (Levinson 2000: 232-36). And, indeed, in their recent rejoinder to Levinson's claims for what they call 'strong pragmatic' effects on truth conditions, King and Stanley (forthcoming) focus entirely on the intrusive constructions. They seem to assume that their task of refuting his position consists of tackling these structures one by one and showing that, in each case, there is a parameter in the linguistic semantics of the construction which is responsible for triggering the pragmatic process in question.

For instance, they discuss the conditional in (31), which has an 'and'-conjunction as its antecedent, and which seems to express the proposition that if Hannah insulted Joe and Joe resigned *as a result of Hannah's insult*, then Hannah is in trouble.

(31) If Hannah insulted Joe and Joe resigned, then Hannah is in trouble.

They argue for a (syntactically covert) parameter (requiring the selection of the 'most relevantly similar worlds in the context set') which is simply part of the semantics of 'if' and which, in this case, is pragmatically fixed as those worlds in the context in which a causal relation holds between the events described in the conjuncts. The details of the analysis do not matter here. My point is that, even supposing it works as they say and so renders the pragmatic effect on the truth conditions of (31) weak rather than strong, it patently does not apply to the cause-consequence meaning as it affects the unembedded conjunction. For this, King and Stanley are content with a standard Gricean account, according to which the proposition expressed (i.e.

the truth-conditional content) is the truth-functional conjunction and the cause-consequence connection, derived via a maxim of manner, is implicated:

> (32)   Hannah insulted Joe and Joe resigned.
>   *Proposition expressed:* HANNAH INSULTED JOE & JOE RESIGNED.
>   *Implicature:* HANNAH'S INSULT CAUSED JOE'S RESIGNATION.

They assume, and assume that Levinson assumes, that in the case of the unembedded 'and'-conjunction the pragmatically derived meaning does not compose into the truth conditions, does not enter into 'what is said'.

This position, whether or not it is the one that Levinson is really committed to, was taken by a number of people, often reluctantly, in the early days of work in the Gricean framework. After discussing a variety of cases, including some essentially the same as (31), Wilson (1975: 153) concluded:

> [...] these non-truth-conditional aspects may figure truth-conditionally when simplex positive sentences in which they occur become embedded or negated. ... This simply means that negating, embedding, disjoining or hypothesising may be based on more than a simple computation over the truth-conditions of the related positive sentences, and the projection rules must accordingly be complicated to allow for this. Clearly an enormous amount of work still needs to be done in this area.

Similarly, Posner (1980: 195), also discussing 'and'-conjunctions embedded as conditional antecedents, says:

> A homogeneous treatment of the sentence connectives seems possible only if we weaken the thesis that in natural language the truth-value of the entire sentence is a function of the truth-value of the constituent sentences. Rather, after each step in the truth-functional deduction, it must be considered whether the resulting conversational suggestions alter the derived truth-value. Each deduction in the value distribution of the complex sentence on the basis of the value distributions of two constituent sentences must be open to reinterpretation according to the context in which the sentence has been uttered. This is certainly not a very elegant solution.

Despite his reservations, Posner felt compelled, in the absence of anything better, to accept this approach.

Grice himself confronted the issue in his discussion of negated conditionals (1967: lecture 4). In certain cases, it seems that what is denied is not what would be said by an affirmation of the conditional (assumed to be equivalent to the truth-functional material conditional); rather, what is denied is a (quite general) conversational implicature of an affirmation of the conditional, concerning some sort of cause-consequence connection between antecedent and consequent, as in the following example: *It is not the case that if John turns up at the party Mary will leave.* Grice was very troubled by this, but could see no solution to it (Grice 1989b: 83). Given his unwillingness to allow conversational principles to play any direct role in determining truth-conditional content, he was left with little option but to concede to the view that what are implicatures of simple sentences (hence non-truth-conditional aspects of utterance meaning) can become aspects of the truth-conditional content of embedding constructions such as negations and conditionals. By the time of his 'Retrospective Epilogue' Grice had accepted this as inevitable: 'It certainly does not seem reasonable to subscribe to an absolute ban on the possibility that an embedding locution may govern the standard nonconventional implicatum rather than the conventional import of the embedded sentence ...' (Grice 1989a: 375). Levinson (2000: 260) puts this quote from Grice at the end of his own chapter on pragmatic intrusions into truth-conditional content, saying that it shows that Grice foresaw the very problem that he (Levinson) has been grappling with in the chapter. Again, then, it looks as if the central issue for Levinson is that what are conversational implicatures of simple sentences can become components of the truth-conditional content of more complex constructions in which the simple sentence is embedded.

I have spent some time (too much perhaps) trying to establish for sure that this is Levinson's position. Anyway, it is certainly a position that has had, and still has, quite a number of adherents. Perhaps its most explicit recent rendering is that given by Mitchell Green (1998: 77), who labels it the '*Embedded Implicature Hypothesis*':

> (33) If assertion of a sentence S conveys the implicatum [implicature]
> that p with nearly universal regularity, then when S is embedded
> the content that is usually understood to be embedded for seman-
> tic purposes is the proposition (S & p).

Green gives (34a) as an example which falls under the hypothesis. It standardly ('with nearly universal regularity') conversationally implicates that the contact lens belonged to the speaker (or, more generally, to the person who has lost it). When this same sentence is embedded in the syntactic scope of a negation, as in (34b), or a disjunction, as in (34c), this 'implicature' is judged to fall within the semantic scope of those operators:

> (34) a. I lost a contact lens in the accident.
> b. I didn't lose a contact lens in the accident, but Mary did.
> c. Either Mary lost a contact lens in the accident or Bob did.

I want to take issue with this embedded implicature hypothesis of Green and (probably) of Levinson. Their examples provide plenty of evidence that pragmatic inference plays a fundamental role in determining the proposition expressed; but this does not have to be taken as entailing that what is an implicature (a propositional form distinct from the proposition expressed) of a simple sentence/utterance changes its status when that simple sentence is embedded, becoming then part of the proposition expressed (the truth-conditional content). I would claim that we have a pragmatic contribution to the proposition expressed in both cases (unembedded and embedded) and an implicature in neither. The interesting fact, established in the previous section, is that some pragmatically derived meaning does fall in the scope of logical operators and some does not, so that we have a test for distinguishing pragmatic contributions to the proposition expressed from conversational implicatures.

4 Arguments and Counter-arguments

In this section, I shall offer two kinds of argument for the view that the only coherent position to take is that pragmatically derived meaning contributes to truth-conditional content in both the simple and the complex cases, and that these pragmatic inferences are not to be thought of as cases of conversational implicature.

4.1 The Valid Argument Argument

Consider the following line of argument:

(35) Premise 1: If someone leaves a manhole cover off and you break your leg, you can sue them.
Premise 2: Someone left a manhole cover off and Meg broke her leg.
Conclusion: Meg can sue them.

I take it that the average person (perhaps not a logician) presented with this line of reasoning would assent to it; in other words, it is an intuitively valid argument. We easily derive the instantiation of the universal in premise 1 which involves Meg and, given that, the inference seems to be a straightforward case of modus ponendo ponens (MPP). But if the Levinson/Green description of the phenomenon is correct, it should not be valid because the truth-conditional content of the antecedent of the conditional and the truth-conditional content of the second premise are not the same, so the MPP deduction does not go through. On that sort of account, while the cause-consequence relation between the conjuncts is an element of what is said by the conditional (an 'intrusive' construction), it is merely an implicature of what is said by the unembedded conjunction in the second premise. On the explicature account, on the other hand, the validity of the argument is explained, since the conclusion follows deductively from the premises, both of which are pragmatically enriched in the same way.

The same holds for the scalar case in (36), where, on the Levinson/Green view, the truth-conditional content (what is said) in the second premise is just that the teams both scored at least three goals, so that again the conclusion cannot be validly drawn, contrary to strong intuitions.

(36) Premise 1: If both teams scored three goals then the result was a draw.
Premise 2: Both teams scored three goals.
Conclusion: The result was a draw.

This seems to me to provide quite a compelling reason for rejecting the embedded implicature hypothesis and adopting an account which recognizes that pragmatic inference contributes to the truth-conditional content of utterances quite generally (not just to a small set of complex 'intrusive' constructions). On this latter sort of account, these pragmatically inferred 'enrichments' of linguistically encoded content are distinguished from conversational implicature, which are those pragmatically derived assumptions communicated by an utterance that do not affect truth conditions. However, Alessandro Zucchi has suggested that, contrary to what I have just claimed, it *is* possible to capture the intuitive validity of the argument in (35) while preserving Levinson's 'embedded implicature' assumptions. His argument is presented next.

4.2 A Defense of the 'Embedded Implicature' Position

For ease of reference, here again are the sentences at issue:

---

[7]Zucchi presented this argument in his role as discussant of my talk 'Semantics and conversational implicature', which was the precursor to this paper (at the Workshop on Context, Genoa, October 2002). He should not be taken, on this basis, to endorse either the Levinsonian position or the embedded implicature hypothesis more generally.

(37)   a. Someone left a manhole cover off and Meg broke her leg.
       b. If someone leaves a manhole cover off and Meg breaks her leg,
       she can sue them.

Zucchi's claim is that the intuitive validity of the argument in (35) can be demonstrated even while maintaining that: [i] an utterance of (37a) conversationally implicates (but does not entail) that Meg broke her leg because someone left a manhole cover off, and [ii] the conditional in (37b) is true only if Meg can sue people in case they leave a manhole cover off and she breaks her leg *because of that*.

To show this, Zucchi adopts Stalnaker's (1974: 1999) account of context: a context is the information shared by the conversational participants (their common ground) and it is represented as a set of possible worlds or situations, that is, the possible worlds in which the shared assumptions are true. The assumptions shared by the interlocutors (hence the context) change as the conversation progresses. When someone asserts that P, and provided the participants accept it, P becomes part of their common ground, that is, the context is updated so as to consist only of worlds where P holds. Zucchi suggests, reasonably, that when an utterance conversationally implicates something, the implicature, as well as the asserted propositional content, becomes part of common ground. So, as a result of uttering (37a) both of the propositions given in (38) are added to the common ground (assuming they are accepted by both participants and do not give rise to any inconsistency):

(38)   a. SOMEONE LEFT A MANHOLE COVER OFF & MEG BROKE HER LEG
       b. MEG BROKE HER LEG BECAUSE SOMEONE LEFT A MANHOLE
       COVER OFF

The approach taken here to the (in)validity question is semantic (rather than formal/syntactic/proof-theoretic), hence given in terms of truth: an argument is valid only provided that the truth of the premises (relative to a context c) ensures the truth of the conclusion (relative to the same context c); that is, all those possible worlds in which the premises hold are worlds in which the conclusion holds. Since the major premise of the argument at issue is a conditional, much hangs on the semantics of conditionals. Zucchi suggests the following truth conditions for indicative conditional statements:

(39) 'If A, then B' is true in a context c iff B is true in all the worlds in c in which A and what A implicates are true.

So (37b) is true provided that all the worlds in which Meg can sue are worlds in which someone left a manhole cover off, Meg broke her leg, and the former is a cause of the latter.[8] The content of a conditional statement is added to the conversational participants' common ground (assuming it is accepted by both of them) so the context is updated as follows:

(40) c' = c + [if A, then B] = the set of worlds in c in which either A and what A implicates are false or B is true.

For instance, when a context c is updated as a result of an utterance of (37b), the new context c' differs from c in that it contains no worlds in which Meg has broken her leg because someone has left a manhole cover off and Meg cannot sue them.

The main point here is that this approach meets the challenge of accounting for the intuitive validity of the argument in (35), repeated here (with the appropriate instantiation of the universal in premise 1), while maintaining Levinson/Green's embedded implicature assumptions:

(41) Premise 1: If someone leaves a manhole cover off and Meg breaks her leg, she can sue them.
Premise 2: Someone left a manhole cover off and Meg broke her leg.
Conclusion: Meg can sue them.

As a result of uttering premise 1, the context c is updated to a new context c' that contains only worlds in which either it is false that Meg breaks her leg because someone leaves a manhole cover off or it is true that Meg can sue them. Then, utterance of premise 2 brings about an update of c' yielding a context c", to which both the content of the assertion AND of the conversational implicature have been added, so worlds in which it is false that Meg has broken her leg because someone has left a manhole cover off have been

---

[8]Zucchi's definition is a bit different from the semantics for indicative conditionals given by Stalnaker (1975): 'an indicative conditional is true iff the consequent is true in all the worlds in which the antecedent is true and which are the most similar, in relevant respects, to the actual world'. There is no mention here of implicatures of the antecedent; however, as noted in section 3, King and Stanley (forthcoming) develop an account of 'pragmatic intrusions' into conditionals using Stalnaker's definition, which turns out to be quite similar to Zucchi's (see also note 11 below).

removed. The result is that c" consists of just those worlds in which Meg can sue; that is, the conclusion is true in c". So we have an account, given in truth-conditional semantic terms, which both reflects Levinson's ('embedded implicature') assumptions about conversational implicatures and the truth conditions of the conditional, and shows why we are inclined to accept (35)/(41) as a valid piece of reasoning.

This is a neat result, apparently solving the problem I raised for the embedded implicature hypothesis. However, I believe it introduces new problems, which make it ultimately untenable, problems arising from the means by which the positive result above is achieved, that is, the implicature-incorporating truth conditions for conditionals and the straightforward untagged adding of implicatures to the common ground. Given the nature of conversational implicatures (their pragmatic, defeasible nature), the account seems bound to overgenerate; that is, to give implicature-infected truth conditions for conditionals when the implicature at issue is, if present at all, independent of the propositional content, and to give predictions of validity for arguments which are intuitively not valid.

4.3 An Overgeneration Argument Against the Defense

First, consider the truth conditions of the conditional given in (39) above. It simply cannot be that any and every implicature of A (the sentence embedded in the antecedent) enters into the truth conditions of a conditional 'If A, then B'. Consider the following conversational exchange:

(42) X: Does Sam like John and Mary?
      Y: He likes Mary.
      Implicature: Sam doesn't like John

The implicature of Y's utterance depends on essentially the same conversational maxim or heuristic as the scalar cases on which Levinson focuses much attention ('some' and the words for cardinal numbers), that is, the Q-heuristic: what is not said (and would be relevant) is not the case. Now, if we apply the truth-conditional schema given in (39) to the conditional sentence in (43a) we get the truth conditions in (43b):

---

[9]Couched as it is in (externalist) semantic terms, I am unsure how closely we should expect this account to mesh with an essentially internalist (syntactic) account of cognitive processes of utterance understanding and mental reasoning. However, in what follows I try to address it on its own terms.

(43) a. If Sam likes Mary, then he'll ask her to his party.
      b. (43a) is true in the current context iff it is true that Sam will invite Mary to his party in all the worlds in the context in which it is true that Sam likes Mary and Sam does not like John.

But these, surely, are not the right truth conditions for (43a). Whether Sam does or does not like John is irrelevant to the truth of the conditional; the conditional is true provided that it is true that Sam will invite Mary to his party in all the worlds in the context in which Sam likes Mary, a potentially broader set of worlds than those specified in (43b).

The next move here would be to qualify the truth-conditional schema in (39) and change 'what A implicates' to 'what A *generally*, or normally, implicates' in an attempt to rule out the more context-sensitive sort of implicature in (42). This would bring the definition more fully into line with the embedded implicature hypothesis as Green (1998) defines it (see (33) above). This is not a possible move for those of us who do not believe that there is any absolute distinction to be made between two kinds of conversational implicatures (context-independent and context-sensitive). However, we will suppose for the moment that the distinction can be drawn so there is a clearly delineated subclass of implicatures (the generalized ones) that play this role in the truth conditions of conditionals. Still, I think, there is a problem of overgeneration, that is, of including in the truth conditions of conditionals certain instances of (generalized) implicature which, according to fairly robust intuitions, result in the wrong truth conditions.

Let's consider several well-established cases of generalized conversational implicature, starting with the example in (44a):

(44) a. John isn't drunk today.
      b. *Implicature:* John might be (expected to be) drunk today.

A number of authors treat utterances of the form 'Not P' as generally implicating 'Possibly P' (Searle 1966; Grice 1967: lecture 1). Presumably, the conversational maxim responsible for this is that concerning relevance. The standard reason for issuing a denial, what makes such an utterance relevantly informative, is that one or other of the conversational participants entertains the possibility that the corresponding affirmative holds. Furthermore, the conditional in (45) with the negative sentence in its antecedent also clearly carries the same implicature:

(45) If John's not drunk today, the lecture will be good.
      Implicature: John might be drunk today.

However, I think most people would agree that the implicature does not contribute to the truth conditions of the conditional; that is, (45) is true iff the consequent (the lecture will be good) is true in all the worlds in which the antecedent (John is not drunk on the day of utterance) is true. The truth or falsity of the generalized implicature, that John might be drunk today, simply has no bearing on the truth or falsity of the conditional.[10]

Disjunctive utterances provide further widely accepted instances of generalized implicature. So an utterance of (46a) has the implicatures in (46b) and (46c), which, as Levinson puts it (2000: 108), are general but defeasible, hence have 'the hallmarks of GCIs':

> (46) a. Sue is a linguist or an anthropologist.
>   b. *Scalar implicature:*
>   Sue isn't both a linguist and an anthropologist.
>   c. *Clausal implicatures:*
>   The speaker doesn't know whether or not Sue is a linguist.
>   The speaker doesn't know whether or not Sue is an anthropologist.

The implicature in (46b) (together with the proposition expressed) gives rise to the common exclusive understanding of a disjunction and is derived by familiar quantity-driven pragmatic reasoning based on the scale <*or, and*>; the choice of a semantically weaker item on the scale is taken to imply the negation of higher items. The so-called 'clausal' implicatures in (46c) express the speaker's uncertainty about the truth value of each of the disjuncts. These latter cases are discussed by Grice (1978/89b: 44-45), where he considers the idea that the word 'or' has a strong sense, such that the meaning of 'A or B' consists of the truth-functional A v B plus a further component to the effect that 'there is some non-truth-functional reason for accepting A v B'. He argues that this second component is a conversational implicature rather than part of the conventional sense of the word 'or', but the fact that the issue of conventional meaning arises at all is indicative of the very general (cross-contextual) nature of the implicature.

Again, however, it seems clear that when the disjunction in (46a) occurs as the antecedent of a conditional, as in (47), the truth or falsity of these implicated propositions has no bearing on the truth or falsity of the conditional, which is true provided just that either it is false that Sue has at least one of the properties: being a linguist, being an anthropologist, or it is true that she is familiar with the linguistic relativity hypothesis.

---

[10] I owe this example and its implications to discussion with Deirdre Wilson.

(47) If Sue is a linguist or an anthropologist, she is familiar with the linguistic relativity hypothesis.

Third, as mentioned at the beginning of section 3, there is a whole host of cases of what Levinson (2000: 38-39, 135-53) calls M-implicatures, that is, generalized implicatures which result from a manner maxim to the effect that if what is said is expressed in an abnormal or marked sort of way then the event described is abnormal in some way. The example in (48) is a standard instance of this phenomenon.

(48) John's action caused the car to stop.
Implicature: There was something abnormal or indirect about the way in which John stopped the car.

However, again, it does not seem that this implicature contributes to the truth conditions of a conditional in which the original sentence occurs in the antecedent:

(49) If John's action caused the car to stop then he is responsible for the crash.

John's responsibility for the crash seems to rest just on his having been the person who was instrumental in stopping the car, not on this together with the implication that the stopping of the car was achieved in some unusual way.

So, even with the class of implicatures restricted to the (allegedly) generalized variety, it looks as if the truth conditions given for the conditional in (39) still result in the prediction of pragmatic effects on the truth conditions of conditional statements where there are none.[11] It is also worth noting that Levinson, who is probably the staunchest advocate of the generalized/particularized distinction, could not consistently support this restriction, since he has pointed out that there are in fact *some* particularized implica-

---

[11] King and Stanley (forthcoming) attempt a somewhat similar account of pragmatic contributions to the truth conditions of conditionals, their main concern, however, being to show that these pragmatic effects are 'weak', that is, they are mandated by elements of linguistic form. This depends on the assumptions: (a) that there is some formal/syntactic reflex in linguistic form of the 'contextually relevant similarity relation' component of Stalnaker's semantics for conditionals (see brief discussion in section 3 above), and (b) that the (allegedly) linguistically triggered search picks up just those elements of pragmatic meaning that do in fact affect truth conditions. Breheny (forthcoming) argues that the account fails in both these respects; in particular, with regard to the second point, he claims that it faces essentially the same problem of overgeneration as the account I am discussing.

tures that can enter into the content of such 'intrusive' constructions as the conditional (see Levinson 2000: 237-39). If this is right, the distinction between those pragmatic inferences that affect truth conditions and those that do not, crosscuts the distinction between generalized and particularized implicatures, so it looks as if there is no way of amending the definition of the truth-conditional content of conditionals so as to capture just those instances of implicature that do intrude.

Let's consider now the issue of (intuitive) argument validity. As we have seen, Zucchi's account does capture the intuitive validity of the argument in (41), while maintaining the 'embedded implicature' view of the utterances in the premises. However, given that there appear to be no constraints (apart from a consistency requirement) on the adding of implicatures to common ground, the account seems bound to overgenerate, that is, to predict some lines of argument as valid when they are not. My strategy here is to take a putative argument which is plainly not valid and show that the aspect of the context-update account which does the work of capturing the validity of (41) leads to erroneous validity predictions in these other cases. Consider the following apparent line of reasoning:

(50) Premise 1: If Sam doesn't like John, he won't invite him (John) to his party.
Premise 2: Sam likes Mary.
Conclusion: Sam won't invite John to his party.

I take it that we would not assent to this, that we intuitively find it to be not a valid argument. Crucially for my point, this seems to be so even in a context resulting from the exchange in (42) (repeated here for convenience):

(42) X: Does Sam like John and Mary?
Y: He likes Mary.
Implicature: Sam doesn't like John.

It just seems that when it comes to arguments (what some might term 'adversarial discourse') we do not allow the intrusion of even quite salient implicatures.

Let's see how (50) works on Zucchi's approach, bearing in mind that the implicature(s) as well as the asserted content of an utterance become part of the common ground. Premise 1 updates the context so that it contains only worlds in which either it is false that Sam dislikes John or it is true that Sam will not invite John to his party. Premise 2 causes an update in which both the proposition expressed *and the implicature* are added to the context, so that all those worlds in which it is false that Sam likes Mary and (crucially) all those worlds in which he dislikes John are thrown out, leaving just worlds in which it is true that Sam will not invite John to his party. So the argument is predicted to be valid.

Now it might reasonably be objected that, just as with the truth conditions of conditionals discussed above, there have to be restrictions on the class of implicatures that enter into judgments of argument validity, that is, the implicatures at issue must be of the generalized variety (occurring regularly across contexts unless specifically blocked). So let's take an argument with the same structure as the previous one but which involves a much less context-sensitive implicature: the inference from a use of 'some of the x' to 'not all of the x', which is, as discussed earlier, usually given as the textbook case of a generalized conversational implicature:

(51) Premise 1: If not all the students pass the exam the teacher will be upset.
Premise 2: Some of the students will pass the exam.
Conclusion: The teacher will be upset.

My own intuitions and those of everyone I have consulted are that this putative argument is not valid; there is a strong sense of a missing premise. However, on the Zucchi account it will come out as valid, since the occurrence of the sentence in the second premise carries a default implicature that not all of the students will pass the exam, and this implicature enters into the common ground (updating it so that worlds in which all students pass the exam are removed) along with the asserted content. Thus the antecedent condition is met (not all the students will pass the exam) and the conclusion (that the teacher will be upset) is true in that context.[12]

Consider another example, one which turns on the generalized implicature carried by a denial of P, namely that it is possible that P:

(52) Premise 1: If it's possible that John is drunk today we should cancel his lecture.
Premise 2: John is not drunk today.
Conclusion: We should cancel his lecture.

---

[12]Breheny (forthcoming) argues convincingly that scalar implicatures never intrude on propositional content, contrary to Levinson's (2000) claims. Since scalar implicatures, in particular those associated with the use of 'some of the x', are the paradigm case of generalized conversational implicatures, Levinson's claim (2000: 259) that their special properties (as allegedly local default inferences) provide us with at least a solid chunk of the solution to the problem of pragmatic intrusion into what is said (Grice's circle) is severely undermined.

As a line of reasoning, this is quite bizarre; the 'conclusion' seems to be virtually the opposite of the one that we would be inclined to draw from these two premises. However, again, validity is predicted if the implicature that generally accompanies denials (so is carried by an utterance of the sentence in premise 2) is added to the common ground, thus ruling out worlds in which the antecedent of the conditional is false and leaving those in which the consequent is true.

My strategy here has been to choose as the antecedent of the conditional premise a proposition whose content is the same as that of a generalized implicature of the minor premise and then trade on the fact that the implicature does not enter into our validity judgements. The procedure could be repeated for any number of other cases involving alleged generalized implicatures (for example, the disjunction cases and the M-implicatures mentioned above).

To conclude this section, although the Zucchi account successfully captures the validity of the particular argument in (35)/(41) while preserving the 'embedded implicature' assumptions, it is liable to make a range of wrong predictions, both about the truth conditions of conditionals and about the (intuitive) validity or invalidity of other arguments. So it looks as if this account cannot be adopted in any general way as a means of saving the embedded implicature position of Levinson, Green and others.

4.4 The Coherent Conversation Argument

Some people are uneasy about the use of natural language in framing logical arguments, considering it to be too imprecise and connotation-ridden for this job, which requires a regimented logical language. There is a worry too about just what intuitive judgements of validity are really judgements of. Although I do not think this is a problem for the arguments above, let us anyway turn to a consideration of more obviously conversational exchanges, where the judgement to be made is not one of (in)validity but of conversational (in)coherence. To get a feel for the property in question, consider C's contribution to the conversation in (53):

(53) A: Does Bill have a girlfriend these days?
B: He visits New York every weekend.
C: No, he doesn't. He goes there to see his ill mother.

There is something noticeably odd/less than fully coherent about C's response. Arguably, the oddness lies with C's disagreeing not with what B has said but with an implicature of B's utterance (that Bill does have a girl-friend). It seems that the implicature does not fall in the scope of the denial.

Consider next the exchange in (54):

(54) A: Mary fell over and hurt her knee.
      B: No, she didn't. She hurt her knee and fell over.

This seems to be a coherent exchange; there is no oddity comparable to that in (53), though, as with (53), there is a pragmatically derived element of meaning, this time concerning the temporal order and the cause-consequence relation of the two events under discussion and it is this that B is disagreeing with. We can explain the difference between the two cases if we assume that B intends the content falling within her negation to be the same as the content of A's utterance, that is, that Mary fell over and *as a result* she hurt her knee. On a relevance-theoretic account, a pragmatic enrichment of the linguistically encoded content of A's utterance (hence an aspect of its truth-conditional content) is being denied by B; this is what distinguishes the example from (53), where it is an implicature that is being denied.

For Levinson, the cause-consequence relation in (54) is a generalized implicature of A's utterance, while the implicature in (53) is particularized. However, he cannot use his GCI/PCI distinction to account for the difference in coherence between the two cases, as the following exchanges show:

(55) A: The teacher's going to be upset unless we pass all the exams.
      B: Yes, that's right. If we pass some of the exams she's going to be upset.

(56) A: John caused the car to stop.
      B: No, he didn't. He stopped the car by braking in the usual way.

Neither of these seems to be a fully coherent exchange. The second part of B's utterance in (55) does not satisfactorily endorse his just expressed agreement with A, even though 'some of the exams' has the very default implicature which should match the content of the antecedent of A's conditional. In (56), B disagrees with the generalized implicature which is carried by A's use of the phrase 'caused the car to stop' (as opposed to the unmarked 'stopped the car'), that is, the implicature that there is something unusual about the way John stopped the car. But it seems, again, that this does not fall in the scope of his explicit denial.[13]

Thus we see that intuitions about conversational (in)coherence, like those concerning argument (in)validity, are not captured by the hypothesis that the generalized conversational implicatures of simple structures fall within the semantic scope of more complex constructions in which the simple sentences are embedded.

5   Conclusion: Pragmatic Enrichment and Conversational Implicatures

The arguments in the previous section, concerning the validity (or invalidity) of arguments framed in natural language, and the coherence (or incoherence) of conversational exchanges, favor an account of the pragmatically derived meaning of the examples under consideration as aspects of their truth-conditional content, both when they are embedded in the scope of a logical operator and when they are freestanding.

What the so-called 'intrusive' constructions do is provide us with a means for sharpening and corroborating our intuitions about the truth-conditional content of simple sentences. They do this because they prompt us to make truth-conditional evaluations of one constituent part with respect to another (the antecedent and the consequent of a conditional; the two states of affairs being compared in a comparative; the state of affairs expressed a denial and by its affirmative counterpart, etc). Hence the usefulness of the Scope Criterion.

Viewed as an application of this criterion, the examples in (55) and (56) show that at least two of Levinson's central cases of generalized implicatures do not contribute to truth-conditional content. Given also that some cases of particularized pragmatic inferences do contribute to truth-conditional content, it seems that we would not get much purchase on the question of what distinguishes the two kinds of pragmatic inference at issue (those that affect truth conditions and those that do not) by buying into the generalized/particularized implicature distinction. On the relevance-theoretic approach, the distinction is between pragmatic enrichments of encoded meaning, on the one hand, and genuine conversational implicatures, on the other, a distinction which is reflected in our intuitions about the content falling in the scope of logical operators, and which the mechanisms of utterance interpretation posited by the theory are set up to model. This approach preserves the original Gricean insight that the distinguishing charac-

---

[13]This argument turning on considerations of conversational coherence is based on similar points made by Breheny (2003, forthcoming).

teristic of implicatures (wherever and however they arise) is that they are non-truth-conditional components of utterance meaning.

References

Bach, K. 1994. Conversational Impliciture. *Mind and Language* 9: 124-62.

Bach, K. 2000. Quantification, Qualification, and Context: A Reply to Stanley and Szabò. *Mind and Language* 15: 262-83.

Bezuidenhout, A. 1997. Pragmatics, Semantic Underdetermination and the Referential/Attributive Distinction. *Mind* 106: 375-409.

Bezuidenhout, A. 2002a. Generalized Conversational Implicatures and Default Pragmatic Inferences. *Meaning and Truth: Investigations in Philosophical Semantics*, eds. J. K. Campbell et al., 257-83. New York: Seven Bridges Press.

Bezuidenhout, A. 2002b. Truth-Conditional Pragmatics. *Philosophical Perspectives* 16: 105-134.

Breheny, R. 2003. On the Dynamic Turn in the Study of Meaning and Interpretation. *Meaning: The Dynamic Turn*, ed. J. Peregrin. Amsterdam: Elsevier.

Breheny, R. forthcoming. On Pragmatic Intrusion into Semantic Content. Ms. RCEAL, Cambridge: University of Cambridge.

Carston, R. 1988. Implicature, Explicature and Truth-Theoretic Semantics. *Mental Representations: The Interface between Language and Reality*, ed. R. Kempson, 155-81. Cambridge: Cambridge University Press.

Carston, R. 1998. Informativeness, Relevance and Scalar Implicature. *Relevance Theory: Applications and Implications*, eds. R. Carston and S. Uchida, 179-236. Amsterdam: John Benjamins.

Carston, R. 2000. Explicature and Semantics. *UCL Working Papers in Linguistics* 12: 1-44. Reprinted 2004 in: *Semantics: A Reader*, eds. S. Davis and B. Gillon. Oxford: Oxford University Press.

Carston, R. 2002. *Thoughts and Utterances: The Pragmatics of Explicit Communication*. Oxford: Blackwell.

Carston, R. forthcoming/2004. Review of Presumptive Meanings: The Theory of Generalized Conversational Implicatures, by S. Levinson. *Journal of Linguistics*.

Cohen, L. J. 1971. Some Remarks on Grice's Views about the Logical Particles of Natural Language. *Pragmatics of Natural Language*, ed. Y. Bar-Hillel, 50-68. Dordrecht: Reidel.

García-Carpintero, M. 2001. Gricean Rational Reconstruction and the Semantics/Pragmatics Distinction. *Synthèse* 128: 93-131.

Green, M. 1998. Direct Reference and Implicature. *Philosophical Studies* 91: 61-90.

Grice, H. P. 1967. *Logic and Conversation*. William James lectures. Harvard University. Reprinted in H. P. Grice 1989b, 1-143.

Grice, H. P. 1975. Logic and Conversation. *Syntax and Semantics 3: Speech Acts*, eds. P. Cole and J. Morgan, 41-58. New York: Academic Press. Reprinted in H. P. Grice 1989b, 22-40.

Grice, H. P. 1978. Further Notes on Logic and Conversation. *Syntax and Semantics 9: Pragmatics*, ed. P. Cole, 113-27. New York: Academic Press. Reprinted in H. P. Grice 1989b, 41-57.

Grice, H. P. 1989a. Retrospective Epilogue. In H. P. Grice 1989b, 339-85.

Grice, H. P. 1989b. *Studies in the Way of Words*. Cambridge, MA: Harvard University Press.

King, J. and J. Stanley forthcoming. Semantics, Pragmatics, and the Role of Semantic Content. *Semantics vs. Pragmatics*, ed. Z. Szabò. Oxford: Oxford University Press.

Levinson, S. 1988. Generalized Conversational Implicatures and the Semantics/ Pragmatics Interface. Ms. University of Cambridge.

Levinson, S. 2000. *Presumptive Meanings: The Theory of Generalized Conversational Implicature*. Cambridge, MA: MIT Press.

Neale, S. 1992. Paul Grice and the Philosophy of Language. *Linguistics and Philosophy* 15: 509-59.

Neale, S. 2000. On Being Explicit. *Mind and Language* 15: 284-94.

Neale, S. forthcoming. *Linguistic Pragmatism*.

Posner, R. 1980. Semantics and Pragmatics of Sentence Connectives in Natural Language. *Speech Act Theory and Pragmatics*, eds. J. Searle, F. Keifer and M. Bierwisch, 168-203. Dordrecht: Reidel.

Recanati, F. 1989. The Pragmatics of What is Said. *Mind and Language* 4: 295-329.

Recanati, F. 1993. *Direct Reference: From Language to Thought*. Oxford: Blackwell.

Recanati, F. 2002. Unarticulated Constituents. *Linguistics and Philosophy* 25: 299-345.

Recanati, F. forthcoming/2003. *Literal Meaning*. Cambridge: Cambridge University Press. Available at website: http://www.institutnicod.org

Searle, J. 1966. Assertions and Aberrations. *British Analytical Philosophy*, eds. B. Williams and A. Montefiore, 41-54. London: Routledge and Kegan Paul.

Sperber, D. and D. Wilson. 1986/95. *Relevance: Communication and Cognition*. Oxford: Blackwell.

Stainton, R. 1994. Using non-Sentences: An application of Relevance theory. *Pragmatics and Cognition* 2: 269-84.

Stalnaker, R. 1974. Pragmatic Presuppositions. *Semantics and Philosophy*, eds. M. Munitz and P. Unger. New York: New York University Press. Reprinted in R. Stalnaker 1999: 47-62.

Stalnaker, R. 1975. Indicative Conditionals. *Philosophia* 5. Reprinted in R. Stalnaker 1999: 63-77.

Stalnaker, R. 1999. *Context and Content*. Oxford: Oxford University Press.

Stanley, J. 2000. Context and Logical Form. *Linguistics and Philosophy* 23: 391-434.

Stanley, J. and Z. Szabò 2000. On Quantifier Domain Restriction. *Mind and Language* 15: 219-61.

Wilson, D. 1975. *Presuppositions and non-Truth-Conditional Semantics*. New York: Academic Press.

Wilson, D. and D. Sperber 2002. Truthfulness and Relevance. *Mind* 111: 583-632.

6

Procedural Meaning and the Semantics/Pragmatics Interface

ANNE BEZUIDENHOUT

1 Introduction

Relevance theorists have argued that we must distinguish between words that encode concepts and those that encode procedures. The latter encode instructions that constrain the inferential phase of verbal communication. (This is explained in more detail below). This raises the question as to how we are to understand the notion of procedural encoding. I will argue that the notion of a procedural unit is something that has a place in an account of language *use*, and hence it belongs to a theory of pragmatic performance and not to a theory of semantic competence.

A very strong statement of this claim would be that the phrase 'procedural semantics' is a contradiction in terms. This paper examines an argument that purports to demonstrate this. The conclusion of the argument is that if one is interested in a theory of language production and understanding (in other words, in a theory of linguistic performance), and one appeals to the notion of procedural knowledge, then one cannot regard such procedural knowledge as embodied in semantic rules without turning it into something with conceptual content, and thus turning it into something that loses its procedural character. In other words, one cannot simultaneously treat something as procedural and as semantic. Something that lies on the procedural side of the procedural/declarative divide is something inherently

The Semantics/Pragmatics Distinction.
Claudia Bianchi (ed.).
Copyright © 2004, CSLI Publications.

pragmatic and belongs to a performance system, and is distinct from the knowledge that is constitutive of a speaker-hearer's semantic competence.

By stating the conclusion in this way, it seems that one must accept that the following distinctions line up with one another:

Semantic/pragmatic

Declarative/procedural

Competence/performance

In the course of critically evaluating the above-mentioned argument against procedural semantics, I will ask whether the parallelism between these three distinctions is ultimately sustainable.

1 The Conceptual/Procedural Contrast

I begin with a description of the contrast between procedural and conceptual encoding. The vast majority of lexical items have conceptual meaning, including common nouns ('chair', 'water', etc.),[1] verbs ('consider', 'leap', etc.), adjectives (e.g., 'red', 'slow', etc.), adverbs ('sadly', 'quickly', etc.), and prepositions ('behind', 'under', etc.). That is to say, these items encode concepts. If a lexical item has conceptual meaning, this meaning can potentially contribute to the truth-conditional content of an utterance containing that lexical item. However, having conceptual meaning does not guarantee that the item will be truth-conditionally relevant, since items with conceptual meanings sometimes play a non-truth-conditional role. Consider the following:

(1) Sadly, John's mother died last night.

(2) John looked sadly at the mess his dog had made.

'Sadly' has some conceptual content, but in (1) it is functioning as a sentence adverbial, and hence its conceptual content does not contribute to the truth-conditional content of the utterance, or at least to the truth-conditional content of the primary proposition expressed by the utterance. Rather, it

---

[1] I set to one side the Putnam/Kripke view about natural kind terms, such as 'tiger' and 'water'. On this view, the concepts associated with such terms are merely part of the stereotypes associated with these terms. These stereotypes are not extension-determining meanings. Instead, what fixes the extension of a natural kind term N is a causal-historical chain of uses of N that can be traced back to some event at which N was first introduced into the language. The extension of N includes all and only those objects whose natures are relevantly similar to the natures of those objects demonstratively or otherwise picked out during this introductory event. Since it is up to science to discover these natures, we must defer to the experts to determine which objects belong to the extensions of our terms. This linguistic division of labor means that we can use these terms even though our associated concepts are not uniquely identifying.

contributes to a higher-level proposition that expresses the speaker's attitude towards the proposition that John's mother died the night prior to the time of utterance. The speaker could have conveyed his attitude to this proposition using non-linguistic means, say by uttering the sentence 'John's mother died last night' in a sad tone of voice. The use of 'sadly' in (1) is in contrast to its use in (2), where 'sadly' *does* contribute conceptual content to the proposition expressed.

In contrast to items such as common nouns, verbs, etc., relevance theorists have claimed that words such as 'but', 'however', and inferential 'so' encode procedures. These items indicate something about the context in which the utterances of which they are a part are to be processed. They guide the hearer towards intended contextual effects,[2] and hence reduce the overall effort required to process the discourse.[3] Consider utterances of sentences such as:

(3) Kathleen is 37 years old but still attractive.
(4) It is winter in Genoa but summer in Johannesburg.

The use of 'but' in (3) is sometimes called the denial of expectation use. See Lakoff (1971). This use of 'but' presupposes that 37-year-old women are generally unattractive. It is possible that the speaker shares this prejudice against 37-year-old women.[4] However, even if the speaker rejects this presupposition, she must be assuming that this assumption is widely held by members of a certain cultural/social community. For instance, (3) could be uttered in response to what the speaker perceives to be Hollywood's prejudice against older women.

---

[2] There are three kinds of contextual effects that result from processing utterances. There might be contextual implications (i.e., ones that follow from what is expressed by the utterance together with assumptions already in the context, but that do not follow from either of these components alone). Second, an existing assumption might be strengthened. Third, an existing assumption might be contradicted.

[3] RT is often accused of emphasizing language understanding and ignoring language production. But the reduction in overall effort mentioned in the text applies equally to speaker and to hearer. If the speaker can rely on her hearer to pick up on her linguistic clues as to how to process her utterances, she can spare herself the effort of explicitly articulating everything she means to convey. Levinson (2000), in the course of defending his default theory of generalized conversational implicature, makes the point that articulation is costly.

[4] Thomas (1995: 57) cites a reaction by the actress Kathleen Turner when she received a movie script that was written for a female character '37 years old but still attractive'. Turner circled the word 'but' in the script and returned it to the movie studio with a note saying 'Try again'. She clearly attributed the presupposition mentioned in the text to the writer(s) of the script and perhaps also to the movie producers and studio executives.

The 'but' in (4) signals a contrast between two sets of implications. It signals that whatever propositions the listener was prepared to infer from the utterance of the first conjunct, he should infer a parallel but opposite set of propositions from the utterance of the second conjunct. For instance, if the listener was prepared to infer from the proposition expressed by the utterance of the first conjunct that anyone traveling to Genoa should pack warm clothes, then he should infer from the proposition expressed by the utterance of the second conjunct that anyone traveling to Johannesburg should *not* pack warm clothes. In addition to the uses illustrated here, there are undoubtedly further uses of 'but'.

Lexical items such as inferential 'so', 'since', 'as' and 'because', and words and phrases such as 'moreover' and 'after all' are also said to encode procedures. Consider:

(5) John wasn't at the party last night. So he must have stayed home.
(6) He was hungry, so he went to McDonalds.
(7) As/since/because John was hungry, he went to McDonalds.
(8) As/since John isn't here, he must still be in his meeting.
(9) John owes me money. Moreover, he owes me a lot.
(10) Have another drink. After all, it's your birthday.

'So' in (5) indicates that the utterance that follows should be processed as a conclusion. It differs from the 'so' in (6), which indicates that John's going to McDonald's is a causal consequence of his being hungry. 'As', 'since' and 'because' may signal that what follows is a cause, as in (7), or a reason, as in (8). 'Moreover' in (9) signals that what follows is an elaboration, and 'after all' in (10) signals that what follows offers justification or support.

Many other lexical items and linguistic constructions, too numerous to survey here, have been said to encode procedural meanings. For discussion see Andersen and Fretheim (2000); Blakemore (1987, 1988); Blass (1990); Fretheim (1998a, 1998b); Giora (1997); Iten (1997, 1998, 2002); Nicolle (1995, 1998); Wilson (1998); Wilson and Sperber (1993).

It is also possible to have items that encode *both* concepts *and* procedures. For instance, consider:

(11) He [gesturing to someone] is the man I saw stealing the car.
(12) The man from the IRS called. He will be here tomorrow.

The use of the pronoun 'he' carries a presupposition of weak familiarity, and hence its use signals to the listener that he should identify the referent of the pronoun with an individual that is salient/accessible in the context. The individual may be one that is salient in the physical context, as in (11), or from the prior linguistic context, as in (12). However, 'he' also carries some (admittedly rather minimal) conceptual/descriptive meaning. It carries person, number, gender, and animacy information (third person singular animate male). This conceptual content may or may not be truth-conditionally relevant. Direct reference theorists, for example, assume that singular referring expressions, including pronouns, contribute nothing but their referents to the propositions expressed with their help. Hence the gender, number and person information encoded by a pronoun such as 'he' would not be part of the proposition expressed by its means, but would simply constrain the search for an appropriate referent. However, if there are attributive uses of such pronouns, as argued by Bezuidenhout (1997), then such conceptual meaning may become truth-conditionally relevant. An example of such an attributive use is: 'He [pointing at a large footprint in the sand] must be a giant'. This arguably expresses the proposition that the male who made the footprint must be a giant.

Wilson and Sperber (1993) argue for the need to distinguish procedural and conceptual encoding, and they suggest at least two ways of doing so:

(a) Conceptual meaning is available to consciousness, whereas procedurally encoded information is not (1993: 16).
(b) Conceptual meaning is compositional, whereas procedurally encoded information is not (1993: 18).

However, both these criteria are problematic. Criterion (a) is problematic because even if we concede, as I think we should, that procedurally encoded information is not available to consciousness,[5] it is not clear that conceptual meanings as conceived of in RT are available to consciousness either. According to RT, conceptual meanings are the lexical concepts that are (potential) constituents of the LF-representations that are the output of linguistic decoding processes. These representations in turn are inputs into the pragmatic processes of enrichment and loosening that result in *ad hoc* concepts. The latter are constituents of the propositional forms (explicatures) of utterances. See Carston (1997, 2002). At best it would be these *ad hoc* concepts (the pragmatically adjusted lexical concepts) that are available to con-

---

[5]Wilson and Sperber think that procedurally encoded information is unavailable to consciousness because we do not have direct access to 'the inferential computations used in comprehension' (1993: 16). This suggests that they are identifying procedural information with *inferential computations*. This is different from the view I will defend in the following sections, according to which procedural meanings are *causal dispositions*. For present purposes this difference between Wilson and Sperber and myself is not relevant, since I would agree that procedural information is not available to conscious awareness.

scious awareness. Thus it is not clear that the consciousness test helps to make a principled distinction between conceptual and procedural encoding.

Criterion (b) is also problematic. It is suggested in the course of a discussion of illocutionary adverbials. Wilson and Sperber claim that these adverbials have conceptual meanings and yet are non-truth-conditional, in the sense of not contributing content to the proposition expressed by an utterance (i.e. to its base-level explicature). Instead, these adverbials contribute content to higher-level explicatures. They indicate something about the speaker's attitude towards the expressed content or about the manner in which the speaker is expressing this content. Consider:

(13) Frankly, he is someone I never liked.
(14) Confidentially, he will not get the job.
(15) Unfortunately, I can't help you.

In (13) the speaker expresses the proposition that the male individual in question is someone the speaker never liked, but she also conveys the proposition that this information is being given in an open manner, that reveals her true opinions. (14) would be analyzed in a similar manner. In (15), the speaker expresses the proposition that she can't help the hearer, but she also conveys the proposition that this fact is something she regrets. In defense of the view that such sentence adverbials should be given a conceptual rather than a procedural analysis, Wilson and Sperber point out that such adverbials can be part of semantically complex phrases, which must be compositionally understood, as shown by (16) - (18) below:

(16) Frankly speaking, he is someone I never liked.
(17) Speaking frankly, though not as frankly as I would like, he is someone I never liked.
(18) In total, absolute confidence, he will not get the job.

However, the lexical items that are treated in RT as encoding procedural information can also occur as a part of semantically complex phrases. Consider the following:

(19) She is interested in our job. But, and this is a big but, we'll have to offer her much more money.
(20) PhotoShop allows us to digitally manipulate photographic images. So, although perhaps not obviously so, photography has become more like painting.

I do not think that the occurrence of these items in semantically complex phrases should deter us from a procedural analysis of these terms. But it does suggest that the compositionality test is not a reliable one for distinguishing the procedural from the conceptual.

In this paper I will not be concerned with deciding which items are to be analyzed in procedural terms and which are to be analyzed in conceptual terms (which to a large extent is what discussions of the conceptual/procedural distinction have been focused on). Rather, I will assume that there are some items that are correctly analyzed in procedural terms, and then ask what it means to say that such terms encode procedures.

1 Rules, Representations and the Procedural/ Declarative Distinction

So, what does it mean to say that lexical items of the sort mentioned above encode procedural information, or as Blakemore (1992: 151) puts it, 'encode instructions for processing propositional representations'? It is natural to assume that it means that the entries for these items in an ideal speaker-hearer's mental lexicon contain these instructions. In other words, to say that the lexical entry for item X contains procedural information is to say that there is a rule or instruction 'written' in the entry for X that specifies that a certain procedure must be followed if certain conditions are fulfilled. Such a rule would be what AI researchers call a *production rule*, which is a condition-action pair, $<C, A>$. It is a rule that says that if a certain condition C is fulfilled, then a certain action A must be performed.

Talk of rules being written under entries is a metaphorical way of speaking. The idea is that the mental lexicon uses a proprietary code for representing semantic information. This code could be Mentalese, which is the system of representation that Fodor (1975) claims is the language of thought. Hence these rules will be written in Mentalese. When the speaker-hearer accesses an item in the lexicon, he or she is able to access the information associated with that item, presumably in some sort of 'look-up' process that allows the entry for that item to be searched for relevant information. If the item encodes procedural information, the look-up process will access a rule. If the item encodes conceptual/descriptive information, the look-up process will access a concept.[6]

If the look-up process accesses a rule, and the condition of the rule is met, a certain action will be performed. Here the action in question is some

---

[6]Some philosophers equate concepts with rules. The concept *red* is a rule that specifies the conditions under which it is appropriate to apply the word 'red' (or whatever word in your language is associated with that concept – 'rouge' or 'rooi' or whatever). This would be to reject the conceptual/procedural distinction as understood within relevance theory, since all lexically encoded meaning would collapse into procedural meaning. So, for the purposes of this paper I will assume that concepts and rules are distinct.

sort of symbol manipulation (i.e. manipulation of Mentalese representations). In other words, given certain representations as input, certain representations will be produced as output. Figure 3.1 illustrates this representationalist picture of how (from the perspective of language comprehension) conceptual and procedural information is embodied at the sub-personal, computational level. On this representationalist conception, concepts and procedures are just two sorts of meanings, and both should be regarded as a part of our semantic competence. With these assumptions in place, it is now possible to state the argument against procedural meaning.

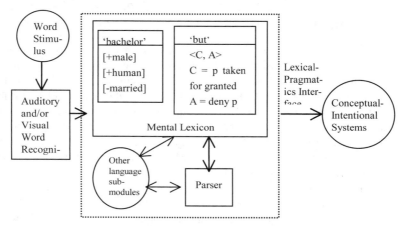

Figure 3.1: The Representationalist Picture of the Mental Lexicon

The argument against procedural meaning thus conceived is very simple to state. It is a version of an argument that is used in a slightly different context by Dennett (1981), and by Kripke (1982) in his discussion of Wittgenstein on rule following. If procedural rules are treated as items that are represented in Mentalese and as items that are listed in lexical entries (which in turn are simply lists of representations – data structures – that can be searched), then we face a form of the rule following paradox. Rules themselves will simply be more symbols along with the symbols they are meant to manipulate. But then it looks as though we'll have to posit another set of rules for instructing us on how to use the original rules. Now, if these new rules are themselves items that are represented in Mentalese, the same problem arises all over again. Clearly we are off on an infinite regress here. Wittgenstein thought that if this regress of rules is to be avoided, there must be some point at which the rules give out. The whole system must therefore be grounded in something other than rules. For Wittgenstein, rules are grounded in actions or practices.

Wittgenstein would not have approved of the sort of computational perspective on language use that I have adopted in this paper, but his insight can be translated into one that applies within this computational perspective. The regress of rules I described can be stopped if at some point rules give way to procedures, where procedures are understood in some *non*-representational or *non*-symbolic way. We should think of procedures as part of the architecture of the performance system. In other words, procedures are embodied as part of the causal structure of the language production and comprehension system, and are not symbols or representations that are manipulated (inferentially or otherwise) within the system. Here I am following Dennett (1981: 50), who contrasts two ways of storing information: storing it in propositional or coded form and storing it tacitly, in the organization of the representational system.

Dennett makes this distinction in the course of a discussion of how our beliefs are stored. We potentially believe an indefinite number of things, but in the course of our lives will only generate some finite number of propositions by means of an extrapolator-deducer mechanism, whose operations Dennett describes as follows (1981: 45-46, his emphases):

> It has the capacity to extract axioms from the core when the situation demands it, and deduce further consequences. To do this, it needs to have an information store of its own, containing information about what items it would be appropriate at any time to retrieve from the core … . Now how will the extrapolator-deducer mechanism store its information? In its own core library of brain-writing sentences? If it has a core library, it will also need an extrapolator-deducer mechanism to act as librarian, and what of *its* information store? Recalling Lewis Carroll's argument in 'What the Tortoise Said to Achilles', we can see that an extrapolator-deducer will be hamstrung by a vicious regress if it must always rely on linguistically stored beliefs which it must retrieve and analyze about what can be deduced from what… .
>
> The conclusion is that writing – for instance, brain writing – is a *dependent* form of information storage. The brain must store at least some of its information in a manner not capturable by a brain-writing model.

One might call the alternative conception of procedures that I am advocating the *dispositionalist* conception, in contrast to the *representationalist* or *rule-based* conception of procedures that I have argued leads to an infinite regress of rules. If we accept this dispositionalist conception of procedures, must we reject the relevance theory distinction between conceptual and procedural encoding? Not at all. However, we will need to understand the distinction in a different way from the one assumed at the beginning of this section. The conceptual/procedural distinction is not a difference in the type of information encoded by a lexical item (concept vs. rule). Rather, the distinction is one regarding how such knowledge is embodied. Conceptual meanings (concepts) are embodied as mental representations/symbols. Procedures are embodied as causal dispositions, as ways in which the system acts on representations.

Blakemore (1992: 148-51) contrasts what she calls a representational with a procedural analysis of expressions like 'so', 'after all' etc. In her discussion, 'representational' is functioning as a synonym for 'conceptual' so that the contrast Blakemore is discussing is just the conceptual/procedural distinction discussed in Section 2. Blakemore attributes a 'representational' (i.e. conceptual) analysis of items like 'so' to Grice. Grice (1989: 362) claims that one can make what he calls a ground floor statement and simultaneously perform a higher-order speech act of commenting in a certain way on the lower-order speech act. Consider 'Our computer is down. So I cannot help you'. On Grice's analysis, this simply asserts that the speaker's group's computer is not functioning and that the speaker cannot help the hearer. But the 'so' communicates the higher-order proposition that the speaker's being unable to help is explained by the computer's being down (i.e. that being unable to help is a causal consequence of the computer's being down). Blakemore construes this analysis of 'so' as a 'representational' one, since she says it amounts to claiming that 'so' has conceptual content (because 'so' communicates a higher-order proposition). Blakemore contrasts this with her own procedural account of 'so', according to which 'so' encodes instructions for processing propositional representations. So Blakemore's use of 'representational' is different from the one in the previous paragraph, which applies not to a particular type of analysis of lexical items such as 'so', but to a particular understanding of what it is for an item to lexically encode a procedure. Blakemore does not address the latter issue. Blakemore (1992: 150) says that when a speaker uses 'so' *the speaker is instructing the hearer* to interpret what follows as a conclusion. But she does not offer any details of a sub-personal, computational account to explain how this personal-level claim can be true. In contrast, my main concern is to offer a computational account that explains how the conceptual/procedural distinction is psychologically realized.

I have argued that procedures must be thought of as part of the causal structure of the *language performance system* (viz., the language production and comprehension system). This is because, on the comprehension side, the sort of procedural knowledge we are concerned with is knowledge of what are appropriate contexts for the interpretation of utterances and knowledge of how to connect utterances so as to produce adequate contextual effects for no gratuitous processing effort. On the production side, it is knowledge of how to guide the hearer to these contexts and how best to organize the discourse so as to make one's communicative intentions clear. So we have moved quite far from the representationalist idea that conceptual and procedural meanings are both stored in the mental lexicon. Procedures are strictly not a part of the lexicon at all, but of the performance system, although presumably the performance system is able to use information from various sources, including conceptual information from the mental lexicon.

Perhaps we've moved too quickly. Perhaps we need to backtrack and assume that procedures and concepts *are* both stored in the lexicon, the former tacitly and the latter explicitly. This would be tantamount to thinking of procedural information as part of the causal structure of the *mental lexicon*, not of the *performance system*. Now I agree that the mental lexicon must have certain information tacitly stored. As the quote from Dennett (1981: 45-46) suggests, *any* cognitive (sub-)system will need to have some sort of extrapolator-deducer mechanism, which is able to manipulate the information that is symbolically represented in that system. If this mechanism is not to be 'hamstrung by a vicious regress', its operation will necessitate a distinction between information that is represented in symbolic form and information that is hard-wired into the architecture of the (sub)-system. This applies just as much to the mental lexicon as it does to the performance system.

Clearly, we must recognize the existence of certain purely lexical processes, e.g. the hypothesized 'look-up' processes mentioned earlier. The lexicon is after all just a store of information and there must therefore be purely lexical processes involving the storage, cataloguing, and retrieval of such information.[7] Moreover, there must be rules governing such processes, and these rules cannot be (or cannot all be) propositionally represented, or else we face a regress of rules. So there must be information tacitly stored in the causal structure of the mental lexicon. But even though we must recognize that some information is tacitly stored in the lexicon, this information is not the procedural information that was described in the previous section.

We must also recognize that there are processes such as sense extension, lexical disambiguation, type coercion, conceptual blending, pragmatic enrichment and loosening, etc. See Asher and Lascarides (1996); Carston (1997, 2002); Copestake and Briscoe (1996); Coulson (2001); Fauconnier (1985, 1997); Fauconnier and Sweetser (1996); Pustejovsky (1995, 1998); Pustejovsky and Boguraev (1996); Sperber and Wilson (1995). Some peo-

---

[7] What information is lexically stored is a matter of some dispute. Some theorists, such as MacDonald et al. (1994), argue that a great deal of information is included in the lexicon. Besides the usual semantic, lexical category and thematic role information that one would expect in a lexical entry, they also think that there is information about possible argument structures and possible phrase structures (X-bar structures) that the item could be a part of. (1994: 688, Figure 3). Moreover, they claim that 'each component of a lexical entry carries information about its frequency of occurrence in the language' (1994: 685).

ple might regard these as lexical processes. However, all of these are processes in which lexical and pragmatic information interact, and so they cannot be thought of as *purely* lexical. Hence the procedures governing these processes cannot be purely lexical either.

For example, Asher and Lascarides (1996) show how discourse level information can interact with lexical information in the process of lexical disambiguation. Asher and Lascarides claim that there are various rhetorical relations that affect the structure of discourse. The rhetorical relations they have in mind are ones such as: *Narration, Elaboration, Explanation, Background, Evidence, Consequence* and *Contrast.* Consider the following two discourses:

(21) The judge asked where the defendant was. His barrister apologized, and said he was at the pub across the street. The court bailiff found him slumped underneath the bar.
(22) The judge asked where the defendant was. His barrister apologized, and said he was at the pub across the street. But in fact the court bailiff found him slumped underneath the bar.

Asher and Lascarides argue that the ambiguous term 'the bar' will be resolved in favor of the pub meaning in case (21), because this is a narrative story, and if we see the sentences in the discourse as connected via the relation *Narration,* we will assume that the events are described in their temporal sequence. On the other hand, the use of 'but' in (22) signals a contrast, and so the events described will be related via the rhetorical relation *Contrast.* In this case the term 'the bar' will be interpreted in its courtroom sense.

These are cases where discourse knowledge helps in lexical disambiguation, so the influence is from pragmatics to lexical semantics. But sometimes the influence is in the opposite direction. Knowledge of semantics determines what sort of discourse relation one will infer. Consider:

(23) Max fell. John pushed him
(24) Max enjoyed a large meal. He ate salmon and devoured lots of cheese.

In the case of (23), one's semantic knowledge that pushing can cause the thing pushed to move will suggest that the second sentence in (23) is to be understood as an explanation for the occurrence reported by the first. In (24), one's semantic knowledge that enjoying a meal involves eating food and that salmon and cheese are types of food will suggest that the second sentence is an elaboration on the event reported by the first sentence.[8]

The main point here is that because processes such as sense extension and lexical disambiguation involve the *interaction* of lexical and pragmatic information, the procedures governing them cannot be thought of as purely lexical. Hence these procedures cannot be thought of as part of the causal architecture of the mental lexicon. Rather, they must be thought of as part of the causal architecture of the performance system more generally. What is true of the procedures governing processes such as sense extension is equally true of the procedures that were described in Section 2, which govern the inferential phase of verbal communication. That the operation of these procedures is not confined to the mental lexicon should be even clearer, for these procedures are not used only to interpret single lexical items, or even single phrases or sentences.[9] They play a role also in the recovery of implicatures and help the hearer to construct discourse-level representations. Hence there is even more reason than in the case of the procedures involved in sense extension, lexical disambiguation, etc. to see these procedures as non-lexical or at least not purely lexical.

So I conclude that conceptual and procedural information are not two types of information both of which are stored in the lexicon, one type explicitly and the other tacitly. Rather, procedural information is not properly speaking a part of the lexicon at all, but part of the causal architecture of the performance system more generally.

Thus far the picture that emerges is that lexical-conceptual meanings are embodied in a different way from the procedural knowledge that is used in inferential communication. To mark this fact that one might invoke Chomsky's distinction between competence and performance. The conceptual meanings that are associated with lexical items constitute an ideal speaker-hearer's *semantic competence*, whereas the ability to use those concepts constitutes the ideal speaker-hearer's procedural knowledge, and this procedural knowledge is what drives language production and understanding (viz.

---

[8]Asher and Lascarides (1996, 1998) offer analyses of discourse within a framework they call Segmented Discourse Representation Theory (SDRT). In SDRT, discourse contexts are represented as recursive, relational structures (SDRSs), which involve discourse representation structures (DRSs) that represent the contents of clauses, but that also represent discourse relations like *Parallel*, *Narration* and *Background*. These relations hold between DRSs and they indicate how the discourse hangs together. So discourse relations that are given a procedural treatment in RT are declaratively represented in SDRT. This declarative approach is not something that Asher and Lascarides attempt to justify.

[9]Sometimes they are used in this way. For example, indexicals such as 'he' encode procedural information, which is used in context to determine the referents of these indexicals. Hence this procedural information is used in the recovery of *explicatures*. On the other hand, lexical items such as 'but' encode information that is used in the recovery of *implicatures*.

linguistic performance). So it appears then that the conceptual/procedural distinction lines up with the competence/performance distinction as well as with the semantic/pragmatic distinction. The notion of a procedural unit is something that has a place in an account of language *use*, and hence it belongs to a theory of pragmatic performance and not to a theory of semantic competence.

1   Objections to the Dispositional Analysis and Replies

One might try to resist the causal/dispositionalist understanding of the procedural element in language by insisting that the procedural knowledge associated with lexical items such as 'but', 'however', etc. *is* rule-based. After all, we can formulate the procedure associated with 'but' as a rule or instruction that has propositional content. Hence to say that we have the procedural knowledge in question is to say that we have mentally represented what the rule specifies (the condition-action pair). If we have mentally represented this condition-action pair, then we should say that this rule is part of our *semantic competence*, and that it is knowledge that is accessed in the course of language production and understanding.

In reply, we need to distinguish what belongs to our *theory* of language understanding and production (viz. our theory of linguistic performance), and what belongs to the performance system itself. As theorists we surely *can* give propositional expression to the procedural knowledge embodied in the linguistic performance system. But if we are to avoid the regress of rules mentioned in the previous section, we cannot conceive of these rules as implemented in the linguistic system in the form of mentally represented rules that are entered in the mental lexicon in the same way that conceptual meanings are.

A second objection to the dispositionalist view is that even if items like 'but', 'so', and 'after all' encode procedural knowledge, this knowledge will still have to be exercised in particular conversational contexts. This suggests that there must be some sort of 'trigger condition' associated with these lexical items that indicates when it is appropriate to exercise the dispositions they encode. Surely such trigger conditions will have to be explicitly represented, so that after all procedural knowledge will have to rest on something declarative. However, like the first objection this confuses what is part of our theory of the performance system and what is part of the system itself. We as theorists can explicitly state the conditions under which a certain disposition will be exercised. But all that is necessary is that there be some situation that triggers the exercise of the disposition in the speaker-hearer. The speaker-hearer need not represent this situation, either explicitly or tacitly.

A third objection to the dispositional view of procedures is a version of an objection that Chomsky (1996) raises against Dummett and Kenny. Chomsky attributes to these philosophers the view that knowledge of language is an ability, and hence that knowing a language is just like knowing how to ride a bike. Linguistic knowledge for these philosophers is knowledge-how rather than propositional knowledge-that. Chomsky objects that abilities or any kind of know-how must be grounded in something non-dispositional. He writes: 'knowing-how involves a crucial cognitive element, some internal representation of a system of knowledge' (Chomsky 1996: 565). So, applying this to the dispositionalist understanding of procedures, one might argue that procedural knowledge presupposes declarative knowledge, and that underlying any procedure is some mentally represented system of propositional knowledge. This would appear to reverse the order of dependence suggested by the regress of rules argument laid out in the previous section. That argument purported to show that propositional knowledge must rest ultimately on something non-representational/proce-dural.

I believe that the regress of rules argument trumps any claim that propositional knowledge is more basic than procedural knowledge. But in any case, I think this objection from Chomsky can be defused, because there is an understanding of Chomsky's point about linguistic abilities according to which it is *not* a challenge to the conclusion of the regress of rules argument. Chomsky's point can be seen as a particular application of a more general argument that has been made in the philosophy of science about dispositional properties, such as the property of being soluble. It has been argued that solubility, say of table salt, cannot be reduced to facts about the behavior of table salt in various types of situations. It is of course true that if table salt is placed in water it will dissolve, and if it is placed in gravy it will dissolve, and so on. But these dispositional facts about table salt must supervene on something more basic. In particular, there must be facts about the microstructure of table salt that explain these dispositional facts.

In a similar vein, Chomsky can be understood as saying that linguistic abilities rest on and are explained by something more basic. Presumably the more basic level here is the computational level. Chomsky describes this as the level at which we can talk of an 'internal representation of a system of knowledge'. This phrase of Chomsky's may seem to commit us to the idea that all linguistic knowledge is encoded in mental symbols. However, the phrase 'internal representation' can be treated as a term covering both explicit and tacit ways of storing information. (See Dennett 1981: 50). Not all information is explicitly mentally represented (i.e. by means of mental symbols). Some is stored tacitly, in the organization of the representational system. On this way of understanding Chomsky, his critique of Dummett and Kenny on linguistic abilities does not contain the seeds of a challenge to the dispositional understanding of procedures, given that we construe the dispositional view as claiming that at least some linguistic information must be tacitly stored, in the organizational structure of the performance system.[10]

A fourth objection is that I've misapplied the regress of rules argument. One might argue that the most that argument shows is that *some* procedural information must be tacitly represented in the causal architecture of the system, not that *all* of it must be. For all the regress argument shows, much of our procedural knowledge is stored in the mental lexicon (along with lexical concepts) in the form of explicit rules. Well, yes, there could be propositionally stated rules in the mental lexicon. But then these fall on the conceptual side of the conceptual/procedural divide, and they are not properly speaking procedural in the sense I intend. They stand in need of interpretation or application just as much as non-propositional lexical concepts do, and in that sense such rules do not drive interpretation. They are things being manipulated, not things doing the manipulating.

A fifth objection is that my view commits me to the claim that there are no procedural symbols in the language of thought. Natural language words that have conceptual meanings correspond to lexical concepts, and these lexical concepts are in effect (a subset of) symbols of Mentalese. So by denying that words such as 'but' correspond to concepts, I am committed to saying that there are no analogs in Mentalese to words such as 'but'. There is no mental symbol in Mentalese that plays the same role that 'but' plays in English. But this is implausible, since one can reason in Mentalese just as one can in English, and surely such non-linguistic reasoning needs markers of structure (like 'so' and 'but') just as reasoning expressed in natural language does? In response one could simply deny that this is so. Procedural markers such as 'but' have evolved to help hearers identify discourse structure, but an individual thinker does not need such aids in order to know how his own reasoning is structured. One possible retort is that a thinker can engage in a mental dialogue with himself, taking first one side of an issue then another, and surely such mental dialogue would stand in need of structural markers? I do not deny that we often rehearse arguments in our minds. But such conscious thought processes are carried out in natural language – English if one is a monolingual speaker of English. And of course such conscious thinking can make use of words such as 'but' and 'so', since these are English words.

---

[10]This does mean stretching the word 'representation' so that it covers both mental symbols and causal structures, and requires a rephrasing of the distinction between what I earlier called the representational and dispositional accounts of procedural knowledge, since even the dispositional view counts as representational in this stretched sense.

But the sort of pragmatic processes that are involved in language comprehension and production are not available to conscious awareness, and these unconscious 'inferential' processes involving the manipulation of Mentalese symbols do not stand in need of symbols that are analogues to natural language structural markers. If there were such symbols, they would just be more mental symbols in need of manipulation, and so the regress of rules argument would apply straightforwardly to show that truly procedural elements cannot be embodied as mental symbols but must be part of the causal architecture of the system doing the reasoning.

A sixth objection is as follows. I have argued that procedural information is not part of the mental lexicon, since it is not stored in the mental lexicon either explicitly (in the form of a propositionally represented rule) or tacitly (in the causal structure of the mental lexicon). It is, I have claimed, stored tacitly as part of the causal structure of the performance system more generally. (This system may of course, as part of its functioning, need to access information stored in the mental lexicon). One might object: 'How could "but" and its ilk not be a part of the lexicon when these are words in the language?'. Obviously I would not deny that 'but' is a word of the language. But I do deny that every word of the language is necessarily associated with an entry in the mental lexicon. Some words trigger procedures and some words are associated with concepts (and some words have dual aspects and so both trigger procedures as well as are associated with concepts). Only words associated with concepts have entries in the mental lexicon. One might respond that so long as I concede that 'but' is a word of the language, I must be committed to there being some place where a mental representation of that word is stored, and where else would that be but the mental lexicon? Yes, I concede there must be a word store, and for all I have said so far, there could be a single store for all words. What I am denying is only that all words have *entries* in the lexicon. In other words, on my picture, even if 'but' (or a representation of it) is stored in the mental lexicon, activating that word will not give access to a data structure. Instead, a disposition to process data structures in a certain way will be triggered.

This leads to a seventh objection. I have said that the role of some words is to trigger procedures, not to give access to concepts in the mental lexicon. So I am committed to there being two classes of words whose roles in processing are very different. But, the objection goes, it is implausible to claim that the roles of words are divided in this way. Implausible as it may seem to common sense, there nevertheless is a fair amount of empirical evidence that supports this view. Psycholinguists have long been interested in a distinction between content words and function words (or open-class versus closed-class words). This distinction does not perfectly line up with the conceptual/procedural distinction, but there is a good deal of overlap. Many of the words regarded by psycholinguists as function words (e.g. determiners, sentence connectives etc.) are given a procedural treatment within RT.[11] The point is that there is evidence that content and function words are not accessed or processed in the same way. See Bradley (1978); Bradley et al. (1980); Friederici (1985); Garrett (1975, 1980, 1981); Koriat and Greenberg (1994, 1996); Joshi (1985); Park et al. (2002); Rapp and Caramazza (1997); Stemberger (1982).[12]

Not all of this work can be discussed here. I will briefly mention some of the findings of these researchers. There is evidence that function and content words participate in different sorts of speech errors. See Garrett (1975, 1980, 1981); Stemberger (1982). Bilingual code-switching data, discussed by Joshi (1985), also indicates that function and content words behave differently. Bradley (1978) found that in lexical decision tasks, where participants must decide whether a stimulus is a word or a non-word, there is a frequency effect for content words but not for function words. That is, there is a significant difference in reaction time on the decision task between high- and low-frequency content words but this difference is not significant for function words. Bradley also found that content and function words behave differently in tests of interference effects in judgments of non-words. Participants are slower to reject non-words when these begin with strings that correspond to real words. (e.g., people are slower to reject TOASTLE than to reject POASTLE). Bradley found this interference effect for content words, but not for function words. Bradley et al. (1980: 278) use such findings to hypothesize that the organization of word-retrieval mechanisms is different for function and content words. This in turn is used to explain the particular sorts of language performance deficits found in people suffering from Broca's aphasia (1980: 281). Broca's aphasics have problems with the

---

[11]One way in which the content/function distinction fails to line up with the conceptual/procedural distinction is that prepositions such as 'down', 'under' etc. are treated by psychologists as function words, whereas these would fall on the conceptual side of the conceptual/ procedural divide, since they clearly encode (fairly rich) conceptual content. Prepositions such as 'down' are more like words such as 'loves', which stand for real world relations, than they are like 'but' or 'after all', which indicate something about the information structure of discourse. Friederici (1985) is aware of this problem, and she is careful to distinguish between what she calls lexical prepositions and obligatory prepositions. These are distinguished precisely by the fact that the former have conceptual content, whereas the latter play a role in identifying the structure of sentences (and presumably also the structure of whole discourses).

[12]There is also work that suggests that content and function words are stored and accessed similarly. See Schmauder (1996); Schmauder et al. (2000). However, Schmauder and her collaborators included prepositions such as 'down' as examples of function words. But as mentioned in note 11, prepositions such as these encode concepts not procedures. Hence the work by Schmauder and her colleagues does not give a pure picture of how truly procedural words such as 'but' are stored and accessed.

functional aspects of language, both in language production and comprehension, although their ability to use content words seems relatively spared. This pattern of dissociation would be explained if content and function words are associated with two distinct recognition routines, one of which is impaired in Broca's aphasics.

Friederici (1985: 135) notes that several attempts to replicate Bradley's frequency effects have been unsuccessful. Nevertheless, Friederici accepts Bradley's claim that there is a processing distinction between function and content words. Friederici thinks that this distinction will not be revealed in the sorts of tasks that Bradley used, in which words were presented in isolation. Instead, Friederici presented function and content words in semantically constraining versus semantically neutral sentential contexts. Participants were given a booklet of target words (one word per page) and then they heard a series of sentences. For each auditory presentation (one corresponding to each target word) participants were instructed to signal as soon as they heard the target word. Friederici found that for normal (i.e. non-impaired) listeners, there was a significant context effect for content words, but not for function words. In other words, for content words, listeners were quicker to identify target words in semantically constraining as opposed to semantically neutral contexts. There was no such benefit for function words. Friederici takes this as evidence that content and function words operate at different processing levels. Function words play a role at the structural level in determining the frame within which content words will be processed, and hence they are relatively insensitive to semantic context.

This conclusion is bolstered by the performance of a group of agrammatics (e.g. those suffering from Broca's aphasia) on Friederici's word monitoring task. Like normal listeners, agrammatics showed a context effect for content but not for function words. But unlike normal listeners, their monitoring times for function words were slower than their monitoring times for content words. Friederici takes this to support the claim by Bradley et al. (1980) that in Broca's aphasics, mechanisms for the retrieval and processing of function words are impaired.

Koriat and Greenberg (1994, 1996) found that in a letter detection task, participants were more likely to skip letters in function words than in content words. Moreover, this is not attributable to the fact that function words are more frequent and/or predictable, so that they tend to be skipped over in reading. Koriat and Greenberg were able to rule out explanations in terms of frequency by using a feature of Hebrew. In Hebrew, function morphemes can appear as prefixes. By using content words that had the same initial letters as words with function prefixes, but where the letters were part of the word stem rather than a prefix, Koriat and Greenberg were able to show that the missing letter effect is greater for function words than for content words.

That is, letters are skipped more often when they are part of function prefixes than when those same letters are part of stems of content words. (These content words were matched for length and frequency with the prefixed words). In English, some words can play a function role in one context and a content role in another. For instance, compare the role of 'on' in 'on his way' with its role in 'on-switch'. Koriat and Greenberg have found that letter skipping is more likely in contexts in which such words are playing a function role.

Koriat and Greenberg argue that their findings support a structural view of text processing. The role of function words is to set a structural frame into which concepts accessed by content words will subsequently be slotted. They argue that once function words have played their role, their representations fade into the background, which explains the missing letter effect. Letter detection is harder for words with degraded representations. They also suggest that the structure revealed by function words is a tool that helps focus the meanings (the concepts) that are accessed via content words. These conceptual meanings are the primary objects of attention and memory (1996: 1194). This is compatible with the view argued for in this paper, where words that encode procedures are treated differently from words that encode concepts. Procedural information is stored as part of the causal architecture of the performance system, and so is indeed a 'tool'. It is what drives interpretation rather than being an object of interpretation.

I would add that my dispositional account of procedural encoding bolsters Koriat and Greenberg's explanation for their missing letter effect. If words like 'but' encode procedures rather than concepts, and procedures do not correspond to propositional representations, then the only representation associated with a word such as 'but' is a word-level representation. Thus, once processing has proceeded to the deeper, conceptual level, the word-level representation will drop out of the picture, and so presumably will fade. Schmauder et al. (2000) found evidence in the eye movement record during reading that readers are more likely to reread function words than content words. This would be explained if the only representation for a function word is the word-level one. Such representations would need to be continually refreshed, since they are not maintained and reinforced by a connection to a conceptual representation that is the object of attention and memory, as is a content word representation.

1 Objections to the Parallelism of the Semantic/Pragmatic, Conceptual/Procedural and Competence/Performance Distinctions

One might object that by locating procedural encoding in the pragmatic sphere and locating conceptual encoding in the lexical-semantic sphere my view commits me to two separate modules, a pragmatics module and a semantics one. However, a commitment to a pragmatics module leads to difficulties with another claim of mine, namely the claim that procedural information is part of the linguistic performance system, whereas conceptual information is part of our linguistic competence. Prince (1985, 1988, 1997) argues that there is a special purpose linguistic-pragmatics module, which interfaces between the language system proper and the system that controls discourse-level processes. This pragmatics module has its own proprietary store of pragmatic knowledge that is declaratively represented and that constitutes what Prince calls the speaker-hearer's *discourse competence*. If we accept the idea of a pragmatic discourse competence, then we will have to concede that the parallelism between the declarative/procedural, competence/performance, and semantics/pragmatics distinctions fails.

But it is by no means clear that we should accept Prince's arguments for the existence of a special purpose linguistic-pragmatics module. Prince argues that in order to explain how people know which linguistic forms are the appropriate ones to use in certain contexts, they must be supposed to have some sort of pragmatic competence. We cannot explain how people are able to make these form-function choices simply by appeal to their knowledge of meaning plus general conversational principles, since cross-linguistic evidence shows that very different linguistic forms serve the same function. Which forms serve which functions is something arbitrary and language-specific, and hence must be specially learned.

For example, in English we use It-clefts to focus certain content, and to put other content into the background. Consider:

(25) The Israelis claimed that it was they who found Eichmann.

(25) presupposes that someone found Eichmann, and so can only be felicitously used in a context where it is shared knowledge that Eichmann has been found. On the other hand, what is in focus position is new information. However, in Yiddish, a completely different syntactic structure is used to focus content:

(26) ... dos hobn zey gefunen aykhmanen

... this have they found Eichmann

This *dos*-construction is used to functionally focus the pronoun 'zey' ('they'). As Prince says: 'What marks the special function of this construction is the presence of a sentence-initial *dos* which is not an argument of the verb' (Prince 1988: 169). It seems that in Yiddish this construction is contrasted with another construction that is syntactically parallel except that it has a sentence-initial 'es' ('it'). This *es*-construction has a different discourse function. It is used when 'the fewest assumptions about shared knowledge are warranted' (1988: 169).

Prince's main point is that there is nothing iconic about any of these constructions (in either English or Yiddish) that would indicate what function they have. Neither can their function be predicted from knowledge of meaning together with knowledge of general conversational principles, such as the Gricean maxims. These constructions must be specially learned. For example, English speakers must learn principles such as 'If you want to focus content, use the It-cleft construction.' Hence the knowledge as to which forms to use for which functions must be declaratively represented and be part of a speaker-hearer's linguistic competence. Moreover, since this is knowledge of language *use* it is pragmatic knowledge, and so is a part of *pragmatic* competence (rather than semantic competence).

However, the same sorts of arguments that were used in Section 3 apply here and show that even if some form-function knowledge is encoded in the linguistic-pragmatics module in the form of principles or rules, not all such knowledge can be represented in this way, since this would lead to a regress of rules. Some such knowledge must be procedural, i.e. tacitly represented in the causal structure of the linguistic-pragmatics module, rather than explicitly represented in whatever proprietary mental code is used by this pragmatics module.

Moreover, it is not clear that Prince has established that *any* form-function knowledge (i.e. knowledge of which form to use for which function) is declarative knowledge that is represented in the proprietary code of some special purpose linguistics-pragmatics module. First, since the sort of knowledge that Prince is concerned about is very similar to the procedural knowledge that relevance theorists and others have described (see Blakemore 1992: 142-45), it is more parsimonious to reject the idea of a special-purpose linguistic-pragmatics module and instead see the special knowledge that Prince is talking about as knowledge that is tacitly stored in the performance system. So there *is* something special about the knowledge that Prince is pointing us to, but what is special about it is that it is procedurally encoded in the performance system, not that it is declaratively represented in a special-purpose linguistics-pragmatics module.

Second, form-function knowledge is not something that we need to invoke just to explain a small set of facts, such as facts about how different languages handle the focusing of content. Probably no pair of languages solves all form-function problems in exactly the same way. For instance, not all languages have definite and indefinite articles (e.g. Russian and Chinese do not). If we assume that the function of the definite article in English is to signal that the following information is already familiar in the context, whereas the indefinite article signals that the following information is new, then Russian and Chinese speakers must be able to signal this familiar/new contrast in some other way. And of course they are able to signal this in a different way. Similarly, Chinese has no distinction between mass and count nouns. So the mass/count distinction must be signaled in a different way than it is in English. And of course it is. Examples like this can be multiplied. The point is that learning a language is acquiring a system of linguistic forms that will constrain in various ways how one is able to convey certain information. It is not as though one learns various forms and then has to learn which of these forms one should use to perform which function. One learns the form *as* the way to perform a certain function. So form-function knowledge cannot belong to a module interfacing between the language system proper and the system handling discourse processes. It doesn't make sense to think that we can process a certain form and only then get to wonder about what function it is intended to perform. Once again, it seems more parsimonious to conceive of procedural/functional elements as being hard-wired into the performance system as ways of processing forms, rather than as declarative rules specifying which forms have which functions.

So, I do not think that we should accept Prince's claim that there is a special purpose linguistic-pragmatics module, and so we do not as yet have a reason to give up the parallelism between the declarative/procedural, competence/performance, and semantics/pragmatics distinctions.

However, the objection can be pushed from the opposite direction. Instead of trying to argue that procedural knowledge is declaratively represented in a pragmatics module (and so is a part of our 'discourse competence'), one can try to argue that procedural knowledge is part of our semantic competence, my assertions to the contrary notwithstanding. After all, one might protest, it is difficult to accept that knowledge of the meaning of 'table' is part of our linguistic competence, whereas the knowledge associated with 'but' is not. Chierchia raised this line of criticism against my view in his comments at the workshop where my paper was originally presented.

Chierchia writes: 'there are a lot of aspects of language that are best understood in terms of what one would want to call pretheoretically "a procedure" and yet we want to say that they are robustly part of our competence. A case in point (of the many that can be made) is that of negative polarity items (NPIs).' (Chierchia, p.c.). NPIs are items such as 'any', which are only grammatical in downward entailing contexts, such as negative contexts or the antecedents of conditionals. NPIs are ungrammatical in positive contexts. This pattern of licensed uses is illustrated for 'any' below:

(27) There isn't any food in the fridge.
(28) If there is any food in the fridge, we can eat at home tonight.
(29) *There is any food in the fridge.

Chierchia goes on to spell out what the 'procedural' meaning of 'any' might be, and offers a very compelling and elegant hypothesis in this regard. This claim of Chierchia's is something that does not challenge my views and that I can (and do) accept. After all, it is a working assumption of my view that some words encode concepts and some encode procedures. That 'any' belongs to the latter class is something I can readily agree to.

Chierchia's real challenge comes when he goes on to list some characteristics of the behavior of NPIs. Chierchia (p.c.) writes:

> The behavior of NPIs has the following characteristics:
> a.   It has to do with the distribution of a certain class of morphemes
> b.   It shows up, in some form, in every language
> c.   It is subject to parametric variations (e.g. in how large is the class of licensors in a particular language, whether Free Choice uses are admitted etc.)
> d.   It is acquired early by native learners
> e.   It interacts systematically with other aspects of core grammar (like locality on extraction, agreement, etc. – cf. the discussion on so called 'Negative Concord')
> The properties in [a. - e.] are typical of core grammar, competence based phenomena (if anything is).

I am unable to completely address Chierchia's challenge (especially points c. and e. above), as I am not a trained linguist. However, I believe the main trust of the challenge can be met. It is compatible with my view to accept that procedural elements such as NPIs show up in some form in all languages, are subject to parametric variations, and are acquired early by native learners. Even though procedural items on my view correspond to causal dispositions rather than to mental symbols, they must be learned. Treating procedural knowledge as part of the causal architecture of the performance system does not preclude one from claiming that learners of all languages acquire such knowledge early. In fact, given the crucial structural role played by procedural elements in language production and comprehension, these causal dispositions would have to be in place early in language development.

Moreover, my view of procedural information is not incompatible with ideas of innateness and parametric variation across languages. It could be that aspects of the causal architecture of the language performance system are innate, and that the fine-grained aspects of this causal structure will only be set once the language learner is exposed to particular linguistic input. This sort of fine-tuning of the performance system could be a matter of parametric variation across language learners, depending on what sorts of linguistic environments they are initially exposed to. (However, my view is incompatible with Chomsky's ideas about innateness, inasmuch as he claims that our innate grammatical competence is completely independent of our communicative system. I claim, on the contrary, that aspects of the performance system are also a part of our innate language endowment. Hence, language development involves a significant interplay between core grammar and the performance system).

The first point Chierchia raises (that the behavior of NPIs has to do with the distribution of a certain class of morphemes) I take to be asserting that procedural items have a certain pattern of use and that this pattern is systematic or rule-governed. I can accept that procedural items have systematic uses, and would appeal once again to the regress of rules argument to establish that talk of rules must ultimately be cashed out in terms of causal dispositions. (See also the fourth objection and my reply in Section 4 above. This is an objection that Chierchia raises against my use of the regress of rules argument).

The fifth point Chierchia raises is the most tricky for me to handle, since I do not fully understand it. It appears to be saying that procedural elements must be part of a language user's semantic competence (and thus be represented as concepts in the mental lexicon) because procedural elements interact with other aspects of core grammar. A further assumption seems to be that these 'other aspects' are themselves represented as mental symbols in the lexicon. However, at least some of the 'other aspects' that Chierchia lists seem to belong to the procedural side of the conceptual/procedural divide (e.g. agreement phenomena, such as number, gender and case markings). Hence it begs the question to assert that these procedural elements are all represented as symbols in the mental lexicon, rather than embodied in the causal architecture of the performance system. But even if these 'other aspects' are all symbolically represented in the mental lexicon, their interaction with procedural elements that are tacitly represented in the causal architecture of the performance system is not ruled out. In fact, interaction is what procedural elements are all about. In the course of the exercise of these causal dispositions, concepts in the lexicon will be accessed (i.e. interacted with). Thus I do not agree that Chierchia's challenge shows that procedural knowledge (e.g. that embodied in NPIs) is part of our semantic competence.

The final objections that I will discuss are ones implicit in the writings of relevance theorists. We saw in Section 2 that relevance theorists claim that procedural items (e.g. determiners such as 'the' or discourse markers such as 'but') encode instructions that constrain the inferential phase of comprehension, and are involved in the derivation of both explicatures and implicatures. Thus procedural items guide interpretive processes, such as the pragmatic enrichment of semantically underspecified terms, and the interpretation of metaphorical and ironic utterances. But they are not themselves subject to processes such as pragmatic enrichment. As Vicente (2003) puts it: 'discourse markers, ... etc. code instructions that constrain the inferential phase of comprehension at both the explicit and implicit levels, but are themselves impervious to contextual contamination, *which places them neatly within the domain of linguistic semantics.*' (My emphases). The objection to my view is implicit in the italicized phrase. Since procedural items are context-independent, Vicente claims they belong in the domain of linguistics semantics. This contradicts my claim that they belong to the domain of pragmatics.

However, it does not follow from the fact that an item is not subject to inferential modulation or contextual contamination that the item belongs in the domain of linguistic semantics. I accept that conceptual meanings belong to the domain of linguistic semantics and are context-invariant.[13] But I deny that all things that are context-invariant belong to the domain linguistic semantics. On the contrary, procedural knowledge as understood in this paper is also something context-invariant (in the synchronic sense – see note 13). It constitutes the stable mental architecture that enables language users to focus on the contentful aspects of verbal communication. To use language one must rely not only on certain invariant meanings but also on certain stable mental structures. The latter are what ground our procedural abilities.

A second objection is implicit in Carston (2002: 11). Carston notes that while some have argued that the semantics/pragmatics distinction lines up with Chomsky's competence/performance distinction, this is not the position adopted within relevance theory. Instead, according to Carston, the semantics/ pragmatics distinction corresponds to the distinction between the decoding and inferential phases of communication. For instance, to comprehend a speaker's utterance, the hearer must first decode the words the speaker uses and then use the decoded information, along with non-

---

[13]They are context-invariant in the synchronic sense that they do not change across contexts at a time. Of course, over time an individual's lexical concepts may be changed (e.g. refined or broadened).

linguistic (e.g. encyclopedic) information, to infer the pragmatically enriched meaning that the speaker intended to convey. What is recovered via decoding belongs to semantics, whereas the pragmatically inferred meanings belong to pragmatics. My main concern has been the distinction between information that is conceptually and procedurally *encoded*. Thus, it seems, I must concede that procedural information lies on the decoding side of the decoding/inference divide, and hence on the side of semantics rather than pragmatics.

In response I would question the idea that the decoding/inference distinction lines up with the semantics/pragmatics distinction. In particular, I would challenge the idea that decoding processes are all alike. Decoding does not always give access to a conceptual entry in the mental lexicon. Sometimes, decoding triggers a procedure. In Section 4, I cited empirical evidence in support of the claim that items that encode concepts and items that encode procedures are not accessed or processed in the same way. If decoding is not a unitary process, then we are not forced to give all decoded information a uniform, semantic treatment.

An objection that combines aspects of the previous two is implicit in Blakemore's writings. After giving some examples involving lexical items such as 'so' and 'moreover', Blakemore (1992: 46) writes:

> However, while it is true that the meanings of these expressions play a role in the way that contextual assumptions are used in the interpretation of the utterances that contain them, there is no reason for saying that this role is itself pragmatically determined. The knowledge of what these words mean is linguistic knowledge, and, as we have seen, this is quite different from the non-linguistic knowledge that a hearer brings to bear on the interpretation of an utterance. In other words, the meanings of these expressions can be represented in pragmatics only at the expense of the modular view of cognition...

The objection would be that by placing procedural knowledge in pragmatics, I have failed to acknowledge its essentially linguistic character and its difference from the sort of non-linguistic, encyclopedic knowledge that is used in utterance interpretation. Presumably the idea is that all encoded information (even that associated with procedural items) belongs to the language module and is accessed via a process of linguistic decoding. Non-linguistic, encyclopedic knowledge in contrast is not confined to a module, but is part of the central system and is processed inferentially.

I would counter this objection by pointing out that on my view procedural knowledge *is* distinguished from encyclopedic knowledge, even though both fall on the side of pragmatics. The latter is conceptual knowledge, whereas the former is tacitly stored in the causal architecture of the performance system. Moreover, my view does not threaten the idea of a language module. On the contrary, I have been assuming that there is a language module and that the concepts entered in the mental lexicon are part of this module. And I agree that these concepts are accessed via a decoding procedure. But I disagree that all decoding processes access concepts. In some cases they trigger procedures, and these procedures are not strictly part of the language system. Their role is to guide an interaction between something that belongs to the language system (lexical concepts) and something that lies outside that system (encyclopedic and other non-linguistic knowledge).

I conclude that there are as yet no compelling reasons for giving up the parallelisms that were postulated in the introduction. That is to say, we have as yet no reason to give up on the claim that procedural knowledge belongs to the language performance system and is pragmatic, whereas lexical conceptual knowledge is declaratively represented and constitutes a speaker's semantic competence. So there is not anything simultaneously procedural and semantic.[14]

References

Andersen, G. and T. Fretheim eds. 2000. *Pragmatic Markers and Propositional Attitude*. Amsterdam: John Benjamins.

Asher, N. and A. Lascarides 1996. Lexical disambiguation in a discourse context. *Lexical Semantics: The Problem of Polysemy*, eds. J. Pustejovsky and B. Boguraev, 69-108. Oxford: Clarendon Press.

Asher, N. and A. Lascarides 1998. The semantics and pragmatics of presupposition. *Journal of Semantics* 153: 239-99.

Bezuidenhout, A. 1997. Pragmatics, Semantic Underdetermination and the Referential/Attributive Distinction. *Mind* 106: 375-409.

Blakemore, D. 1987. *Semantic Constraints on Relevance*. Oxford: Blackwell.

---

[14]I would like to thank Claudia Bianchi and Carlo Penco for inviting me to participate in the Workshop on Context 2002 and to thank Claudia for encouraging me to publish this paper. Thanks also to Gennaro Chierchia, who was assigned as the commentator on my paper at the workshop, probably because I earlier indicated that I would be discussing Gennaro's work on dynamic semantics. However, I took an early fork in the road and it led somewhere completely different. But Gennaro rose to the occasion and provided penetrating criticisms at the workshop, as well as extensive written comments later. I know that I will not have answered his criticisms to his satisfaction, but I have done my best. Thanks also to my colleagues Raffaella De Rosa and Otavio Bueno, who let me do a trial run of my workshop presentation and gave me valuable feedback. Finally, special thanks go to Begoña Vicente, who read an early version of my manuscript and subjected it to rigorous scrutiny. Although I am sure the final product will still dissatisfy her, the paper is much improved due to her attentions.

Blakemore, D. 1988. 'So' as a constraint on relevance. *Mental Representations: The Interface Between Language and Reality*, ed. R. Kempson, 183-95. Cambridge: Cambridge University Press.

Blakemore, D. 1992. *Understanding Utterances*. Oxford: Blackwell.

Blass, R. 1990. *Relevance Relations in Discourse: A Study with Special Reference to Sissala*. Cambridge: Cambridge University Press.

Bradley, D. 1978. Computational Distinctions of Vocabulary Type. Doctoral dissertation, MIT.

Bradley, D., M. Garrett and E. Zurif 1980. Syntactic deficits in Broca's aphasics. *Biological Studies of Mental Processes*, ed. D. Caplan, 269-86. Cambridge MA: MIT Press.

Carston, R. 1997. Enrichment and loosening: Complementary processes in deriving the proposition expressed? *Linguistische Berichte* 8: 103-27.

Carston, R. 2002. *Thoughts and Utterances: The Pragmatics of Explicit Communication*. Oxford: Blackwell.

Chomsky, N. 1996. Language and problems of knowledge. *The Philosophy of Language*. 3rd ed., ed. A. Martinich, 558-77. Oxford: Oxford University Press.

Copestake, A. and T. Briscoe 1996. Semi-productive polysemy and sense extension. *Lexical Semantics: The Problem of Polysemy*, ed. J. Pustejovsky and B. Boguraev, 15-67. Oxford: Clarendon Press.

Coulson, S. 2001. *Semantic Leaps: Frame-Shifting and Conceptual Blending in Meaning Construction*. Cambridge: Cambridge University Press.

Dennett, D. 1981. Brain writing and mind reading. *Brainstorms*, 39-50. Brighton: Harvester Press.

Fauconnier, G. 1985. *Mental Spaces: Aspects of Meaning Construction in Natural Language*. Cambridge MA: MIT Press.

Fauconnier, G. 1997. *Mappings in Thought and Language*. Cambridge: Cambridge University Press.

Fauconnier, G. and E. Sweetser eds. 1996. *Spaces, Worlds, and Grammar*. Chicago: University of Chicago Press.

Fodor, J. 1975. *The Language of Thought*. New York: Crowell.

Fretheim, T. 1998a. Intonation and the procedural encoding of attributed thoughts: The case of Norwegian negative interrogatives. *Current Issues in Relevance Theory*, ed. V. Rouchota and A. H. Jucker, 205-36. Amsterdam: John Benjamins.

Fretheim, T. 1998b. A relevance-theoretic account of *if* and *in case*. *Proceedings of the 14th Eastern States Conference on Linguistics,* ed. J. Austin and A. Lawson, 58-69. Ithaca: CLC Publications.

Friederici, A. 1985. Levels of processing and vocabulary types: Evidence from on-line comprehension in normals and agrammatics. *Cognition* 19: 133-66.

Garrett, M. 1975. The analysis of sentence production. *The Psychology of Learning and Motivation: Advances in Research and Theory*, vol. 9, ed. G. Bower, 133-77. New York: Academic Press.

Garrett, M. 1980. Levels of processing in sentence production. *Language Production*, ed. B. Butterworth, 177-220. London: Academic Press.

Garrett, M. 1981. Production of speech: Observations from normal and pathological use. *Normality and Pathology in Cognitive Functions*, ed. A. Ellis, 19-76. London: Academic Press.

Giora, R. 1997. Discourse coherence and theory of relevance: Stumbling blocks in search of a unified theory. *Journal of Pragmatics* 27: 17-34.

Grice, P. 1989. *Studies in the Way of Words*. Cambridge, MA: Harvard University Press.

Iten, C. 1997. Because and although: A case of duality? *UCL Working Papers in Linguistics* 9: 55-76.

Iten, C. 1998. The meaning of although: A relevance theoretic account. *UCL Working Papers in Linguistics* 10: 81-108.

Iten, C. 2002. Even if and even: The case for an inferential scalar account. *UCL Working Papers in Linguistics* 14: 119-56.

Koriat, A. and S. Greenberg 1994. The extraction of phrase structure during reading: Evidence from letter detection errors. *Psychonomic Bulletin and Review* 1: 345-56.

Koriat, A. and S. Greenberg 1996. The enhancement effect in letter detection: Further evidence for the structural model of reading. *Journal of Experimental Psychology: Learning, Memory, and Cognition* 22: 1184-95.

Kripke, S. 1982. *Wittgenstein on Rules and Private Languages*. Oxford: Basil Blackwell.

Lakoff, R. 1971. Ifs, ands and buts about conjunction. *Studies in Linguistic Semantics*, ed. C. J. Fillmore and D. T. Langendoen, 115-50. New York: Holt Rinehart and Winston.

Levinson, S. 2000. *Presumptive Meanings: The Theory of Generalized Conversational Implicature*. Cambridge, MA: MIT Press.

MacDonald, M., N. Pearlmutter and M. Seidenberg 1994. Lexical nature of syntactic ambiguity resolution. *Psychological Review* 101: 676-703.

Nicolle, S. 1995. Conceptual and procedural encoding: Criteria for the identification of linguistically encoded procedural information. Paper presented at the University of Hertfordshire Relevance Theory Workshop, Hatfield Peverel, UK.

Nicolle, S. 1998. *Be going to* and *will*: a monosemous account. *English Language Linguistics* 2: 223-43.

Park, G., M. McNeil and P. Doyle 2002. Lexical access rate of closed-class elements during auditory sentence comprehension in adults with aphasia. *Aphasio-logy* 16: 801-14.

Prince, E. 1985. Fancy syntax and 'shared knowledge'. *Journal of Pragmatics* 9: 65-81.

Prince, E. 1988. Discourse analysis: a part of the study of linguistic competence. *Linguistics: The Cambridge Survey*, vol. 2, ed. F. J. Newmeyer, 164-82. Cambridge: Cambridge University Press.

Prince, E. 1997. On the functions of left dislocation in English discourse. *Directions in Functional Linguistics*, ed. A. Kamio, 117-43. Amsterdam: John Benjamins.

Pustejovsky, J. 1995. *The Generative Lexicon*. Cambridge, MA: MIT Press.

Pustejovsky, J. 1998. The Semantics of Lexical Underspecification. *Folia Linguistica* 32: 323-47.

Pustejovsky, J. and B. Boguraev eds. 1996. *Lexical Semantics: The Problem of Polysemy*. Oxford: Clarendon Press.

Rapp, B. and A. Caramazza 1997. The modality-specific organization of grammatical categories: Evidence from impaired spoken and written sentence production. *Brain and Language* 56: 248-86.

Schmauder, R. 1996. Ability to stand alone and processing of open-class and closed-class words: Isolation versus context. *Journal of Psycholinguistic Research* 25: 443-81.

Schmauder, R., R. Morris and D. Poynor 2000. Lexical processing and text integration of function and content words: Evidence from priming and eye fixations. *Memory and Cognition* 28: 1098-108.

Sperber, D. and D. Wilson 1995. *Relevance: Communication and Cognition*, 2nd ed. Oxford: Blackwell.

Thomas, J. 1995. *Meaning in Interaction*. London: Longman.

Vicente, B. 2003. Meaning in relevance theory and the semantics/pragmatics distinction. Ms.

Wilson, D. 1998. Discourse, coherence and relevance: A reply to Rachel Giora. *Journal of Pragmatics* 29: 57-74.

Wilson, D. and D. Sperber 1993. Linguistic form and relevance. *Lingua* 90: 1-25.

7

Assertion and the Semantics of Force-Markers*

MANUEL GARCÍA-CARPINTERO

1 Introduction

In recent work, Williamson (1996/2000) has defended an account of assertion that I find suggestive. It fits with the anti-reductionist account of knowledge he has also independently argued for. Williamson claims that the following norm or rule (the *knowledge rule*) is constitutive of assertion, and individuates it:

(KR) One must ((assert p) only if one knows p)

Williamson is not directly concerned with the semantics of assertion-markers, although he assumes that his view has implications for such an undertaking; he says: 'in natural languages, the default use of declarative sentences is to make assertions' (1996/2000: 258).

In this paper I will explore Williamson's view from this perspective, i.e., in the light of issues regarding the semantics of assertion-markers. I will end up a slightly different account, on which, rather than KR, what is constitu-

*I would propounding like to express my gratitude to the participants in the LOGOS seminar, 2001-2 and to the participants in the Genoa WOC 2002 conference for valuable comments that led to improvements. I am particularly indebted to my commentator, Carlo Penco, and also to Robyn Carston, Max Kölbel and François Recanati. Research for this paper has been funded by the Spanish Government's MCYT research project BFF2002-10164, the Catalan Government grant SGR2001-00018, and a *Distinció de Recerca de la Generalitat, Investigadors Reconeguts* 2002-8.

The Semantics/Pragmatics Distinction.
Claudia Bianchi (ed.).
Copyright © 2004, CSLI Publications.

tive and individuating of assertion is an audience-involving *transmission of knowledge* rule:[1]

> (TKR) One must ((assert *p*) only if one's audience comes thereby to be in a position to know *p*)

I will argue that TKR, of which KR is an illocutionary consequence (but not the other way around), has all the virtues that Williamson claims for his account and no new defect.[2] I will argue in addition that TKR, in contrast to KR, has the outstanding merit of fitting better in a neo-Gricean account of linguistic meaning of the kind I have argued for elsewhere.[3]

The paper has the following structure: in the next section, I justify my resort to the phrase 'semantics of force-indicators', which in many usages is oxymoronic; in the third I present the main features of Williamson's view; in the fourth, I criticize purely truth-conditional views of meaning; in the fifth, I defend my semantic proposal; in the sixth and final section I locate it in the context of debates between Austin, Grice and others about the relative place of intention and convention in speech acts.

2   The Constitutive Account of the Semantics/Pragmatics Distinction

The phrase 'semantics of force-indicators' is prototypically oxymoronic in the usage of people who take it that semantics has only to do with truth-conditional contents and their compositional determination, and nothing to do with speakers' acts. Sometimes this is because they think of linguistics and semantics as a quasi-mathematical enterprise, only concerned with theoretically characterizing the abstract languages that Lewis (1975: 163) contrasts with those actually in use: 'a function, or set of ordered pairs of strings and meanings'. There is no point in quarrelling about this, merely stipulatory usage. I will just note that my interest in an accurate semantics-pragmatics distinction arises from a concern with natural languages, things in use in our spatiotemporal surroundings like English, Spanish or Catalan. As a result, on the stipulation I find expedient 'language' will henceforth

---

[1]My proposal develops Evans' (1982:310) point: 'communication is *essentially* a mode of the transmission of knowledge'. It is also in agreement with Coady (1992: 42) proposal to characterize testimony, if we take, as I do, assertions as *prima facie* acts of testifying.

[2]A content C with force F, F(C), is an *illocutionary consequence* of contents $C_1 \ldots C_n$ with forces $F_1 \ldots F_n$ iff any speaker committed to each $F_i(C_i)$ is thereby committed to F(C). Given a natural understanding of the primitive *commitment*, if an argument is deductively valid, then the conclusion taken with assertoric force will be an illocutionary consequence of the premises also taken with assertoric force. See Green 2000: 444-7.

[3] See García-Carpintero 2001.

refer to them, and semantics will be a part (together at least with phonology and syntax) of a theoretical account thereof; it will also refer to the subject-matter of such an account.

In a series of recent writings Bach (1999, 2002) has clearly articulated why, given our concern with natural languages, it is wrong to state the semantics-pragmatics distinction in terms of an alleged contrast between the determination of truth-conditions on the one hand, and features of what expressions mean that depend on speaker's acts or their context of use on the other. This constitutes a taxonomically and theoretically inadequate conception of languages, as the facts about indexicals and demonstratives make clear. It is a given in the present discussion that semantics aims to provide an explanatory systematization of the validity of English arguments like (1):

(1)   The tallest person is hungry

    ∴   Someone is hungry

By the same token, semantics has to include in its explanatory systematization the validity of arguments like (2)-(4):

(2)   He is hungry

    ∴   Some male is hungry

(3)   That pot is empty

    ∴   Some pot is empty

(4)   You are angry

    ∴   Someone in the audience is angry

But there simply is no way of ignoring context and speakers' acts in accounting for the validity of arguments like (2)-(4). This is so if, following the views of the leading researcher in these matters, Kaplan (1989a), we distinguish the validity of (1) from that of (2)-(4). For this distinction depends on the fact that indexicals, like proper names, are 'directly referential'; their truth-conditional import is just their referent. As a result, (2)-(4) are not valid in the sense in which (1) is: it is not the case that the truth-conditions of their conclusions are satisfied in all possible circumstances in which those of their premises are. The validity of (2)-(4) is 'character-validity': given contexts in which their premises, if uttered there, would all signify truth-conditions satisfied there, their conclusions would signify truth-conditions similarly satisfied if uttered in the very same contexts. On this view, character-validity, even though a semantic phenomenon, is not simply a matter of ordinary truth-conditions, and depends on speakers' acts and their contexts.

Kaplan is aware of the need for a semantics-pragmatics distinction that goes beyond the traditional one that Bach questions. More so in that he is not only a direct-reference theorist about indexicals and demonstratives, but also a Millian about proper names. A Millian rejects the view that proper names are linguistically associated with descriptive contents – even in the way in which an utterance of 'you' must be linguistically related to a description like *the audience in the context in which the utterance of 'you' occurred* to account for the semantic nature of the character-validity of (4). In particular, Kaplan wants to reject the idea that the validity of (5) is a semantic matter, in contrast to that of (2)-(4):

(5)   Kaplan is hungry

∴   Someone called 'Kaplan' in the baptism supporting its use in this context is hungry

To set apart the merely pragmatic validity of (5) from the properly semantic (character-) validity of (2)-(4), Kaplan (1989b: 573-4) made a distinction between *semantics* and *metasemantics*, in terms reminding of the Lewisian distinction:

> The fact that a word or phrase *has* a certain meaning clearly belongs to semantics. On the other hand, a claim about the *basis* for ascribing a certain meaning to a word or phrase does not belong to semantics. 'Ohsnay' means *snow* in Pig-Latin. That's a semantic fact about Pig-Latin. The *reason* why 'ohsnay' means *snow* is not a semantic fact; it is some kind of historical or sociological fact about Pig-Latin. Perhaps, because it relates to how the language is *used*, it should be categorized as part of the *pragmatics* of Pig-Latin (though I am not really comfortable with this nomenclature), or perhaps, because it is a fact *about* semantics, as part of the *Metasemantics* of Pig-Latin (or perhaps, for those who prefer working from below to working from above, as part of the *Foundations of semantics* of Pig-Latin).

Stalnaker (1997: 535), motivated by a similar Millian concern, follows Kaplan's final suggestion and distinguishes *descriptive* from *foundational* semantics: 'A descriptive semantic theory is a theory that says what the semantics for the language is without saying what it is about the practice of using that language that explains why that semantics is the right one. A descriptive-semantic theory assigns *semantic values* to the expressions of the language, and explains how the semantic values of the complex expressions are a function of the semantic values of their parts.' Foundational theories, in contrast, answer questions 'about what the facts are that give expressions their semantic values, or more generally, about what makes it the case that the language spoken by a particular individual or community has a particular descriptive semantics.' Both Kaplan and Stalnaker would like to argue that the validity of (5) is a foundational (pragmatic) matter, not a semantic one, as is the validity of (1) *and* also that of (2)-(4).

Is the Kaplan-Stalnaker line adequate to characterize the semantics-pragmatics distinction for natural languages? I myself disagree with the Millian view, and have argued elsewhere that something like (5) is valid in the same terms that (2)-(4) are, and that proper names are to that extent linguistically associated with ('reference-fixing') descriptions. This issue is not our present concern, but can be used to expose the inadequacy of the Kaplan-Stalnaker characterization. (Incidentally, I think that it has been drawn in that particular way to discard from semantics proper the ascription to names of metalinguistic descriptions.) All parties to the dispute accept that many historical sociological and psychological facts about, say, how 'ohsnay' came to be used in Pig-Latin with the meaning it did lack any semantic import. The issue is whether all do; what we need is a principled way to distinguish those that are from those that are not, and a little reflection shows that neither Kaplan's nor Stalnaker's proposals offer one.

According to Kaplan's and Stalnaker's views, a semantic value of an utterance of 'I' by Kaplan is its referent, i.e., Kaplan himself. This is (in part) what such an utterance means; it is a semantic value that a descriptive semantics should ascribe to it, in order to determine the semantic values of more complex expressions of which it is part. However, a *reason* why such an utterance means that semantic value is that it was Kaplan *who uttered it*. This is a fact about English that fits Kaplan's characterization of what metasemantics is about: that he was *the utterer of that case of 'I'*; for it is a reason why such a case means him. However, by Kaplan's own lights, this particular linguistic fact, this particular reason why the expression means him, falls under the theoretical concerns of semantics, not metasemantics. Similarly, although the fact in question can be described perfectly well as one of those that give the expression (the case of 'I' that Kaplan uttered) its semantic value – i.e., as one in virtue of which the language spoken by a community has a particular descriptive semantics – Stalnaker should not want to count it as belonging to a foundational theory of English, but rather to a descriptive theory. It thus transpires that Kaplan's and Stalnaker's characterizations do not give us what we need; for they do not allow us to distinguish reasons why expressions have certain semantic values which belong in a semantic account from those that do not. As a result, although their characterizations suggest that descriptions linked to proper names like the metalinguistic one used in the conclusion in (5) do not belong in a semantic account of natural languages, they cannot establish it.

The preceding discussion had two goals: to bring Lewis' distinction between abstract and used languages to bear on our problem, and to expose the difficulties of a relatively popular line also invoking it to state the semantics-pragmatics distinction, compatibly with the results of contemporary research on the widespread context-dependence of natural language semantics. Part of what motivates my own proposal is that it captures some of the intuitions that that line tries to articulate.

In advancing linguistic theories, as in advancing theories of any other phenomena, we are sensitive to the distinction between what is constitutive of or essential to our subject-matter, natural languages, and what is merely accidental. I take this notion of what is constitutive of a given object as primitive, irreducible to modal notions like metaphysical or epistemic necessity (see Fine 1994). I assume that we have a sufficient intuitive grasp to ground more theoretical articulations; such a grasp manifests itself in the indicated sensitivity. Following Schiffer (1993), we might usefully put the issue in terms of Lewis' distinction, as concerning the nature of *actual-language relations*. What makes it the case that a particular abstract language is in fact the language used by a given population? What relation should exist between the language and the population, for that to be the case? When we characterize a language aiming thus to describe a fragment of a natural language, we may well fail in our goal, but we at least succeed in characterizing thereby one of Lewis' abstract languages; for the requirements for success in this undertaking are settled only by our pretheoretical conception of languages. The way Lewis describes abstract languages thus gives an idea of the very minimum that is assumed *a priori* to be constitutive of natural languages: they at least should have an (abstract) phonology, determining a stock of well-formed expressions (Lewis' 'strings'), and an equally abstract semantics, determining meanings for some of them. To move beyond this in characterizing what it is that makes a given abstract language the natural language we are trying to characterize (the language actually used by a given population) thus providing a richer characterization of what is constitutive of natural languages requires adopting potentially controversial theoretical decisions; but this is as it should be, here as elsewhere.

Thus, for instance, although some abstract languages lack any substantive syntax, being just a finite set of ordered pairs of strings and meanings, I think we are justified in believing that none of them is appropriate to characterize a natural language, i.e., that it is constitutive of natural languages to have a substantive syntax. For, on the basis of correct information about the nature of the languages they use, ordinary speakers are able to understand strings that differ from any of those that have allowed them to acquire that information; any abstract language capable of counting as a natural language will in fact be infinite. And there simply is no alternative explanation for this than that the object of the speakers' informational state has a compositional semantics, which the informational state correctly represents;[4] some of the compositional rules constitutive of natural languages are recursive, helping thus to determine an infinite number of meaningful strings. It is true that the number of strings that ordinary speakers are able to understand is finite; but I think we are justified in taking this to be explained by accidental properties of natural languages (by features of the psychology of speakers irrelevant to the identity of the languages they use).

My proposal regarding the proper way to capture the semantics-pragmatics distinction is then as follows. As we have seen, a semantic component is uncontroversially constitutive of languages; among other explanatory roles, such an uncontroversial component of linguistic theories accounts for the validity of some arguments, like (1); it also accounts for synonymy relations, ambiguities, analyticities, etc. As we have just seen, what is in general constitutive of natural languages and of the semantic component in particular will depend on substantive matters, to be theoretically settled, regarding the actual-language relation. Thus, if a Chomskian reductively psychologistic view of what is constitutive of natural languages were correct, and languages were just the end products in the mind/brain, internalistically understood, of a biologically determined language faculty, it would make some sense to think of semantics as really a form of syntax, as Chomsky himself has repeatedly insisted. On the sort of neo-Gricean view of what is constitutive of natural languages that I consider correct, that is definitely wrong.[5] Languages are fundamentally conventional resources socially designed to implement the sort of communicative intentions that Grice took to be constitutive of non-natural meaning. I take this to be compatible with some aspects of the Chomskian picture; among other things, a proper account of the facts about compositionality accepted as constitutive of natural languages in the previous paragraph require I think that unconscious psychological facts like those contemplated by Chomsky and his fol-

---

[4]I am not at all persuaded by Schiffer's (1993) efforts to argue for the opposite, but it will take too much space to indicate why. Of course, particular precise versions of the principle of compositionality can be disputed.

[5]García-Carpintero (2001) outlines the view and indicates what is neo-Gricean in it, i.e., distinct from the Gricean view as it is usually understood.

lowers be also constitutive of them.[6] What is wrong in the Chomskian view is its reductive internalist psychologism. For reasons like those given by Kaplan for the case of indexicals, the semantic component will I think ascribe to some expressions environment-involving propositions.

If this view is correct, there are psychological third-personal features that are constitutive of natural languages, i.e., involved in the determination of the actual-language relation, while others are not. Now, I take pragmatics to deal with features of natural languages of the same kind that the semantic component of a theory of a given natural language deals with (the ascription to expressions of propositional contents and forces, intended to explain some validities, ambiguities, etc.), where the former differ from the latter in that they are not constitutive of that natural language. Particularized conversational implicatures and non-literal uses like creative metaphors, irony, etc., as understood by Grice (1975), are the prototype that I have in mind for what pragmatics is about. For, on Grice's view, the fact that implicated meanings are ascribed to expressions can be accounted for in virtue of facts that are not constitutive of the language in question, or of any other particular natural language for that matter. They can be accounted for on the basis of practical principles that follow rationally from the nature of communicative purposes; and these purposes are in themselves independent of any specific natural language. To put it in a nutshell, helping ourselves to a prior conception of meaning: semantics deals with meaning-features of expressions constitutive of specific natural languages; pragmatics deals with those of their meaning-features not constitutive of any particular natural language.

The present proposal captures what is intuitively correct in the proposals by Kaplan and Stalnaker considered earlier. Semantics attempts to characterize the meaning-properties constitutive of specific natural languages. This is why semantics is compositional, as Stalnaker simply takes for granted without any justification arising from his own elucidation. Foundational theories give an account of those linguistic facts that, even if empirically important to establish that a population uses a given language, are not constitutive of it. As we said earlier, psychological facts determining performance, as opposed to competence, belong in this category. The same applies to meaning-facts like those which the present proposal would count as pragmatic, like conversational implicatures or non-literal meanings that speakers of any given language convey. Similar points about the semantics and pragmatics of illocutionary forces will be made later.

---

[6]Davies (2000) supports a compatibilist view that takes Chomskian third-personal, unconscious features of psychological states to be constitutive of languages, in addition to the consciously available, first-personal features that a Gricean picture focuses on.

In addition to being supported by the intuitions motivating Kaplan's and Stalnaker's characterizations, the present proposal allows us to count as semantic the descriptive aspects of the meaning of indexicals accounting for the character-validity of (2)-(4), without provoking the doubts I raised for those accounts. Even if we agree, as I do, with the direct-reference view that the truth-conditional contribution of indexicals is exhausted by their referents, to the extent that there are good reasons to contend that indexicals are associated with certain descriptions as a matter of their constitutive natures in a given language we can still count the association as a semantic phenomenon. It would then be a further problem to articulate the nature of that association, semantic but distinct from the association between expression and referent.[7] On this proposal, the basic disagreement between Millians and anti-Millians concerns whether the link between names and some descriptions, like the metalinguistic descriptions accounting for the validity of (5), is constitutive of the semantics of names in natural languages, irrespective of whether the link is such that the truth-conditional import of proper names in natural languages is thereby identical to that of the relevant descriptions.

The present proposal agrees with this claim by Bach (2002: 287): 'For me the distinction applies fundamentally to types of information. Semantic information is information encoded in what is uttered – stable linguistic features of the sentence – together with any linguistic information that contributes to the determination of the references of context-sensitive expressions.' As Bach says, a merit of a proposal along these lines is that it helps prevent a widespread confusion concerning the relevance of psycholinguistic facts to these issues. It is a clear commitment of my proposal that there is a substantive distinction, among the undifferentiated meaning-facts concerning the expressions of a given natural language, between those that are the concern of linguistic theories (semantics) and those that are not (pragmatics). This sets it apart from the views of many contemporary writers, including Bezuidenhout, Carston, Recanati, Schiffer, Sperber and Wilson, and Travis. Just to give an example, the present proposal provides a principled justification to put Grice's generalized implicatures in the pragmatic basket; later I will touch upon similar cases, indirect speech acts and explicit performatives. Even though there is a form of linguistic conventionality (standardization) involved in these cases, it is arguable whether the conventions at stake are among those constitutive of the relevant languages; in addition to appealing to Grice's Modified Occam's Razor, considerations like

---

[7]García-Carpintero (2000) argues that it is a form of presupposition.

those marshaled by Levinson (2000) could be invoked to argue that they are not.

Now, those writers I just mentioned argue for what in my view is a mistaken blurring of the semantics-pragmatics distinction on the basis of certain psychological assumptions.[8] They assume, for instance, that the semantic meaning of a sentence should easily come to the conscious awareness of speakers untrained in theoretical linguistics. Or they assume that the processing of the semantic content of a given sentence should finish before the processing of the pragmatic content starts. On the present proposal, these assumptions are unwarranted. A given meaning of a sub-sentential expression (say, the temporal connotations of disjunction) may well be pragmatic, i.e., non-constitutive, even if the processors of the typical speaker in the typical context compute it previously to deriving the interpretation of the sentences in which they occur.[9] Similarly, it is compatible with the present proposal to classify a meaning as pragmatic, even though it is the first that comes to mind to the conscious awareness of the ordinary speaker, and even if it takes some effort to bring what is properly the semantic meaning of the relevant expression to the conscious awareness of such a speaker. It is not, as I have insisted, that on the present proposal the languages for which we trace the semantics-pragmatics distinction are entities fully independent of the psychology of speakers. To think of actual-language relations as settled in part by which conventions are in place to perform communicative acts entails in my view that languages are constitutively psychological, the psychological features constitutive of them including conscious and unconscious features.

Bach (1999: 64) makes a claim about the distinction with which I disagree: 'semantic information pertains to linguistic expressions, whereas pragmatic information pertains to utterances and facts surrounding them'. The context makes it clear that 'expression' here is expression-type; in my previous discussion of facts concerning indexicals, as henceforth in the rest of the paper, by that term and related ones like 'sentence', 'phrase', etc., I mean expression-cases or expression-tokens.[10] Given my proposal, this is unwarranted. It is true that a language is on my view essentially conventional, and also that linguistic conventions are associated to types: to adopt a convention relative to an expression entails potential regularities in behavior involving the expression, which therefore should be something repeatable, i.e. a type. But this is compatible with thinking of natural languages as

---

[8]García-Carpintero (2001) discusses further the matter, and provides references.

[9]See Levinson (2000) for many illustrations that this is the case.

[10]See García-Carpintero (1998) for justification and further clarification. Levinson (2000: 23-4) appears to make an assumption similar to Bach's.

classes of actual and possible concrete utterances. In my view, a proper understanding of indexicality requires this. For an analogy, consider the case of a symbolic system like traffic signals. It is essentially conventional; signals acquire their meaning in part in virtue of their instantiating certain types. But it is also essentially designed so that their meanings are ascribed to signals in virtue of some of the physical properties they have, like their spatial and temporal location. Thus, it does not seem correct to describe the meaning-features constitutive of this system as merely pertaining to types. The same applies to natural languages, and this fact is even much more deeply widespread in that case. If, for instance, Kripke and Putnam are right about the semantics of natural kind terms, as I think they are, semantic information pertains essentially to natural kind term-tokens.[11]

Under the present proposal, speaking of the semantics of force-markers is not immediately oxymoronic. In the fifth section we will consider the reasons why it not only makes sense, but is actually justified. A more immediate concern now is to be clear about what the meaning of force-indicators might be, putting aside whether it is constitutive of natural languages, in some cases at least, the signification of illocutionary forces; i.e., whether the signification of forces is a semantic or rather a pragmatic matter. One of the many merits of Williamson's (1996/2000) discussion is that it gives a clear account of the nature of assertoric force. Let me now briefly summarize his account.

3 Williamson's View

Like other speech acts, assertions are praised and criticized in many respects: as relevant or not, impolite or not, sincere or not, clumsily phrased or not, etc. Say that any respect in which the performance of an act can be praised or criticized is a *norm* or *rule* for that act; assertions are subject to many norms. The same applies to many social activities, like games, for instance, or musical performances. Among norms governing these activities we should distinguish those that are constitutive of them from those that are not, including Rawls's (1955) and Searle's (1969) *regulative* rules. Constitutive norms for a given type of act are essential to it: necessarily, the rule governs every performance of the act. Regulative norms are thus not essential, although they might be ordinarily involved in appraisals of the act. Thus, for instance if one promises p and does not then bring p about, or brings it about but not for the reason that one promised – perhaps having forgotten all about it – one breaks the constitutive rule of promises. One is then subject to blame, even if the act can be praised from utilitarian or other

---

[11]*Abstract* languages are so only in being possibly non-instantiated in the actual world.

teleological considerations. And the other way around: the promise is constitutively correct if it is kept, even if it can be criticized on utilitarian grounds. The utilitarian or teleological considerations constitute merely regulative rules. As Rawls emphasizes, this leaves open the appeal to utilitarian considerations in justifying the *existence* in the actual world of the institution of promising with its defining constitutive obligations.

Thus, for instance, we can think that the composer of a musical work M specifies a constitutive norm that is to govern performances of that work. He states his composition on a score Σ, indicating pitches, rhythms, harmonies, dynamics, timbres and so on. We can think of the composer as thereby specifying a constitutive norm of this form:

(MW) One must ((perform M) only if one instantiates in so doing Σ)

The combination: one performs M, although in so doing one does not instantiate Σ, is taken to be possible, otherwise there would be no point in forbidding it. Under this view, there could be incorrect performances of M: acts consisting in producing sounds that do not instantiate the score, but still count as performances of the work – incorrect ones. Perhaps most performances of M are incorrect. On this view, the production of sounds instantiating the score is not an essential property of the act of performing the musical work, one without which the work is not really performed. What is essential is that those acts are regulated by the norm invoking the score; the score thus serves as a criterion of correctness.

This is just offered here by way of illustration of the intuitively correct distinction between the constitutive character of a norm involving a given criterion, in contrast to the non-constitutive character of the criterion itself. A similar account of games would, intuitively correctly, allow for cheating; violations of their constitutive rules could still count as instances of the game. As Wolterstorff (1980: 33-105) indicates in defending an account of musical works along these lines, it agrees better with the way we speak than Goodman's contrasting view that the score is an essential property of performances of a musical work, and therefore no performance that does not instantiate the score *really* counts as a performance of the work. On the other hand, the analysis counterintuitively counts as performances of a given work even those that diverge wildly from the score; an intuitively correct account of what is constitutive of musical works should classify those that diverge very much from the score as at most failed attempts. Thus, filling out the schema MW does not appear to suffice to define what counts as a performance of a musical work.

Speech acts are supposed to be defined by illocutionary forces, and to have propositional contents. There is a well-known ambiguity, such that 'illocutionary force' may refer both to types of illocutionary forces (asserting, promising, ordering, questioning and so on), but also to the combination of one of these types with a given propositional content (or, in cases like wh-questions, with a propositional function as content). Here I will mostly follow the first usage; when I do not, context should make it clear. Given that speech acts necessarily have contents, in characterizing illocutionary forces we need to schematically mention them. By a *simple account* of an illocutionary force like assertion Williamson means one according to which the force is defined (uniquely characterized) by a constitutive rule, which invokes as constitutive criterion a property of the asserted proposition. Williamson's account in terms of the *knowledge rule* KR, repeated below, is a case in point; one in terms of the *truth rule* TR is another:

(KR) One must ((assert p) only if one knows p)

(TR) One must ((assert p) only if p is true)

As before in the examples of musical works or games, violation of what these rules forbid (i.e., that one asserts false propositions, or propositions that one does not know) is on simple accounts understood to be possible. It is even compatible with accounts of this kind that this is what, as a matter of fact, happens most frequently. What simple accounts propound is that one such rule is constitutive of the act: necessarily, any performance of the act is governed by it; also, that one such rule individuates the act: assertion is necessarily the unique force of which the relevant rule is the unique norm. Any further norm applying to the act can be derived from the constitutive rule and considerations not specific to it.

Simple accounts are normative; they define forces in terms of norms. They might well be false; remember that for Williamson assertion is supposed to be the act that, by default, we perform in uttering declarative sentences. This is vague, but still allows for his proposal to be mistaken. Perhaps forces are not normatively defined. Perhaps they are normative, but no constitutive rule of the indicated kind is individuating by itself; as suggested before for the example of musical works, it may well be that further additional conditions are required, even if some constitutive norm is also part of the defining character of the relevant force. Nevertheless, Williamson's compellingly made case for a simple account based on KR is worth considering as a starting point. It is of course no objection to such an account that there are assertions whose producers lack knowledge of the contents they assert. The claim is not that knowledge by the asserter (or truth, for that matter) of the asserted proposition is essential; the claim is rather that being subject to blame if knowledge (or truth) are missing is essential. I will not present here Williamson's elegantly and economically presented arguments for his view; I will just outline what I take to be their main elements, referring the reader to his work for elaboration.

First, conversational patterns favor the account: we challenge assertions politely by asking 'How do you know?', or more aggressively 'Do you know that?' (252).[12] Second, the account explains what is wrong in a version of Moore's paradox with 'know' instead of 'believe': *A, and I do not know that A* (253-4). Third, mathematics provides for formal situations where the speaker's sensitivity to the norms of assertion is highlighted; in those situations, being warranted to assert *p* appears to go hand in hand with knowing *p*. Fourth, an account based on TR seems at first sight preferable: given that the truth rule is satisfied whenever the knowledge rule is, but not the other way around, it provides for a practice with fewer violations of its governing rule; some evidential rule could then be explained as derived from TR, and considerations not specific to assertion. However, the truth rule does not individuate assertion; alternative speech acts like conjecturing, reminding or swearing also involve a truth rule (244-5). Moreover, reflection on lotteries (cases in which, knowing that you hold a ticket in a very large lottery, I assert 'your ticket did not win' only on the basis of the high probability of the utterance's truth) question the validity of any such alleged derivation (246-52). Finally, intuitions about many cases in which we assert without knowing can be made compatible with the view. In some cases, it is reasonable for us to think that we know, even if we do not; what we do is not permissible, but it is, as we feel, exculpable. In some cases, additional values (putting someone out of danger, enjoying a relaxed conversation) are at stake, allowing again for exculpation based on their contextual relative strength (256-9).

---

[12] Austin (1962: 138) appears to have this in mind when he says: 'It is important to notice also that statements too are liable to infelicity of this kind in other ways also parallel to contracts, promises, warnings, &c. Just as we often say, for example, "You cannot order me", in the sense "You have not the right to order me", which is equivalent to saying that you are not in the appropriate position to do so: so often there are things you cannot state – have no right to state – are in no position to state. You *cannot* now state how many people there are in the next room; if you say "There are fifty people in the next room", I can only regard you as guessing or conjecturing'. Austin seems to be contemplating a situation in which the utterer lacks knowledge of the number of people in the next room; I think that he says that in that case the assertion is not permitted, and that, those facts being fully in the open, the most natural thing is to interpret the speaker as (indirectly) doing some weaker act.

4   Are Forces Linguistically Encoded?

The following words used by Harnish (1994: 417) summarize our previous proposal about the semantics-pragmatics distinction: 'Semantics is the study of linguistic meaning – meaning encoded into expressions of a language'. As we saw, a formulation along these lines allows for semantics to go beyond truth-conditions (whether characterized in terms of possible-worlds, or *à la* Davidson, by means of Tarskian truth-definitions) and their compositional determination. Williamson's account of assertion elaborates on what it is for meanings to transcend truth-conditions. The indication that an act governed by KR is being performed goes beyond the asserted truth-conditions. Is this encoded by expressions of natural languages?

That meaning in general, and in particular meaning encoded by expressions of natural languages, reduces to truth-conditions is the core of what Austin (1962) deplored as the *declarative fallacy*. Initially Austin appears to argue for his reproof of that fallacy by contrasting *constative* utterances, whose meaning is constituted by descriptive contents amenable to truth-conditional analyses, with *performative* utterances, which, not being truth evaluable, do not allow for a truth-conditional treatment. It soon transpires, however, that Austin is justifiably not satisfied with this way of putting the matter, and ends up arguing instead that utterances of the two kinds have a locutionary aspect, characterizable in truth-conditional terms, and an illocutionary force not so characterizable.[13] On the assumption that a proposal along Williamson's lines appropriately characterizes this non-truth-conditional element, Austin's view appears to provide an answer to our question: forces are encoded in language.

Unfortunately, matters are not so simple. Austin mainly discussed explicit performatives, sentences like 'I bequeath you my Ferrari', 'I promise to come', 'I declare war on Zanzibar'; his own proposals to characterize non-truth-conditional meanings by felicity conditions (which in the final section I will compare to my own) are designed with that paradigm in mind. However, the best treatment of explicit performatives has it that, in uttering those sentences, one (*tactically*, to put it in terms of Dummett's (1993) happy metaphor) asserts that one is at the same time promising, or christening, or declaring war, and (*strategically*, to go on with Dummett's metaphor) thereby additionally does these things.[14] Even though it is the second, strategic goal that is consciously salient to ordinary speakers, the constitutive account of the semantics-pragmatics distinction suggests that it is in fact

---

[13]Levinson (1983, ch. 5) offers a clear presentation of the Austinian dialectic.

[14]Ginet (1979) provides an excellent defense of this view.

only their tactical means for it, namely the assertion, which is linguistically encoded. There is a conventional, standardized mechanism by means of which the assertion that one is bequeathing leads to the bequest; but arguably the conventions in question do not count among those constitutive of natural languages; and if so the phenomenon is not semantic but pragmatic on the present view. On the Gricean view languages are conventional devices to put forth communicative intentions; the needs accounting for the practices at stake (declaring war, promising, bequeathing and so on) go beyond those basic communicative intentions for whose satisfaction we would expect a community to develop conventional resources. As a result, we would expect the phenomenon to occur in every community where the practices exist, no matter what natural language they use; this is in fact the case.

The fact that we do not need to count as semantic the signification of the illocutionary forces ultimately intended by explicit performatives may fuel the hopes of those who think that truth-conditions exhaust the meanings encoded in natural languages. Aside from explicit performatives, grammatical moods (imperative, interrogative, and the indicative mood of full sentences) are the obvious candidates for the role of force-encoders in natural languages. The suggestion to sustain a truth-conditionalist view would then be to treat the utterances in question as linguistically mere surface variants of the appropriate explicit performatives. Proposals along these lines differ mainly on how they treat indicatives. On a *symmetric* view, the indicative is treated symmetrically: semantically, an utterance of 'I am hungry' has the truth-condition of 'I hereby assert that I am hungry', and is therefore true to the extent that, in making it, I indeed assert that I am hungry at the time, whether or not I am in fact hungry. On the more popular alternative *asymmetric* proposal of Lewis (1970) and Davidson (1979), indicatives are unique in not being taken as equivalent to the corresponding explicit performative.

These proposals are not correct. The first and philosophically most important point to make against them is not that they fail to provide a proper account of the linguistic meaning of utterances in non-indicative moods, although this criticism is also valid. The main problem is that they fail to account even for the linguistic meaning of utterances in the indicative mood. Frege pointed out that an indicative has the same propositional content both when it is uttered as a full sentence and is thereby asserted, and when it occurs as part of longer sentences, in particular as the antecedent of a conditional. Frege's point thus accounts for the validity of *modus ponens*. Although 'Mallory climbed Mt. Everest' does not have the same meaning, broadly speaking,[15] than it has in 'If Mallory climbed Mt. Everest, Irvine did so too', this 'ambiguity' is still compatible with the validity of inferring 'Irvine climbed Mt. Everest' from them: the validity of the inference depends on relations among propositional contents. Now, it is at most propositional contents that are captured in the theories we are considering, in terms of truth-conditions.[16] When we are first exposed to these theories, it is perhaps obscured to us that only contents of that kind are according to them *linguistically* encoded by indicatives, or any other utterance. The linguistically encoded meaning of (6) is therefore represented by (7); according to proponents of the symmetric view the linguistic meaning of (8) is represented by (9), and according to proponents of the asymmetric view by (10):

(6) Did Mallory climb Mt. Everest?

(7) That I ask you if Mallory climbed Mt. Everest

(8) Mallory climbed Mt. Everest

(9) That I assert that Mallory climbed Mt. Everest

(10) That Mallory climbed Mt. Everest

Of course, proponents of the views under consideration would admit that (10) (or (9), if they countenance the symmetric view) does not capture all that is communicated in uttering (8); for they admit that speakers also convey assertoric force. Their view is that this is not *linguistically* encoded.

This claim obviously contradicts our intuitions.[17] But this is only the most conspicuous symptom of what is really wrong with them. Notice first that, even if forces are never linguistically encoded, Austin's claim still remains unchallenged as a point about the theory of meaning in general, if not about semantics – i.e., about linguistically encoded meanings. Even if it is only the content that I am performing a bequest with a certain content that is

---

[15]I.e., leaving aside whether the extra element is linguistically encoded or not, not to prejudice the present debate.
[16]I say 'at most', because these proposals also fail to capture, I think, presuppositional elements that are also part of linguistically encoded meanings.
[17]Dummett (1993: 207-8) makes this point.

linguistically encoded in 'I hereby bequeath you my Ferrari', while the bequest itself is a merely pragmatic implication, a general theory of meaning should still have to provide an analysis of the latter, even if under the 'pragmatics' label; and there is no hope of doing that merely in truth-conditional terms.[18] Bequests, like promises, orders and so on ought to be characterized in part in normative terms, in terms of something like the norms we have so far considered for assertion, in addition to the truth-conditional characterization of their contents. Given that irreducibly normative forces are in any case meant, the claim that they only occur in linguistically encoded meanings as they do in (7) and (9), as constituents of propositional contents suitable to be antecedents of conditionals, needs a justification based on a general conception of language.

On the neo-Gricean view of natural languages espoused here, the truth-conditional view is unsupported. If languages are conventional devices to help implement communicative intentions, it is only to be expected that forces themselves will be signified, not just as part of propositional contents; propositional contents will be signified only in so far as, together with forces, they contribute to characterize the distinctive objects of linguistically fundamental communicative intentions. This prediction of Gricean views is confirmed by our intuitions about the unsuitability of (9) and (10) to characterize all that is linguistically encoded in (8). Defenders of the views I am questioning should provide an alternative view of natural languages well supported enough to dismiss that intuition.

A usual objection to the views I am criticizing is that they counterintuitively make implicit performatives in non-indicative moods, like (6), true or false (Harnish 1994: 418). I should warn at this point about a small inadequacy in my previous classifying together of Lewis and Davidson, the only two defenders of the view that I have referred to. For the latter (1979: 114-5) proudly claims that his proposal is not subject to this criticism, and in fact criticizes Lewis' on this very account. This is because Davidson does not

---

[18]Some writers in the symmetric division appear to think that their proposal of taking, say, the interrogative force of (6) as a content-constituent, as in (7), does provide an explanation of its nature; this would be a motivation for the symmetric treatment of (8), as in (9). This is a philosophically misguided suggestion, which obviously engenders an infinite regress. For, as the representation of the ascribed meanings by (7), (9) and (10) makes perfectly clear, even if the proposal is correct as a view about what is linguistically encoded, it still leaves aside some force with which explicit performatives are meant. To account for it under the present suggestion, we would need to think of them as part of the content of further explicit performatives with one more level of embeddings, like 'I assert that I ask if ...' for (7); and this, of course, is just the starting point of a regress. Writers in the asymmetric division do not make this mistake; Davidson (1979: 120-1) makes it clear that his view is not intended to account for assertoric force, which he takes to be a pragmatic matter, a matter of what speakers do.

analyze non-indicative implicit performatives like (6) as synonymous with the corresponding explicit performative. He instead provides a 'paratactic' analysis, by which (6) would come out under analysis as the juxtaposition of the *mood-setter* 'My next utterance is interrogative in force' and the *core* 'Mallory climbed Mt. Everest'. This is in my view essentially indistinguishable from Lewis' proposal; Davidson can only contend the opposite because he stipulates *à la* Humpty-Dumpty that, when a sentence comes out after analysis as the paratactic juxtaposition of two, it is neither true nor false, even if the juxtaposed sentences have truth-values (1979: 121). This is an *ad hoc* maneuver, recommended only for the distinction it allows between Davidson's and Lewis's proposals; as Harnish (1994: 420) says, there is no good reason to think that the paratactic juxtaposition of two truth-evaluable sentences is not truth-evaluable.[19] It proves to be ultimately futile. Davidson (1979: 115) criticizes Lewis' account thus: 'simply reducing imperatives or interrogatives to indicatives leaves us with no account at all of the differences among the moods … mood is as irrelevant to meaning as voice is often said to be'. This criticism is fair, but it applies to Davidson's view too. In his account (1979: 121), moods only occur in linguistic meanings as constituents of the propositional content (truth-conditions) of the mood-setter; they occur in essentially the same way in Lewis' account. This is not enough to capture the intuitive *linguistic* differences between the moods.[20]

What, then, of the usual objection to these views that they counterintuitively make true or false implicit performatives in non-indicative moods, like (6)? A variant of this is the criticism by proponents of the asymmetric view of proponents of the symmetric view, that they provide incorrect truth-conditions for ordinary indicatives: in giving (9) as the linguistic content of utterances of (8), they make those utterances much more easily true than we intuitively think. Whether or not what we linguistically say obtains is only, according to the symmetric view, a matter of whether, in making the utterance, we really make the relevant assertion; it does not depend at all on what happened on Mount Mt. Everest on a day in June, 1924.[21] Intuitively, this is

---

[19]Davidson (1969) proposes a similarly paratactic analysis of propositional attitudes reports; but he does not absurdly conclude from this that they are not truth-evaluable.

[20]Segal (1991: 104-7) presents another criticism of Davidson's and Lewis' proposal.

[21]Lewis (1970: 224) gives this as his reason to adopt the asymmetric variant. Of course, he faces then a contrasting problem, namely, that of justifying the asymmetric treatment of implicit performatives in the indicative mood. The desire to evade this problem perhaps accounts for the incoherent justification that Davidson provides for the asymmetric view. With the elusiveness typical of his argumentative ways, he declares (1979: 119): 'Indicatives we may as well leave alone, since we have found no intelligible use for an assertion sign'. To 'leave indicatives alone' is here to forgo providing for them the paratactic analysis, which would produce a theory essentially equivalent to the symmetric view that they also are 'transformations'

not what we assert: we assert something whose truth depends on what happens on the mountain; the corresponding present point is that, similarly, with (6) we do not intuitively assert anything susceptible of truth or falsity. This criticism is in my view correct, but it should be understood in light of the first and conceptually most important. I would like to present the point, also by way of summary of what has gone so far, by analogy with one that Dummett has been pressing since his classic paper on truth: that purely disquotational accounts of truth miss something crucial (the 'point' or 'significance' of truth, he says), which can only be accounted for by thinking of the bearers of truth as objects of assertions.[22]

We apply 'true' to propositional contents, like those represented by (7), (9) and (10), and also to assertions like that made with (8). Let us reserve 'obtains' for the former use to simplify the exposition. 'Obtains' applies indifferently to what is linguistically encoded by utterances in different moods. It applies also to moodless sentences that occur as parts of longer sentences, and it is thus what is needed, say, to give the semantics of truth-conditional connectives. 'True' does not apply so indifferently; it applies to utterances in the indicative, but not to utterances in other moods. A disquotational theory of truth is adequate as an account of what we here mean by 'obtains', but it does not suffice to account for the invidious 'true'; Dummett's contention is that a proper account of truth requires to embed an account of the former in an account of the latter. Now, the main objection to the theories that we have been discussing is not that they count as truth-evaluable (6), for there is this ambiguity in 'true', and it is a difficult intuitive question whether or not, in uttering (6), we convey the corresponding explicit performative, whose content indeed counts as true at least in the sense of 'obtain'. The objection is that they only ascribe as *linguistic* meanings to utterances things that can obtain or not; but they do not ascribe to them, as theories of this kind intuitively should, things only some of which can be true or false. In doing this, they fail to give a proper account both of the meanings linguistically encoded by non-indicative moods, and, what is

---

of corresponding explicit performatives. The phrase 'we have found no intelligible use for an assertion sign' alludes to Davidson's argument against the possibility of a conventional indication of assertion, which I will discuss in the main text presently. Davidson, however, is clear that the argument allegedly establishes *also* that there could not be either conventional indications of commands or questions. Consistency would then require that the other moods were also 'left alone'. That would be compatible with a theory along the lines of Stenius (1967); but not with Davidson's own.

[22]See, for instance, Dummett (1973), ch. 10, 'Assertion'.

conceptually a more fundamental failure,[23] of those linguistically encoded by utterances in the indicative mood.

On a Gricean view of natural languages, it is to be expected that there exists an asymmetry between meanings linguistically encoded that cannot be evaluated as true or false, and those that can. This is just the asymmetry in 'direction of fit', separating communicative acts into two classes by their criteria of correctness or regulating norms: those, on the one hand, for which how the world is independently of them constitutes a criterion of correctness (because they are constitutively intended as its faithful representations); and those, on the other, for which how the world is independently of them does not constitute such a criterion (because they are constitutively intended to change it in ways dependent on them). Communicative acts are essentially overt on a Gricean view; it is thus to be expected that some indication of which of these two groups a given speech act belongs to be conventionally marked. This renders dogmatic the views we are questioning, which allow for linguistically encoded meanings to be appraised only in terms of the indifferent 'obtains'. They are dogmatic because they should justify their contrasting view on the basis of an alternative conception of natural languages, but so far as I know they have not done so.[24]

We have thus found reasons for an affirmative answer to the question with which we began this section; some illocutionary forces are linguistically encoded in natural languages, as expected on our conception of what they are, and moods appear to be conventionally designed for this purpose. Conventionality by itself is not enough; there is a form of conventionality, standardization, in the signification of force by explicit performatives, but one can nonetheless resist the view that forces explicitly mentioned in them are *linguistically* encoded. In that case, however, we have an explanation of how they are conveyed, compatible with their non-linguistic nature. Con-

---

[23] It is more fundamental firstly in that it is not on the surface: because of the ambiguity in the ordinary use of 'true', it may seem at first sight that these views provide an acceptable account of utterances in the indicative. Secondly, because it is explanatorily more basic: it is only after one appreciates the reasons why they do not account for indicatives, that one really understands why they do not properly account for non-indicatives either.

[24] A more ambitious criticism, closer to Dummett's, would be that only by assuming linguistically encoded meanings properly including the normative element can we have a correct view about the other component of linguistic meaning, truth-conditions. The identification of truth and warranted assertability is not part of the agreement expressed here with Dummett's view that a philosophical theory of truth should be embedded in a theory of assertion. Cf. Williamson's (1996/2000: 242-3) distinction between realist and anti-realist accounts of assertion along the lines of his, and his critical remarks on Brandom's (1983, 1994) anti-realist but otherwise congenial view (*ibid.*, 258 fn.).

ventionality is a good *prima facie* indication, which, together with the previous reflections, does support the claim.[25]

Davidson (1979: 114) has argued against this as follows: 'mood is not a conventional sign of assertion or command because nothing is, or could be, a conventional sign of assertion or command'. His argument for this is based on the Humpty-Dumptyesque tactic of stipulating a new meaning for 'convention'. He first reminds us that sentences in the indicative mood can be used to perform speech acts different from assertion; the same of course can be said of the other moods. Thus, with 'in this house, we remove our shoes before entering' a command is typically indicated; indicative sentences are also indirectly used in jokes, fiction, or in theatre. He then derives the previous conclusion from this point, as a corollary of what he calls *the autonomy of linguistic meaning*, that 'there cannot be a form of speech which, solely by dint of its conventional meaning, can be used only for a given purpose, such as making an assertion or asking a question' (*ibid.*, 113-4). If 'convention' is used in any ordinary way, the conclusion obviously does not follow from this. It is no objection to there existing in a given country a convention of driving on the right that morally unconcerned suicides bend it to their own goals by driving recklessly on the left. Not much about conventions in the ordinary sense can follow from what we may call *the autonomy of driving*, that there cannot be a form of driving which, solely by dint of its conventional regulation, can be used only for a given purpose, such as arriving safely or quickly to one's destination.

Cases like those that Davidson calls to our attention should, I think, be treated in a similar way to the one suggested earlier for dealing with explicit performatives; i.e., as pragmatic meanings derived basically through a mechanism analogous to the one involved in the conversational implicatures, as theorized by Grice (1975). It cannot be exactly that, for Grice's appeal to the maxims of quantity and quality manifests that he mostly had in mind implicatures derived from assertoric meanings; but other writers have developed proposals along similar lines.[26] Having recourse to Dummett's (1993) metaphor mentioned above, we should distinguish the speaker's *strategic* intent (ordering his audience to remove his shoes, or, in the case of fiction or play, leading his audience to imagine certain states of affairs) from

---

[25]Pendlebury (1986), Belnap (1990) and Green (2000) provide additional reasons. Pendlebury and Belnap point out that there also are conventional contrastive forms to report in indirect discourse questions (indirect yes/no and wh-questions questions), commands and assertions. Green points out that parenthetical remarks, like 'as I conjecture' or 'as I suggest' conventionally serve to indicate illocutionary commitments additional to the one that might be indicated by the mood of the main clause.

[26]See, for instance, Searle (1975). Dummett (1993: 209) makes a similar suggestion.

the *tactical* role that his indicative utterance plays; the fact that with that utterance a certain assertion would be made if used literally according to its semantics is still essential to its performing this strategic role.

5   Assertions as Transfers of Knowledge

Davidson's argument does point to real problems for an account of the semantics of moods, though. Harnish (1994) documents well how variegated their use is. Thus with imperatives, in addition to issuing commands, we commonly plead ('let me go!'), give advice ('be strong!'), permission ('help yourself!'), warn ('don't trip on that wire'), wish ('have a good time!'), and so on. With indicatives, in addition to asserting, we remind, conclude from previous premises, answer exams, confess, address indifferent, incredulous or inattentive audiences, soliloquize, and so on. The uses of interrogatives are at least as variegated.

There are two options, in view of this, for a semantics of moods. The one chosen by Harnish (1994) is to reduce conventionally signified forces to an unspecific minimum, compatible with most of the typical uses, leaving to context (to pragmatics) the selection of a specific force compatible with the conventional one. This could be understood by analogy with the case of indexicals and demonstratives. A token-reflexive linguistic rule associated with the type 'this glass' in English descriptively relates every token of the expression to a glass salient when the token is uttered. Knowing this descriptive character is typically not sufficient to understand a token; overhearing one uttered in a kitchen from another room is not sufficient to understand what the speaker means, it is also required in addition to gain through perception further knowledge identifying the glass referred to. Similarly, in the case of indicative utterances with content p the conventionally conveyed force-element could be the indication that the force of the utterance is such that part of its defining normative requirement is that the speaker believes p; in the case of imperatives, the indication that the force is to be such that part of its defining normative requirement is that the audience desires p to be the case. Context would then indicate additional elements sufficient to individuate the specific force meant by the speaker.

Williamson suggests an alternative when he says: 'in natural languages, the default use of declarative sentences is to make assertions' (2000: 258). On the alternative view, we would provide a specification of a given force as the *default* for utterances in the relevant mood. In a minimal context (a context without more information than that derived from the presumption that the participants know the language), that force would be unconditionally signified, all things considered; but the default assumption could be overridden in other contexts by an open-ended list of conditions: that the alleged assertion has been made after 'once upon a time', or after 'let me remind you of the following', or 'therefore', or in an exam, or includes parentheticals like 'I surmise'. By default the utterance of a full sentence in the indicative mood signifies according to Williamson's proposal that the act is subject to the rule KR; the counterexamples would be dealt with by taking into account the operation of some condition overriding the default assumption.

I think that the second option is better, for reasons to be given presently. Practically speaking, perhaps there is not much difference. We still end up ascribing a disjunctive, and to that extend unspecific, conventional meaning to mood, leaving to context the specification of which force is meant. Theoretically, however, a proposal along these lines agrees better with the neo-Gricean conception of language, in committing itself, as the default for each mood, to meanings in accord with the view of natural languages as social devices designed to help implement communicative intentions. Or, rather, that would be so if what individuates the default assertoric force is the token-reflexive rule TKR instead of Williamson's KR:

(TKR) One must ((assert p) only if one's audience comes thereby to be in a position to know p)

I follow Williamson's (2000: 95) use of 'being in a position to know': 'To be in a position to know p, it is neither necessary to know p nor sufficient to be physically and psychologically capable of knowing p. No obstacle must block one's path to knowing p. If one is in a position to know p, and has done what one is in a position to do to decide whether p is true, then one knows p. The fact is open to one's view, unhidden, even if one does not yet see it. Thus, being in a position to know, like knowing but unlike being physically and psychologically capable of knowing, is factive: if one is in a position to know p, then p is true'.

I have recourse to this notion in order to characterize assertion in terms of an audience-oriented norm of knowledge-transmission that does not contradict clear pre-theoretic intuitions regarding which assertions are wrong. Intuitively, cases in which we assert p but fail thereby to transfer knowledge of p to audiences who already know p do not count as such as violations of norms constitutive of assertion. Nor do analogous cases in which we fail to transfer knowledge to an audience who is not paying attention, or who has beliefs defeating our testimony, perhaps overzealous skeptical doubts. Like Williamson's KR, the norm still requires an existing truth-maker for the contents of acceptable acts of assertion, and that the act be connected with the truth-maker so as to allow for knowledge.

What arguments are there in favor of TKR? In the next section I will argue that assertion, the default speech act indicated by declarative mood, is conventional in the sense that, necessarily, a community has the practice of asserting only if it has the practice of using conventional devices to execute it, as a matter of fact we do. But it is only a practice defined by TKR, as opposed to one governed by KR, that one would expect to be conventional in that sense. Silence is enough to obey both KR and TKR, which is I think O.K. However, in contrast to TKR Williamson's rule is also obeyed by a community of individuals who assert what they know, but only in soliloquy. It would be hard to explain why a community would find a use for a convention to signify that an act governed by such a rule is intended.

Williamson (2000: 267-9) considers reasons to justify the existence of conventions to signify assertion, individuated by KR, as opposed to, for instance, a speech act individuated by the truth rule TR. The main difference lies in that, in the latter case, the rule could be obeyed just by accident: one asserts p though one is very far from knowing p, but p just happens to be the case. Williamson argues that it is socially more useful to have a device to indicate an act governed by the stronger rule, because it requires of the asserter to ensure that there exists the non-accidental relation needed for knowledge between the act and its truth-maker. He compares the relation between bringing about p on the one hand and merely desiring p when in fact p obtains on the other, to that of knowing p on the one hand and merely believing p when in fact p obtains on the other. The first members of the two relations are distinguished from the others by their requiring a non-accidental relation between act and truth-maker. Williamson suggests that it makes more social sense to institute a device to indicate an act regulated by a norm requiring these stronger, non-accidental relations.

This argument works better to justify the conventional indication of an act governed by the stronger TKR vis-à-vis TR than the weaker KR. What does make social sense is the indication of a communicative act, by which someone with authority confers a responsibility to bring about p on someone else; not just the indication that the act will be correct if it brings about p. What we expect is not a device for the conventional indication of an act regulated by the norm that its performance brings about p; but rather that the audience thereby brings about p. In line with this, if we advanced accounts of the speech acts that are the default uses of interrogatives and imperatives of the kind envisaged by Williamson, the norms we would end up with would be audience-oriented, like TKR. The same, *mutatis mutandis*, applies to assertion. In issuing a command, someone confers responsibility on someone else to thereby make p the case; the norm constitutive of commands requires of the former to have the authority to confer this responsibility, and of the latter to discharge it by thereby bringing about p. By default, imperatives conventionally signify an act subject to this norm. In issuing an assertion, someone confers a responsibility on oneself *relative to someone else* for the truth of p; the norm constitutive of assertion requires of the former to have the epistemic authority to discharge this responsibility, by putting thereby the latter in a position to know p. The latter can challenge the epistemic authority of the former; but, if he does not, p will be rightfully taken afterwards as common knowledge. By default, declaratives conventionally signify an act subject to this complex of normative relations.[27]

Can we not explain TKR as a non-constitutive norm of assertion, derived from KR as its constitutive rule and considerations not specific of assertion? No proposal along these lines that I know works. One obvious candidate that comes to mind is an appeal to Grice's maxim of *relevance*. However, such a proposal would work only by smuggling in the conception of the relevance at stake the view about assertion that the TKR proposal embodies. If we tried to elaborate an account of the indirect speech acts made with interrogatives or imperatives, along the lines of Grice's theory of conversational implicatures (which was designed with implicatures made with declaratives in view), we should replace the submaxims of quality and quantity by others adequate to commands and questions, the acts conventionally made by default with those other moods. At first sight, we should not do the same with the submaxim of relevance; but this is only because we wrongly assume a conveniently unspecific understanding of relevance.[28] Properly understood, what is relevant is relative to the goals at stake; there is thus a form of relevance appropriate to the constitutive point of assertions, and a different one appropriate when the constitutive goals of commands and questions are at stake. Now, if we only consider the sort of relevance appropriate to acts regulated by KR, I cannot see how we can obtain TKR (or anything audience-involving) as a derivative rule. We can only do that, as far as I can see, by assuming the kind of relevance adequate when it is an act regulated by TKR that is intended; but that would be a viciously circular way of establishing TKR as a derivative rule.

---

[27] The present account suggests an elucidation of the claims by Burge (1993) regarding the apriority of the epistemic justification of belief based on testimony, as just a particular case of the apriority of analyticity. Davis (2002) provides a detailed account, based on Burge's views, of how such an account of the conventional meaning of declarative mood can be used to justify the transfer of knowledge from speaker to audience in particular cases. Taken together with that elaboration, the present account thus supports the dynamic picture of assertion provided by Stalnaker (1978). It could also be usefully developed on the basis of the detailed elaboration by Brandom (1983, 1994) of the outlined normative relations.

[28] Levinson (2000) criticizes such an unspecific understanding of relevance.

These considerations provide the reason alluded to before to prefer, of the two considered possibilities to deal with the fact that moods have common uses for different speech acts, the view that a specific one is conventionally a default. If it is only conventional for moods the indication of the unspecific constraint on forces proposed by Harnish, it is left to the rationality of speakers to infer in each context the specific force on the basis of their knowledge of language. It seems to me to agree better with the way language is taught and acquired that it is rather the conventional relation with a specific force that is constitutive of natural languages, leaving only to the reasoning of individual speakers to work out in non-default contexts which other forces are intended.

One of the reasons that Williamson gives to support KR vis-à-vis TR is that it provides a more properly individuative rule than TR, because the latter does not discriminate assertion from other speech acts, like conjecturing or swearing. A similar consideration supports TKR vis-à-vis KR. Presupposing is another speech act, which is as much subject to KR as asserting; what characteristically distinguishes the former from the latter is that presupposings are not subject to TKR. On the contrary, what is presupposed is typically taken for granted as constituting common knowledge.

In addition to these considerations in favor of the TKR proposal, we can see that it also has the merits that Williamson claims for KR. The conversational patterns he mentions also support TKR; and there are others specifically in its favor, like a usual criticism of assertions based on their inaptness to transfer knowledge ('I already knew that, thanks'). The TKR account also explains what is wrong with the modified version of Moore's paradox, for, typically, in order for an assertion of p to put the audience in a position to know p, the asserter should know p.[29] The practices of mathematics and formal testimony in court manifest as much sensitivity to KR as to TKR. Finally, any feeling we may have that one should not be blamed in cases in which one asserts what one knows but does not thereby put an audience in a position to know can be handled by means of Williamson's strategy for corresponding objections to his own view: we can argue that what one does in those cases is not permissible, but it is exculpable.[30]

---

[29]Lackey (1999) shows that there are exceptions, cases in which an assertion puts the audience in a position to know even though the speaker does not know. They include cases where one transmits knowledge acquired from knowledgeable sources that one does not trust; and cases where speakers' lack of knowledge derives from their having defeaters that are not transferred to their audiences together with their testimony.

[30]Although the proposal advanced in this section on the conventional meaning of the indicative mood does not coincide with Dummett's own, it should be clear that it is in the spirit of his views on this matters, when contrasted with the views of truth-conditional theorists like Davidson which we considered and rejected in the previous section.

6 Intention and Convention in Speech Acts

In claiming that illocutionary force is an irreducible aspect of meaning overlooked by previous theorists, Austin (1962) argues for a social, anti-individualistic conception of meaning; nothing is more opposed to the Austinian vision than the view of meaning that Searle (1983) has ended up propounding. Austin wants to oppose traditional views of linguistic meaning in general, and assertion in particular, that take it to aim at the mere expression of independently characterized inner states, like beliefs or judgments. To pursue this ambition, Austin distinguishes constitutive from non-constitutive features of the *felicity conditions* by means of which he hopes to characterize illocutionary forces, and then follows a two-pronged strategy. Firstly, he suggests that the existence of a specific conventional procedure is the central constitutive feature of forces; secondly, he contends that the inner states associated with acts of meaning figure in merely non-constitutive sincerity conditions.

Opposing the first prong in a classical defense of a Gricean individualistic view according to which only communicative intentions are essential to non-natural meaning, Strawson (1964) rebutted some of Austin's claims. Austin says: 'there cannot be an illocutionary act unless the means employed are conventional' (Austin 1962: 119). This appears to be the very strong claim that there cannot be an illocutionary act, unless the means employed to perform it are conventionally intended for such an undertaking; this is also suggested by his claim that the existence of a conventional procedure is the main constitutive felicity condition of illocutionary forces. As Strawson points out, however, illocutionary acts that we ordinarily perform by using non-conventional means, like warnings made with declarative utterances and so on, disprove the claim so understood.[31] Austin himself did not appear to have much confidence in the view, as witnessed by the extremely weak characterization he provides of the conventionality of forces at other places; thus, a warning is conventional 'in the sense that at least it could be made explicit by the performative formula' (Austin 1962: 103).

However, Strawson's criticism leaves open the question of whether conventions are necessary in a stronger sense for the linguistically basic speech acts that we have taken to be conventionally signified by moods, like assertions. They could be conventional in the stronger sense that a community

---

[31] The point applies also to the speech acts constituting, on the present view, the default meanings of moods, like questions, commands and assertions. Thus, in 'Some Advice for poets', *New York Review of Books* XLIX, 14, James Fenton says that the way poets refute the death of the sonnet 'is not by argument, but by assertion. My sonnet asserts that the sonnet still lives' (*ibid.*, 67). To produce a sonnet is not a conventional means for asserting that the sonnet still lives (unless, of course, the sonnet says so, which is not Fenton's point).

could not have instituted the practice of performing acts subject to the rules constitutive of them, except by having conventional devices to indicate so. This sense is stronger than the one Austin provides in the passage just quoted in that, unlike the latter, it is incompatible with the individualistic ambitions of Grice's program. As far as I can see, conventions are constitutive in that stronger sense, which is what accounts in part for my describing the view that this paper contributes to articulate as merely *neo*-Gricean. Non-natural meaning constitutively involves communicative intentions; but the relevant communicative intentions are in part individuated relative to conventions operating in the social environment and accounting for the meaning-contribution of the semantic units of the expressions one has put together to produce one's utterance. Dummett (1973: 311, 354) argues for this in the case of assertion. His argument relies on the fact that, except for a very limited range of cases, we cannot make sense of the attribution of the inner state (belief, knowledge or judgment) that the act verbalizes independently of its regulating function in the performance of the relevant linguistic acts. This is certainly the case for the complex higher-order mental states characteristic of Gricean accounts.

In this regard I find some remarks by Williamson about the relation between conventions and constitutive rules potentially misleading. He argues as follows: 'Constitutive rules are not conventions. If it is a convention that one must ϕ, then it is contingent that one must ϕ; conventions are arbitrary, and can be replaced by alternative conventions. In contrast, if it is a constitutive rule that one must ϕ, then it is necessary that one must ϕ ... a rule will count as constitutive of an act only if it is essential to that act: necessarily, the rule governs every performance of the act' (Williamson 2000: 239). Although Williamson does not say so, this might suggest that there cannot be the kind of necessary connection between assertion and convention defended in the previous paragraph, because they have contrasting modal properties. Assertions are defined by constitutive norms, which are essential to them; norms related to conventions, on the other hand, are contingent.

This rough argument can be questioned on several grounds, and it is not my intention to attribute it to Williamson. But his argument may well confusingly suggest something like it; and, in any case, I think it is wrong: any sense in which norms related to conventions can be said to be contingent is such that the corresponding norms for assertions can also be said to be contingent; and vice versa, to the extent that assertions are related to constitutive norms that are essential to them, conventions are also related to constitutive norms essential to them. Intuitively, this is what should be the case. For conventions are tacit or explicit agreements regulating a potentially indefinite number of cases; these agreements are exchanges of conditional promises, by which one commits oneself to do something in certain recurring situations on condition that others keep corresponding promises;[32] and promises are just the sort of thing to be defined by constitutive norms. Thus, for the sake of the argument, let us consider the status of the following norm associated to the convention of driving φ on the right:

> (DR) One must ((convene with others on driving on the right) only if one thereby drives on the right while others do likewise)

Is Williamson's a good reason not to count DR as a constitutive rule of the convention to drive on the right? He argues that conventional obligations are contingent, because conventions are arbitrary. However, notice that, in the case of, say, an assertion that snow is white, the obligation that he takes to be constitutive, necessarily governing any instance of the assertion, has acts of asserting in its scope; it forbids asserting that snow is white, when one does not know that snow is white: 'The rule is to be parsed as 'One must ((assert p) only if p has C)' ... The rule unconditionally forbids this combination: one asserts p when p lacks C' (Williamson 2000: 241). The arbitrariness of conventions is surely compatible with the claim that DR is a constitutive rule of the convention of driving on the right, understood as Williamson proposes here for the case of assertion. The convention's constitutive rule unconditionally forbids convening with others on driving on the right, and then driving on the left while other parties to the convention comply with it. The arbitrariness of conventions must be compatible with counting this prohibition as necessarily governing any such case of convening. At least, the following seems to be the case: to the extent that assertions are essentially governed by the kind of norm that Williamson contemplates, conventions can be equally governed by similar norms.

'If it is a convention that one must φ, then it is contingent that one must φ; conventions are arbitrary, and can be replaced by alternative conventions': surely this is platitudinous. But, to the extent that this is platitudinous, there is a corresponding platitude true of assertions. It is contingent that a particular convention has in fact been adopted; another convention (or none at all) could have been adopted instead, for instance that of driving on the left. But the obligation defining the convention of driving on the right would still be in place in the counterfactual situation; for it would still forbid convening on driving on the right, and then proceeding to drive on the left. What is contingent is the existence of an obligation to drive on the right, given that the convention determining it could well not have been adopted;

---

[32] An exchange of promises of a peculiar kind; see Gilbert, 1993.

this does not make contingent the obligation DR, constitutive of the convention in the view parallel to the one Williamson holds regarding assertion. In the very same sense, the obligations related to assertions are contingent. If any given assertion were not made, the knowledge-obligation imposed by what Williamson takes to be its constitutive rule would not exist. No act of assertion might exist, and then none of the knowledge-commitments imposed by that rule would exist either. It would still be the case in those subjunctive situations that the obligations constitutive of assertion (as Williamson defines it) obtain.

Thus, the arbitrariness of conventions does not posit any special difficulty for the view that linguistically fundamental forces like assertion, although defined by constitutive rules, are necessarily conventional in the sense previously outlined; and this vindicates in part the Austinian position in the debate about the place of intention and convention in speech acts.

The view of assertion defended here should also help appraise the other prong of Austin's anti-individualistic strategy, namely, his counting as non-constitutive the felicity conditions concerning the presence of mental states that, on individualistic views, the utterances merely voice. Gricean critics correctly pointed out that some relation between forces and mental states should also be constitutive; because part of what distinguishes asserting from commanding is that the former is related to doxastic states in a way in which the latter is rather related to conative states, even granting that the existence of specific conventional procedures also distinguishes them.

Discussions of these matters have been in my view obscured by a confused idea of what a constitutive rule is, held both by Austin and by his critics; the preceding considerations should help clarify the issues. A norm constitutive of an act, in contrast to a mere regulative rule, is essential to the act; necessarily, every performance of the act is subject to the rule. However, the essential character of the norm should not be confused with an essential character of the criteria invoked in the norm. It is a constitutive norm of commands that whoever issues them has the required authority. But it is confused and fruitless to debate whether a command has been really issued by someone who utters an imperative merely pretending to have the relevant authority for it. What is clear is that the act counts as a flawed order, an act made in violation of a norm constitutive of ordering. As with the similar case of cheating in games, one can well say that it is because it was an order that it can be described as a flawed one; it is because it was still a game of football that the goal was scored illegally, the forward having deceitfully used his hand. As Williamson insists, it does not count as an objection to the present view that many assertions are made in violation of the rule here claimed to be constitutive, by ignorant speakers or to inattentive audiences.

What is claimed to be constitutive of assertions is their being subject to the norm, not its satisfaction.

Part of Rawls' (1955) aim in distinguishing constitutive and regulative norms was to put the vindication or rejection of utilitarianism in its proper place. The view of utilitarianism as a reductionist form of naturalism goes hand in hand with thinking of all norms as regulative, as generalizations summing up useful consequences that follow from recurring situations. This gives rise to a confused view of the kind of obligation applying to particular instances of practices, acts subject to norms like promises or punishments. The anti-reductionist view that there are constitutive norms prevents these confusions; and, as Rawls suggests, it still allows a place for utilitarian considerations, now directed at establishing which practices defined by constitutive rules should be in fact adopted, and thus which irreducible obligations should thereby exist in the actual world.

A similar point could be made regarding the social character of linguistic representation, as presented in this paper. It is not that the norms associated with illocutionary forces merely sum up uses of representational devices with socially beneficial consequences; this view will only lead to a confused interpretation of the obligations accruing to performances of speech acts. However, among all forces existing in the Platonic Heaven, all of them equally imposing their constitutive norms on their instances, it makes natural sense (i.e., it is compatible with a scientific view of the place of rational beings in the natural world), in addition to being confirmed by our intuitions as competent speakers, to think that the conventional signification of some of them is constitutive of natural languages; this is in a nutshell the main reason given in the previous section to think that some specific forces are conventionally signified, even if only as defaults, by devices like moods. It makes natural sense to think so of those forces whose existence would confer socially beneficial consequences – like one whose instances count as correct to the extent that they allow the transfer of information from a truthful speaker to a trustful hearer. This is, in a nutshell, the main reason given here to think of TKR rather than KR as the constitutive rule of the type of speech act conventionally signified by default by the declarative mood.

References

Austin, J. 1962. *How to Do Things with Words*. Oxford: Clarendon Press. (2nd ed. issued as an Oxford U.P. paperback, 1989, to which page references are made.)

Bach, K. 1999. The Semantics-Pragmatics Distinction: What It Is and Why It Matters. *The Semantics-Pragmatics Interface from Different Points of View*, Ken Turner (ed.), 65-84. Oxford: Elsevier.

Bach, K. 2002. Semantic, Pragmatic. *Meaning and Truth*, eds. J. Keim Campbell, M. O'Rourke and D. Shier, 284-92. New York: Seven Bridges Press.

Belnap, N. 1990. Declaratives Are not Enough. *Philosophical Studies* 59: 1-30.

Brandom, R. 1983. Asserting. *Noûs* 17: 637-650.

Brandom, R. 1994. *Making it Explicit*. Cambridge MA: Harvard U.P.

Burge, T. 1993. Content Preservation. *Philosophical Review* 102: 457-88.

Coady, C.A.J. 1992. *Testimony*. Oxford: Clarendon Press.

Davidson, D. 1969. On Saying That. *Synthèse*, 19: 130-46. (Reprinted in his *Inquiries into Truth and Interpretation*, 1984, 93-108. Oxford: Clarendon Press).

Davidson, D. 1979. Moods and Performances. *Meaning and Use*, ed. A. Margalit, Dordrecht: D. Reidel; reprinted in his *Inquiries into Truth and Interpretation*, 1984, 109-21. Oxford: Oxford University Press, to which I refer.

Davies, M. 2000. Persons and their Underpinnings. *Philosophical Explorations* 3: 43-62.

Davis, S. 2002. Conversation, Epistemology and Norms. *Mind and Language* 17: 513-37.

Dummett, M. 1973. *Frege: Philosophy of Language*; 2nd ed., 1981, from where I quote, London: Duckworth.

Dummett, M. 1993. Mood, Force, and Convention. In his *The Seas of Language*, 202-23. Oxford: Oxford University Press.

Evans, G. 1982. *The Varieties of Reference*. Oxford: Clarendon Press.

Fine, K. 1994. Essence and Modality. *Philosophical Perspectives* 8, *Logic and Language*, ed. J. Tomberlin, Atascadero CA: Ridgeview.

García-Carpintero, M. 1998. Indexicals as Token-Reflexives. *Mind* 107: 529-563.

García-Carpintero, M. 2000. A Presuppositional Account of Reference-Fixing. *Journal of Philosophy* XCVII (3): 109-147.

García-Carpintero, M. 2001. Gricean Rational Reconstructions and the Semantics/Pragmatics Distinction. *Synthèse* 128: 93-131.

Gilbert, M. 1993. Is an Agreement an Exchange of Promises? *Journal of Philosophy* XC: 627-649.

Ginet, C. 1979. Performativity. *Linguistics & Philosophy* 3: 245-65.

Green, M. 2000. Illocutionary Force and Semantic Content. *Linguistics and Philosophy* 23: 435-73.

Grice, H. P. 1975. Logic and Conversation. *Syntax and Semantics*, eds. P. Cole and J. Morgan, vol. 3, New York: Academic Press. Also in Grice, H.P., *Studies in The Ways of Words*, 22-40. Cambridge MA: Harvard U.P.

Harnish, R. 1994. Mood, Meaning and Speech Acts. *Foundations of speech act theory*, ed. S. L. Tsohatzidis, London: Routledge.

Kaplan, D. 1989a. Demonstratives. *Themes from Kaplan*, eds. J. Almog, J. Perry and H. Wettstein, 481-563. Oxford: Oxford University Press.

Kaplan, D. 1989b. Afterthoughts. *Themes from Kaplan*, eds. J. Almog, J. Perry and H. Wettstein, 565-614. Oxford: Oxford University Press.

Lackey, J. 1999. Testimonial Knowledge and Transmission. *Philosophical Quarterly* 49: 471-490.

Levinson, S. 1983. *Pragmatics*. Cambridge: Cambridge University Press.

Levinson, S. 2000. *Presumptive Meanings*. Cambridge MA: MIT Press.

Lewis, D. 1970. General Semantics. *Synthèse* 22: 18-67; in his *Philosophical Papers, vol. 1*, 1983, 189-229. Oxford: Oxford University Press, to which I refer.

Lewis, D. 1975. Languages and Language. *Language, Mind and Knowledge*, ed. K. Gunderson, Minnesota: University of Minnesota Press; in his *Philosophical Papers, vol. 1*, 1983, 163-88. Oxford: Oxford University Press, to which I refer.

Pendlebury, M. 1986. Against the Power of Force: Reflections on the Meaning of Mood. *Mind* 95: 361-72.

Rawls, J. 1955. Two Concepts of Rules. *The Philosophical Review* 64: 3-32.

Schiffer, S. 1993. Actual-language Relations. *Philosophical Perspectives 7: Language and Logic*, ed. J. Tomberlin, 231-58. Atascadero CA: Ridgeview.

Searle, J. 1983. *Intentionality*. Cambridge: Cambridge University Press.

Segal, G. 1990/1. In the Mood for a Semantic Theory. *Proceedings of the Aristotelian Society* XCI: 103-18.

Searle, J. 1969. *Speech Acts: An Essay in the Philosophy of Language*. Cambridge: Cambridge University Press.

Searle, J. 1975. Indirect Speech Acts. *Syntax and Semantics*, eds. P. Cole and J. Morgan, vol. 3, 59-82. New York: Academic Press.

Stalnaker, R. 1978. Assertion. *Syntax and Semantics* 9, ed. P. Cole, 315-32. New York: Academic Press.

Stalnaker, R. 1997. Reference and Necessity. *A Companion to the Philosophy of Language*, eds. C. Wright & B. Hale, 534-54. Oxford: Blackwell.

Stenius, E. 1967. Mood and Language-Game. *Synthèse* 17: 254-74.

Strawson, P. 1964. Intention and Convention in Speech Acts. *Philosophical Review* 73: 439-60.

Williamson, T. 1996/2000. Knowing and Asserting. *Philosophical Review* 105: 489-523; included with some revisions as chapter 11 of his *Knowledge and Its Limits*, 2000. New York: Oxford U.P., to which I refer.

Wolterstorff, N. 1980. *Works and Worlds of Art*. Oxford: Clarendon Press.

8

The Syntax and Pragmatics of the Naming Relation

KENNETH A. TAYLOR

1 Preliminaries

Philosophers of language have lavished attention on names and other singular referring expressions. But they have focused primarily on what might be called lexical-semantic character of names and have largely ignored both what I call the lexical-syntactic character of names and also what I call the pragmatic significance of the naming relation. Partly as a consequence, explanatory burdens have mistakenly been heaped upon semantics that properly belong elsewhere. This essay takes some steps toward correcting these twin lacunae. When we properly distinguish that which belongs to the lexical-syntactic character of names, from that which belongs to the lexical semantic character of names, from that which rests on the pragmatics of the naming relation, we lay to rest many misbegotten claims about names and their presumed semantic behavior. For example, though many believe that Frege's puzzle about the possibility of informative identity statements motivates a move away from a referentialist semantics for names, I argue that the very possibility of Frege cases has its source not in facts about the lexical-semantic character of names but in facts about the lexical-syntax of the naming relation. If I am right, Frege cases as such are insufficient to justify the introduction of the distinction between sense and reference. In a similar vein, I offer a new diagnosis of the widely misdiagnosed felt invalidity of the substitution of co-referring names within propositional attitude contexts.

The Semantics/Pragmatics Distinction.
Claudia Bianchi (ed.).
Copyright © 2004, CSLI Publications.

That felt invalidity has been taken to justify the conclusion that an embedded referring expression *must* be playing some semantic role either different from or additional to its customary semantic role of standing for its reference. I argue, to the contrary, that failures of substitutivity have their source not in the peculiar semantic behavior of embedded expressions but entirely in certain pragmatic principles.

2   On the Lexical-Syntax of the Naming Relation

I begin by exploring the lexical-syntactic character of the linguistic category NAME. The contrast between the lexical-syntax and lexical-semantics is meant to distinguish lexically governed or constrained word-word relationships, on the one hand, from lexically governed and constrained word-world relationships, on the other. My central claim about the lexical-syntax of NAME is that names are a peculiar sort of anaphoric device. In particular, I claim that if N is a name, then any two tokens of N are guaranteed, in virtue of the principles of the language, to be co-referential. I will say that co-typical name tokens are *explicitly co-referential*. Explicit co-reference must be sharply distinguished from what I call *coincidental co-reference*. Two name tokens that are not co-typical can refer to the same object, and thus be co-referential, without being explicitly co-referential. For example, tokens of 'Hesperus' and tokens of 'Phosphorus' co-refer but are not explicitly co-referential. The fact that tokens of 'Hesperus' one and all refer to Venus is entirely independent of the fact that tokens of 'Phosphorus' one and all refer to Venus. Indeed, I take it to be a correlative truth about names, a truth partly definitive of the lexical-syntactic character of names, that when m and n are distinct names, they are *referentially independent*. Referential independence means that no structural or lexical relation between distinct names m and n can *guarantee* that if m refers to o then n refers to o as well. To say that any distinct names are always interpretationally and referentially independent, is not to say that distinct names must fail to co-refer. Indeed, we can directly show that two names are co-referential via true identity statements. But referential independence does mean that when two distinct names m and n do co-refer, their co-reference is a mere coincidence of usage.

   The referential independence of distinct names and the explicit co-reference of tokens of the same name type partially defines the lexical-syntactic character of the category NAME. Part of what it is to be a name is to be an expression type such that tokens of that type are explicitly co-referential with one another and referentially independent of the tokens of any distinct type. If one knows of e only that it belongs to the category NAME, then one knows that, whatever e refers to, if it refers to anything at all, then tokens of *e* are *guaranteed* to be co-referential one with another and referentially independent of any distinct name *e'*, whatever *e'* refers to.

A name (type) is, in effect, a set of (actual and possible) name tokens such that all tokens in the set are guaranteed, in virtue of the rules of the language, to co-refer one with another. Call such a set a *chain of explicit co-reference*. It is, I suspect, a linguistically universal fact about the lexical category NAME that numerically distinct tokens of the same name will share membership in a chain of explicit co-reference and numerically distinct tokens of two type distinct names will be members of disjoint chains of explicit co-reference – even if the two tokens are coincidentally co-referential.[1]

My claims about lexical-syntactic character of NAME is entirely consistent with competing theories of the lexical-semantic character of NAME, but once we appreciate the true lexical-syntactical character of the naming relation, I shall argue, it is easy to see that certain phenomena that have been

---

[1] At the conference at which a version of this paper was originally presented, Diego Marconi objected that the twin properties of explicit co-referentiality of co-typical name tokens and referential independence of type-distinct name tokens does not distinguish names from certain other sorts of expressions. For example, he notes that according to a popular account all tokens of the type 'tiger' refer (rigidly) to the species 'tiger'. Similarly with the word 'yellow'. So, Marconi worried that my account fails to pick out any *distinctive* property of names. In response, it should be noted that my claim is only that explicit co-referentiality and referential independence *partially* characterize the syntactic category NAME. Names are also expressions that, for example, may well-formedly flank the identity sign and may well-formedly occupy the argument places of verbs. Some totality of such properties jointly constitute a broader, still syntactically characterized class of expressions, the class of SINGULAR TERMS. The category NAME is a distinguished subclass of that class, however exactly the broader class is defined. Included in the class of singular terms are also demonstratives and indexicals – the anaphoric properties of which I discuss below. What I claim, in effect, is that the category NAME consists of the set S of *singular term types* such that: (a) if a term t is a member of S, then tokens of t are explicitly co-referential and (b) if t and t' are members of S such that t ≠ t' then t and t' are referentially independent. So my approach requires an antecedent analysis of singular termhood. I haven't offered such an analysis here, at least not a full-blown one. But see Taylor (forthcoming-a). The account of singular terms offered therein bears a certain affinity to that offered in Brandom (1994). The twin properties of referential independence of type distinct tokens and explicit co-referentiality of co-typical tokens does, I think, serve to distinguish names from other singular terms. Another distinguishing feature of the anaphoric character of names is that names may dominate anaphoric chains, but are never dominated within any such chain. Contra Marconi, then, it wouldn't bother me at all if there were other expressions in, say, the category PREDICATE or the category COMMON NOUN that had somehow 'correlative' syntactic properties. This wouldn't, though, suffice to make predicates be names or obliterate the important syntactic distinction between names and predicates. But I stress again that it is not my goal here to offer a full blown and explicit analysis of the very idea of a singular term.

widely thought to motivate Fregean and neo-Fregean theories of the lexical-semantic character of names do nothing of the sort. Instead, they point to facts about the peculiar lexical-syntactic character of names. Consequently, though my approach does not *entail* referentialism, it does remove certain obstacles that have widely been thought to stand in the way of referentialism.

2.1 Frege's Puzzle and the Lexical-Syntax of the Naming Relation

Consider Frege's puzzle about the possibility of informative identity statements. Frege wondered how possibly a statement of the form $\ulcorner a = a \urcorner$ may differ in cognitive value from a true statement of the form $\ulcorner a = b \urcorner$. Statements of the former sort are always trivial, while statements of the latter sort may contain new information. Yet, if a is identical with b, then a statement asserting the identity of a with b merely purports to assert the identity of an object with itself. But that, it seems, is precisely what the trivial statement $\ulcorner a = a \urcorner$ purports to assert. How can the one statement be trivial and the other informative when the two statements seem to assert the very same thing about the very same object?

Frege introduced the notion of sense partly in order to answer this last question. Names have two distinguishable, though related, semantic roles. Beside the semantic role of denoting its reference, a name also has the semantic role of expressing a sense. A sense was supposed to be or contain a mode of presentation of a reference and to serve as a constituent of the thought or proposition expressed by any sentence in which the relevant name occurred. Because names that share a referent may differ in sense, co-referring names need not make identical contributions to the thoughts expressed by sentences in which they occur. And it is this fact that is supposed to explain the very possibility of informative statements of identity. Once it is allowed that names that share a reference may differ in sense and allowed that thoughts or propositions are composed out of senses and only senses, it is a short step to conclude that the thought content expressed by a statement of the form $\ulcorner a = a \urcorner$ is distinct from the thought content expressed by a statement of the from $\ulcorner a = b \urcorner$ even when a just is b.

The real explanation of the very possibility of informative statements of identity turns not on the fact that type distinct names are referentially independent, while numerically distinct tokens of the same name are explicitly co-referential. Because the co-reference of type distinct names is not directly guaranteed by the language itself, an identity statement explicitly linking two distinct, and therefore referentially independent names can have an informative feel. By contrast, an identity statement linking numerically distinct tokens of the very same name purports to make manifest only what is already directly guaranteed by the language itself. The difference in felt significance between informative and trivial identity statements is due entirely to the fact that when one repeats a name by issuing another token of that very name, one *explicitly* preserves subject matter.

So, for example, if Jones says 'My Hesperus looks lovely this evening!' and Smith wishes to express agreement with Jones, Smith can make her agreement explicit by using again the name that Jones originally used. She can utter a sentence like 'Yes, you are right. Hesperus does look lovely this evening!' Suppose, by contrast, that Smith continues the conversation by using a co-referring, but referentially independent name like 'Phosphorus' to refer to Venus. Perhaps she responds as follows, 'Yes you are right, Phosphorus does look lovely this evening!' Though Smith has expressed agreement with Jones – in the sense that she has predicated the very same property of the very same object – she has not done so in a manifest manner. Indeed, it is *as if* Smith has either shifted the subject matter of the conversation or has somehow implicated that 'Hesperus' and 'Phosphorus' co-refer. At a minimum, by shifting to a referentially independent name, the co-reference of which with 'Hesperus' is not explicit, Smith has left open the question whether she has, in fact, preserved the subject matter. She can close that question by stating that Hesperus is Phosphorus. In stating that Hesperus is Phosphorus she puts on display the fact that 'Hesperus' and 'Phosphorus' are co-referential.

My claim is not that the official propositional content of the assertion that Hesperus is Phosphorus is really the metalinguistic proposition that 'Hesperus' and 'Phosphorus' co-refer. Frege was right to deny that *what we say* when we say that Hesperus is Phosphorus is about the signs 'Hesperus' and 'Phosphorus'. But it does not follow that the official propositional content of the statement that Hesperus is Phosphorus must be distinct from the official propositional content of the statement that Phosphorus is Phosphorus or the official propositional content of the statement that Hesperus is Hesperus. One will be tempted by this mistaken view only if one commits what John Perry (2001) calls a subject matter fallacy. One commits a subject matter fallacy, roughly, when one supposes that all the information conveyed by an utterance is information about the subject matter of the utterance.

Despite committing a subject matter fallacy, Frege was onto something. We can give due deference to Frege's underlying insight by granting that there are many different ways of putting forth the content shared by these statements, that is, many different sentential vehicles that express that very same content. By putting forth that content in one way rather than another, via one sentential vehicle rather than another, one 'puts on display' different facts. When one uses a sentence like 'Hesperus is Phosphorus' which contains two referentially independent names to state the identity of Hesperus with itself, one puts on display the coincidental co-reference of two referentially independent expressions. Though this way of looking at matters affords Fregean senses no role in solving Frege's puzzle, it acknowledges and applauds Frege's recognition, however dim, of the very possibility of referentially independent but coincidentally co-referential names. He erred only in the ultimate explanation of the possibility. It is not, as he imagined, that each name is associated with a determinate and independent mode of presentation of its referent as part of its sense. Where Frege sees two names, sharing a reference, but differing in sense in such a way that it cannot be determined a priori that they share a reference, there are really just two names that are referentially independent, but coincidentally co-referential. Where Frege sees a reflection of the lexical-semantic character of names, there is really the influence of the peculiar lexical-syntax of the naming relation. What Frege failed to see is that from a lexical-syntactic perspective names are quite distinctive referring devices. To repeat a name is *ipso facto* to repeat a reference. To refer again to the same object, but using a different name is, in effect, to refer *de novo* to the relevant object, that is, in a way not 'anaphorically' linked with the previous act of reference.

I am not claiming that the complete story about Frege's puzzle begins and ends at the lexical-syntax of the naming relation. So far, my arguments are primarily aimed at explaining why informative statements of identity are possible at all and not, primarily, at explaining the nature and significance of the information carried by a true and informative statement of identity. Though I have said that such statements may put on display reflexive or meta-representational information, it is not my claim that such information exhaust what is potentially conveyed by an informative statement of identity. Elsewhere, I have embedded the story I have been telling about the lexical syntax of names in a larger and more complex story about the semantics of names and about the psychological organization of the referring mind.[2] That larger story explains what sort of psychological impact knowledge of informative identities can have on the referring mind. Though I lack the space to detail that story here, an important clue to its outline comes below in my discussion of what I call *in-the-head-co*-reference.

2.2 How to Type-Individuate Names

I have argued that tokens of the same name type are explicitly co-referential. And I have claimed that a name type can be identified with a chain of explicit co-reference. But I have not yet said what it takes for two name tokens to be members of the same chain of explicit co-reference and thus to count

---

[2]See the essays collected in Taylor (2003).

as tokens of the same name type again. It might be supposed that if m and n are merely spelled and/or pronounced in the same manner, then n is the same name again as m. Sameness of spelling and pronunciation are clearly not jointly sufficient to guarantee co-reference, however. So I must deny that names are type-individuated merely by pronunciation and spelling. Some will want to take issue with that denial. And they will want to insist that tokens of the 'same name' need not be co-referential at all, let alone explicitly co-referential (Perry 2001, Recanati 1993).

In the end, however, there is little at stake between views like mine and views like those of Perry or Recanati. That is because, whatever one's pre-ferred approach, one needs something rather like my notion of disjoint chains of co-reference, if one is to do full justice to the peculiar lexical-syntax of the naming relation. If one insists on type individuating names by spelling and pronunciation, then my claims about referential independence and explicit co-reference can simply be read as claims about the lexical-syntactic character of fully disambiguated names. Our current worry about how to segregate name tokens in to chains of co-reference remains. The claim would then be that it is a linguistically universal fact that when names are *fully disambiguated* tokens of the same name are guaranteed to be co-referential. To disambiguate a name would be precisely to segregate tokens of a certain sound/shape pattern into disjoint chains of explicit co-reference such that it is guaranteed that all the tokens in a given class co-refer with one another and are at most only co-incidentally co-referential with tokens in any distinct class. One way to see this is to see that we might use the same sound pattern twice to refer to the same object, without knowing that we are doing so. Even if there is just one John, we might, for example, mistakenly think that one set of tokenings of 'John' co-refer to a different object from that to which a distinct set of tokenings of 'John' co-refer. In such a situa-tion, despite the co-incidental co-reference of tokens in the two 'John' streams, we would still need to segregate the totality of 'John' tokenings into disjoint chains of explicit co-reference. If we succeeded in doing so, we would thereby have a way of tracking when we are engaged in independent acts of reference to what is coincidentally the same object again and when are engaged in anaphorically linked acts of explicit co-reference. So the distinction I have promoted to center stage is both needed and important, no matter how one cares to type-individuate names.

My central claims and arguments will go through on either way of indi-viduating names. Moreover, a cleaner, more elegant theory results from my own approach. So on f theoretical aesthetic grounds alone, I feel entitled to the assumption that the type individuation of names is not simply a matter of pronunciation and spelling. If not, a name token need not wear its type-identity on its morphological and phonological sleeves. So what criteria do determine when a token counts as the re-occurrence of the same name again? To a rough first approximation, two tokenings are co-typical just in case the occurrence of a given (or similar or at least systematically connected) shape/sound pattern again is a further episode in connected history of such tokenings. To turn this rough idea into a systematic theory, we would have to say just when two tokenings of the same or similar shape/sound pattern does and does not count as a further episode in the same continuing history of tokenings. For the present, I will simply say that two tokenings count as tokenings of the same name again when they are linked via what I call a mechanism of co-reference. A mechanism of co-reference links a system of tokenings one with another in such a way that the tokens produced are guaranteed to co-refer. Mechanisms of co-reference bind tokenings together into what I earlier called chains of explicit co-reference.

I have so far told you only what a mechanism of co-reference does, not the means by which it does that. Here it may help to notice that that there are many ways of marking and displaying co-reference. Explicit anaphora is one way. The identity sign is another. Identity and explicit anaphora are ways of displaying as co-referential expressions which are not directly given, in virtue of their bare type identity, as co-referential. We can, of course, flank the identity sign by tokens which are already given as explicitly co-referential, but it is precisely then that the relevant identity will be trivial and uninformative.

Now the mechanisms of co-reference that link tokenings into a chain of explicit co-reference will be of a rather different character from either explicit anaphora or the identity sign. They do not operate locally, sentence by sentence, or discourse by discourse, to link what are by their type-identity, otherwise linguistically unconnected expressions. Name constituting mechanisms of co-reference have a more global, less formal character. It would not be entirely wrong to think of such mechanisms as being founded on the interlocking and interdependent referential intentions of a community of co-linguals, a community which may be extended in time and spread through space. When I token the sound/shape pattern 'Cicero' I typically do not intend to be tokening something brand new under the sun. Rather, I typically intend to be tokening again what others have tokened before. I intend thereby to refer again to what others have referred to before. And I intend that others recognize that I so intend. It is tempting to think that it is just such a budget of co-referential intentions which makes my tokening of the sound/shape pattern 'Cicero' count as a retokening of the name 'Cicero'. Though there is something to be said for this approach, nothing I say depends on it turning out to be true. I need only the rather more modest claim that absent the intention to either continue or launch a chain of explicit co-reference, a speaker would not even count as using, or even intending to use, a given sound/shape pattern as a name at all. What it is to intend to use an expression as a name is to use that expression with the intention of either launching or continuing a chain of explicit co-reference, however exactly such chains are ultimately constituted and marked.

Despite the fact that I have offered no positive theory of just what makes a tokening of a given sound/shape pattern count as a further episode in this rather than that continuing history of such tokenings, we should not lose sight of the deeper point that the category NAME, together with its defining features of explicit co-referentiality and referential independence, is a linguistic universal, that may be differently realized in different languages. If that category is to be realized in the language of a speech community, then that community must have some practice or other that serves to bind name tokens together in chains of explicit co-reference. In the absence of any such practice, the language of a community would simply contain no instances of the category NAME.[3]

Though it is not part of our current burden to say precisely how the practices of a speech community work to bind name tokens together into chains of explicit co-reference, it is not hard to imagine some ways matters might go. It would be a nice result, for example, if name tokens were bound together into chains of explicit co-reference by some tractable property guaranteed to be epistemically manifest to the merely linguistically competent. A manifest syntactic or formal property would serve nicely in that role. Unfortunately, natural languages are not so nicely designed, though one can easily imagine augmenting our language with a system of co-indexing subscripts to serve as a syntactic marker of explicit co-referentiality. Alternatively, one can imagine a system in which distinct names were never spelled

---

[3]It is sometimes objected to this approach that since I appeal to history and intentions to do the work of segregating tokens into chains of explicit co-reference, my account can no longer be said to be an account of lexical syntax and is really a semantic approach after all. But this criticism is simply confused. UG makes available a certain syntactic category – NAME – partially defined by the explicit co-referentiality of co-typical name tokens and the referential independence of type-distinct name tokens. In order to populate that category with expressions the linguistic community has to *do* something – introduce names into the language. UG doesn't tell you, perhaps, exactly how to do that – at any rate, no story about exactly how that it is done is intended to be on offer here. What UG does tell you, in effect, is what you've achieved once you have succeeded in introducing a name into a language. In particular, you've introduced an expression type such that its tokens are guaranteed to co-refer, merely in virtue of the fact that it is an expression of the relevant type. Nothing in the story I've told *prevents* a community from 're-using' a certain sound shape pattern to initiate new, disjoint chains of explicit co-reference. But my story does imply that if we do re-use an old pattern to initiate a new chain of explicit co-reference, we have, in effect, introduced a new name. Nothing in this story has anything so far to with any *disputed* semantic property of names of the sort, for example, that divide referentialist from anti-referentialists.

the same.[4] Either system would have the effect of introducing a manifest syntactic marker of explicit co-reference. Some of this already goes on in our language just as it stands. The phenomena of surnames, middle names, the whole system of modifiers like 'junior', 'senior' 'the first' 'the second', 'the elder' 'the younger' are all ways of making it more syntactically explicit and epistemically manifest when we are given the same name again and when, despite the same or similar spelling and pronunciation, we are given distinct names, and thus distinct chains of explicit co-reference. Because our language, as it stands, is not fully explicit in this regard, it is not possible to tell by mere inspection *which* name a given tokening of a certain sound/shape pattern is a tokening of. We typically rely on context to achieve the effect of making explicit co-reference more epistemically manifest. Context provides information that enables the hearer to determine whether the tokening of a given sound/shape pattern is intended as a further episode in this chain of explicit co-reference or that chain of explicit o-reference and thus whether it counts as a further tokening of this or that name.

2.2.1 Things sometimes go wrong

Sometimes, for example, we mistake numerically distinct tokenings of the same name again for tokenings of two distinct name types. That is, we mistake what are really links in the same chain of explicit co-reference for links in disjoint chains of explicit co-reference. Just such a mistake seems to be one source of a well known and philosophically interesting puzzle about belief due to Saul Kripke (1979). Imagine an agent Smith. Suppose that unbeknownst to Smith opinions are divided among his co-linguals about the beauty of London. Some think that London is a city of outstanding beauty;

---

[4]Something similar in spirit is suggested by Fiengo and May's (1998) in the guise of what they call the singularity principle:
Singularity Principle: If co-spelled expressions are co-valued, they are co-indexed.
Fiengo and May presuppose a distinction between names and expressions that can, I think, be reconstructed in terms of my distinction between what I call a sound/shape pattern and what I call a chain of explicit co-reference. I disagree with May and Fiengo, however, in thinking that even if two expressions are 'co-valued' and are spelled and/or sounded the same, then they are *ipso facto* explicitly co-referential. Perhaps this is true for a fully disambiguated language, but it is not true for our language as it stands. May and Fiengo seem aware of this worry and attempt to get around it by appeal to the notion of an assignment. For they allow that co-spelled and co-referring expressions can have different 'assignments'. In all frankness, I can't make out what they mean by an assignment, however. Clearly, they can't mean that two expressions have the same assignment just in case they share a reference. They seem – though this is just a guess – to be looking for something intermediate, some sense-like entity to play the role of assignment. It does occur to me that their notion of assignment might well be assimilated to what I call 'in-the-head-co-reference'. This is a kind of 'co-reference' that need not track actual co-reference. But again, this is just a guess.

others think that it is horrendously ugly. Imagine that the name 'London' is first introduced into Smith's referential repertoire via interaction with a collection of apparently knowledgeable people, all of whom think that London is one among the more beautiful cities of the world. He acquires the word 'London', intending in his use of it to co-refer with his co-linguals. Since Smith is inclined to believe what knowledgeable people say, he comes to believe that London is a city of outstanding beauty. Subsequently, Smith comes in contact with other apparently knowledgeable people. These apparently knowledgeable people believe that London is one of the more ugly cities in the world. Once again, since Smith is inclined to take knowledgeable people at their words, he comes to believe that London is a horrendously ugly. Because Smith mistakenly, but not irrationally, believes that knowledgeable people in a single community are unlikely to hold such divergent opinions about one and the same city, he reasons that the apparently knowledgeable people encountered later and the apparently knowledgeable people encountered earlier are not talking about one and the same city.

Kripke's puzzle is a puzzle about beliefs in cases like the above. It seems true to say that Smith believes that London is beautiful and not ugly. Yet it seems equally true to say that Smith believes that London is ugly and not beautiful. Moreover, it would seem a mark of incoherence and irrationality to simultaneously believe and disbelieve the very same proposition, as Smith apparently does. But the story we just told about Smith would seem to support only the conclusion that he is *mistaken*, and not the conclusion that he is either incoherent or irrational in believing as he does. What, in the end, shall we say about Smith, his beliefs, and his rationality or lack thereof?

We are not yet in a position to answer this question fully, but we can say a bit more about just how Smith's confusion comes about and what it consists in. Notice that Smith would surely be surprised to learn 'London is London', as he might put it. Of course, he would be no more surprised to learn this fact than the average Babylonian would have been to learn that Hesperus is Phosphorus. Indeed, his surprise would seem to be surprise of the very same character as the surprise of the average Babylonian who learns that Hesperus is Phosphorus. This suggests that part of Smith's problem is that he treats the sound/shape pattern 'London' *as if* it is associated with two distinct and therefore referentially independent names which just happen to be spelled and sounded the same. If that is right, then at the base of Smith's confusion about the city London is a confusion about the name 'London'. Indeed, Smith's confusion about the *name* 'London' seems deeply implicated in whatever confusion he has about the *city* London.

Let us look more closely at Smith's use of the sound/shape pattern 'London'. It will help to distinguish two (sub)communities of Smith's co-linguals: the A-community and the B-community. The A-community consists of those who think that London is among the most beautiful cities in the world. The B-community consists of those who think that London is horrendously ugly. Suppose further that we distinguish two sequences of Smith's tokenings of the sound/shape pattern 'London' – an A-sequence and a B-sequence. A tokening is a member of the A-sequence when Smith produces it intending to conform to the usage of the A community. Now Smith intends, by conforming to the usage of the A community, to be conforming to the usage of the community at large. Similarly, a tokening is a member of the B sequence when Smith produces it intending to conform to the usage of the B community. Again, Smith intends, by conforming to the usage of the B community, to be conforming to the usage of the community at large.

Now each tokening in Smith's A-sequence is a link in a chain of explicit co-reference that includes tokenings by members of the A-community. In each such tokening, Smith intends to be co-referring with the members of the A community. If we take Smith's intentions as our guide, it would seem to follow that Smith's A-sequence 'London' is explicitly co-referential with the 'London' of the A-community. Similarly, Smith B-sequence tokenings of the pattern 'London' would seem to be links in a chain of explicit co-reference that connects them with tokenings of the pattern 'London' by the B-community. Again, taking Smith's immediate intentions as our guide, it would seem to follow that Smith's B-sequence 'London' is explicitly co-referential with the 'London' of the B-community. Are Smith's A-sequence tokens explicitly co-referential with Smith's B-sequence tokens? On the one hand, we want to say that members of the A and B communities are joint masters of the one word 'London'. The members of the A-community and the B-community take themselves to be disagreeing about a common subject and to be engaging in anaphorically linked acts of co-reference, not referentially independent acts of co-reference. And this fact implies that the A-community's tokenings of 'London' and the B-community's tokening of London are links in a single chain of explicit co-reference. Moreover, each time Smith tokens the sound/shape pattern 'London' he intends merely to be continuing a chain of co-reference already initiated by others. He intends merely to be tokening again what others have tokened before. He thereby intends to assure that what others have referred to before, he refers to again.

Unfortunately for Smith, his usage fails to reflect the explicit co-referentiality of the 'London' of the A-community and the 'London' of the B-community. We might say that although the 'London' of the A-community and the 'London' of the B-community are, in fact, explicitly co-referential they are not in-the-head-co-referential *for Smith*. It is the fact that Smith's A-sequence 'London' and his B-sequence 'London' are not in-the-head-co-referential for Smith that makes it plausible to say that Smith does not quite succeed in doing what he originally intended. Though he intends to use 'London' in conformity with the usage of his community, he somehow manages to use one name as if it were two. That is, he uses the sound/shape pattern 'London' as if the set of tokenings of that pattern formed two disjoint chains of explicit co-reference. Consequently, in Smith's thought and talk tokening 'London' is not simply a way of repeating and co-referring with 'London'.

2.3 Names Contrasted with Deictics

In this section, I contrast names with deictic expressions. Within the class of singular terms, deictics are, in certain respects, the dual of names. Just as it is a (partially) defining fact about the linguistic category NAME that tokens of the same name are explicitly co-referential, so it is a defining fact about the linguistic category DEICTIC that tokens of the same deictic are referentially independent. When tokens of the same deictic do co-refer, the co-reference will be a mere coincidence of usage, rather than a direct consequence of the fundamental linguistic character of deictic referring expressions. Because token deictics of the same type are referentially independent, they are also interpretationally independent. From the would be interpreter's perspective, an episode of deictic reference involves reference *de novo* to the relevant object – at least relative to any numerically distinct deictic. Consequently, each token of a given deictic type must by interpreted by a would-be interpreter 'from scratch'. And this is so even when two token deictics turn out to refer to the very same object.[5]

To say that token deictic reference always involves, relative to any numerically distinct token, reference *de novo* is not to deny the possibility of what we might call discourse deixis. In an episode of discourse deixis, a token deictic refers to an object raised to salience by some earlier chunk of discourse, as in:

> Because of that kick *a coconut* dropped. Because *that nut* dropped *a turtle* got bopped. Because *he* got bopped *that turtle* named Jake, fell on his back with a splash in the lake.

Nor am I claiming that co-referring and co-typical deictic tokens can never be interpreted as co-referential. There are in fact sentences in which it seems all but mandatory that two co-typical deictic tokens be interpreted as co-referential. But I want to suggest that the source of any such mandate is neither lexical nor structural but purely pragmatic. Consider the following:

---

[5]Elsewhere, I put the lexical-syntactic distinction between names and deictics to help explain the pragmatics of what I call mode of reference selection. See Essay V in Taylor (2003).

(1) Ted saw that man and Bill saw that man too

(1') Ted saw (that man)$_i$ and Bill saw him$_i$ too

(2) John hates that man because that man is a cad

(2') John hates (that man)$_i$ because he$_i$ is a cad.

On the default reading, an utterance of (1) would seem to be roughly equivalent to an utterance of (1'). Similarly, on the default reading, an utterance of (2) is roughly equivalent to an utterance of (2'). It may be tempting to conclude that there can indeed obtain a relation of anaphoric dependence between subsequent and antecedent deictic tokens of the same type.

But this temptation should be resisted. What we really have here is co-reference through what I call demonstration sharing. Co-reference through demonstration sharing occurs when a speaker intends that the reference fixing demonstration associated with an 'antecedent' deictic serve also to fix the reference for a subsequent deictic. When two token deictics share a demonstration, there will obtain a kind of mandatory co-reference between those tokens. But co-reference through demonstration sharing is a purely pragmatic phenomenon that resembles co-incidental co-reference more than it resembles explicit co-reference. Explicit co-reference is lexically or structurally guaranteed co-reference. Coincidental co-reference, by contrast, is neither lexically nor structurally guaranteed, but depends entirely on the coincidences of further usage. Since co-reference through demonstration sharing depends precisely on the speaker's entirely optional intention to, in effect, mount the same demonstration twice, it counts as a species of coincidental co-reference rather than a species of explicit co-reference.

A speaker can convey to the hearer that token deictics are intended to co-refer through demonstration sharing in a number of ways. She can openly fail to mount an independent demonstration for the subsequent deictic. Alternatively, she can select a sentence type that 'semantically forces' the relevant deictics to be interpreted as co-referring. (1) above involves such semantic forcing. The presence of the 'too' in (1) renders incoherent interpretations of (1) on which the deictics do not co-refer. On pain of semantic incoherence, the token deictics *must* be interpreted as co-referring. Notice that the threat of incoherence is absent if the 'too' is absent as in:

(1'') Ted saw that man and Bill saw that man.

To be sure, if the first deictic receives greater stress than the second, then even here the preferred interpretation of (1'') involves co-reference through demonstration sharing. On the other hand, if the second deictic receives greater stress than the first then an interpretation on which the deictics do not co-refer through demonstration sharing will be preferred.

Pragmatics also explains the imputation generated by an utterance of (2) that one and the same object is both a cad and is hated by John. In particular, our shared background expectations that, absent special circumstances, people typically do not hate one person because of another person's character, raises the salience of the interpretation of (2) according to which the deictics co-refer through demonstration sharing. Compare (2) with (3):

(3) John hangs out with that man, because that man is a cad.

In an utterance of (3), the deictics may also co-refer through demonstration sharing, but because it is not unusual for a person to hang out with one person partly in response to a different person's character, there will be less pressure to interpret the two deictics as co-referring through demonstration sharing. Though it is surely possible for a speaker to convey via an utterance of (3) the proposition that John hangs out with a certain man because that very man is a cad, there is nothing about (3) as a type that renders such an interpretation of any given utterance of (3) more salient or available than an interpretation according to which the two demonstratives do not co-refer through demonstration sharing.

2.4 Names and Principle C

The interaction of names with other referring expressions in the context of more local anaphoric chains bears brief mention. The entire subject of anaphora is, of course, a large and vexed one, involving many subtle and complex phenomena. I do not pretend even to scratch the surface of that complexity and subtlety here. Still, I want to take brief notice of what I take to be a central and characteristic fact about the role of names in sentence and discourse level anaphoric chains. It is characteristic of names that though they may anchor local anaphoric chains, they may never occupy the role of anaphoric dependent within any such chain. For example, although 'he' can (but need not) be interpreted as referentially dependent on 'John' in (4), (5) and (6) below, there is no interpretation of (7) or (8) below in which 'John' is *bound* to share a referent with 'he:'

(4) John$_i$ just arrived at the party and he$_i$ is already drunk.
(5) Although he$_i$ just arrived at the party, John$_i$ is already drunk.
(6) John$_i$ just arrived at the party. He$_i$ is already drunk. He$_i$ had better behave himself$_i$.
(7) He$_i$ kicked John$_j$.
(8) A man$_i$ just arrived at the party. He$_i$ is already drunk. John$_j$ had better behave himself$_j$.

Of course, 'he' and 'John' in either (7) or (8) could *turn out* to be co-referential. Imagine, for example, that Smith utters (7) while pointing to John, but without knowing that it is John to whom she is pointing. Similarly, imagine that the drunk man who just arrived at the party is none other than John himself, but that the speaker does not know that John is the drunk man who just arrived at the party. Again the co-reference of 'he' with 'John' would be at most coincidental. It is simply not permissible for 'John' to be explicitly co-referential with any 'antecedent' expression except 'John' itself.

This last remark will seem to some to need some qualification, since there are well-known cases in which a name is apparently prohibited from taking even itself as an antecedent. Consider, for example:

(9) John$_i$ kicked John$_j$.

On the default reading of (9), the two occurrences of 'John' are not explicitly but at most only coincidentally co-referential. Indeed, Principle C of the principles and parameters binding theory predicts that with the two occurrences of 'John' co-indexed (9) is straightforwardly syntactically ill-formed and therefore, presumably, not directly interpretable at all (Chomsky 1981, 1995). Since there are contexts in which an utterance of (9) could convey the relevant proposition, Principle C as more or less standardly stated isn't quite correct. Still, it is true that a speaker who utters (9) would defeasibly be interpreted as referring to two distinct Johns and not to the same John twice. This fact gives rise to a prima facie difficulty for my approach. Since the strong default interpretation has it that the two occurrences of 'John' in (9) are referentially independent, it follows, on my approach, that the two occurrences of 'John' should count not as the occurrence of the same name twice, but as the occurrence of two distinct, and therefore referentially independent names. But if to repeat a name is to repeat a reference, why should (9) default to a reading on which the two occurrences of 'John' are occurrences of two referentially independent names?

My answer is that the fact that (9) strongly defaults to a reading on which the two occurrences of 'John' are referentially independent reflects an *independent fact* about the means by which the grammar permits a single name to claim simultaneous occupancy, as it were, of the multiple argument places of a single verb. It is evident that the strongly preferred way of saying that John is simultaneously the agent and patient of a single kicking is to deploy the reflexive pronoun as in (10):

(10) John$_i$ kicked himself$_i$.

Indeed, though a non-reflexive pronoun can often be explicitly co-referential with an antecedent name, explicit co-reference is not possible here. If we substitute a such a pronoun for 'himself' in (10) we get:

(11) John$_i$ kicked him$_j$.

As with (9), on the default reading of (11) 'John' and 'him' are referentially independent. Indeed, Principle B of the binding theory predicts that (11) is syntactically ill-formed when 'John' and 'him' are co-indexed and thus explicitly co-referential (Chomsky 1981, 1995). Again, this constraint does not rule out the possibility that 'John' and 'him' can co-refer in an utterance of (11), but they can do so only if the co-reference is coincidental rather than explicit. These data strongly suggest that, to a first approximation, a single name can simultaneously 'control' multiple argument places of a single verb only through anaphoric dominance of a reflexive pronoun. It is as if a name is defeasibly forbidden from serving as its own referential doppelganger within single argument structure. Within a single argument structure a name cannot be anaphorically dominated *even by itself.*

The prohibition against self-domination within a single argument structure is not a general prohibition against explicitly repeating a reference by repeating a name within a single sentence or single discourse. A name may serve as its own referential doppelganger, for example, when it simultaneously occupies argument places in 'distinct' verb phrases or when one occurrence of the name is merely a constituent of an argument of a given verb phrase and the other occurrence occupies some other argument place of the very same verb phrase. Consider, for example:

(12) Mary$_j$'s kicking of John$_i$ upset him$_i$.
(13) Mary$_j$'s kicking of John$_i$ upset John$_i$.
(14) Mary$_j$'s kicking of John$_i$ upset her$_j$.
(15) Mary$_j$'s kicking of John$_i$ upset Mary$_j$.
(16) Mary$_j$'s kicking of herself$_j$ upset her$_j$.
(17) Mary$_j$'s kicking of herself$_j$ upset Mary$_j$.

Although the relevant names and pronouns in each of (12) - (17) can be interpreted as referentially independent, they need not be. There is nothing like the strong default in favor of interpreting what looks like the same name again in each of (13), (15) and (17) as referentially independent occurrences of two distinct names. Rather, the default interpretation of each of these sentences involves exactly one John and exactly one Mary. Contrast (12) - (17) with:

(18) Mary's kicking of Mary upset her.
(19) Mary's kicking of Mary upset Mary.

For both (18) and (19), at least two, and possibly three Mary's are involved and each sentence is ambiguous as to whether it is the kicking Mary, the kicked Mary or some third person who is upset by the kicking.

Finally, consider (20) - (22), in which we have explicit co-referentiality across different clauses:

(20) If Bill$_i$ hopes to finish his$_i$ dissertation soon, he$_i$ had better get to work.
(21) If Bill hopes to finish his$_i$ dissertation soon, Bill had better get to work.
(22) If Bill hopes to finish Bill's dissertation soon, Bill had better get to work.

(21) strongly – and (22) less strongly – defaults to a reading in which one and the same Bill is denoted by each occurrence of 'Bill'. On the default reading, (21) and (22) each expresses more or less the same proposition as (20), when it is co-indexed as above. Moreover, for each of (23) - (29) below, where the reflexive occupies object position, the weakly or strongly preferred interpretation involves one Bill, rather than multiple Bills. Correlatively, where either a name or a non-reflexive pronoun occupies the direct object position, there is a default to a two person reading of the sentence:

(23) If Bill hopes to earn an A, then he had better watch himself.
(24) If Bill hopes to earn an A, then Bill had better watch himself.
(25) If Bill hopes to earn an A, then he had better watch Bill.
(26) If Bill hopes to earn an A, then Bill had better watch Bill.
(27) If Bill hopes to earn an A, then Bill had better watch him.
(28) If he hopes to earn an A, then he had better watch Bill.
(29) If he hopes to earn an A, then Bill had better watch himself.

What is the source of the prohibition against a name's self-domination within a single argument structure? Is it just a brute fact? Is there a deeper reason why this should be so? Such questions are better left to linguists. My approach is consistent with any answer your favorite syntactic theory is likely to have on offer. The mere fact that a name is defeasibly prohibited from functioning as its own referential doppelganger within a single argument structure spells no deep trouble for my central claim that tokens of the same name type are explicitly co-referential. My view neither predicts that such a prohibition should obtain nor predicts that no such prohibition should obtain. But given independent grounds for this prohibition on the repeatability of a name within a single argument structure, my approach does offer a way of saying just what the prohibition comes to and what it entails. From our current perspective the prohibition against self-domination within a single argument structure entails that when what looks like the same name occupies multiple argument places within a single argument structure those apparently identical names will be defeasibly interpreted as referentially independent and thus as distinct and therefore at most coincidentally co-referential names.

3   The Pragmatic Significance of the Naming Relation

In this section, I explore some aspects of what I call the pragmatic significance of the naming relation. I claim that entirely independently of any particular thesis about the lexical-semantic character of names, we can explain certain aspects of the *use* of names. Such explanations turn partly on facts about the lexical syntax of the naming relation partly on pragmatic facts about the various kinds of language games we play with names. I focus, in particular, on the behavior of empty names in the context of what I call non-veridical language games and on the apparent failure of co-referring names to be intersubstitutable in the context of propositional attitude contexts. I show that a large dose of pragmatics is needed in both cases.

3.1 Referential Fitness and Non-Veridical Language Games

I begin by distinguishing what I call merely referentially fit linguistic representations from what I call referentially successful linguistic representations. Referentially fit representations are those that are, as it were, syntactically fit for the job of standing for an object. By and only by playing an appropriate role in a syntactically interlocking system of representations is a linguistic representation made fit to refer. No isolated representation, all on it's own and independently of its connection to other representations, can be 'fit' for the job of standing for an object. To a first approximation, referentially fit expressions are those that can well-formedly flank the identity sign, well-formedly occupy the argument places of verbs, and well-formedly serve as links of various sorts in anaphoric chains of various sorts. Names, demonstratives, indexicals, variables, and pronouns are the paradigmatic examples. Now I have already argued there are important distinctions among the lexical-syntactic characters of the various kinds of referring expressions. The lexical-syntactic character of the category NAME, for example, is partially defined by twin properties of explicit-co-referentiality for co-typical name tokens and referential independence of type distinct names. The lexical syntactic character of the category DEICTIC, on the other hand, is partially defined by the fact that tokens of the same deictic type are referentially independent. Differences in the lexical-syntactic characters of different categories of singular terms amount to so many different ways of being referential fit.

It is important to distinguish mere referential fitness from referential success. A referentially successful expression is one that is both fit for the job of standing for an object and, in addition, *actually* stands for an object. A representation can be referentially fit without *actually* standing for an object, without, that is, being referentially successful. I will sometimes say that representations are referentially fit, but not referentially successful, are merely *objectual* without being fully *objective*. Merely objectual representations have, as it were, the form and function of objectivity despite the fact that they fail to carry out that function. Elsewhere, I argue that referential fitness or objectuality is a precondition for referential success or objectivity, that no object can be *successfully designated* except by an expression that already occupies the fitness-making role in a system of interlocking representations (Taylor, forthcoming a). This fact reflects the small grain of truth in holism about reference. But the holist fails to appreciate that referential success is not itself a matter of occupying the fitness-making role. Only referentially fit representations that stand in some *further* relation to some actual existent are referentially successful. I hold, but will not argue here, that that further relation is a distinguished causal relation.[6] That is to say, a referentially fit expression e will refer to an object o, and thus be referentially successful, just in case o-involving events play a distinguished causal role in the production of instances of e. Clearly, an adequate theory must explain just *what* causal role an o-involving event must play in the production of instances of e if e is to count as referring to o. I do not pretend to offer such an explanation here, but if I am right, referential success involves the interaction of two independent factors: the intra-representational factors, whatever exactly they are, that suffice for referential fitness and the extra-representational factors, whatever exactly they are, that suffice, when added to referential fitness, for referential success.

Correlative with the distinction between referential fitness and referential success is a further distinction between what I call veridical language games and what I call non-veridical language games. Veridical language games are dialogic games paradigmatically played with singular representations that are presumptively fully objective or referentially successful.

---

[6]But see Taylor (forthcoming a) wherein I defend at some length a two-factor theory of reference.

Moves in such games are typically governed by a concern for truth, a concern for getting things right, as things go in the world. Non-veridical language games, on the other hand, are often played with singular representations that are merely objectual. The governing concerns for such games are various – coherence, consistency, fealty to some truth-like notion that is not yet truth. Pure fiction is one case in point. When we engage in the construction, consumption, and criticism of fiction we play dialogic language games governed by a concern for getting things right, as things go in appropriate stories. But getting things right as things go in a story is not a matter of getting at a peculiar species of truth – truth in a fiction. Granted, we use such expressions as 'It is true in the Holmes stories that...' or 'It is true according to the Santa myth that....' But neither truth in a story nor truth in a myth is a species of genuine truth. To be sure, such expressions may play a dialogic role similar to the dialogic role of genuine truth talk. The predicate '...is true' functions in discourse as a device for claiming entitlement to make assertoric moves in dialogic games of inquiry, argument, and deliberation. One who asserts that p is true, for example, thereby claims an entitlement to put forth p as a candidate for mutual acceptance in a dialogic game of inquiry, argument or deliberation. Expressions like "true in the story" may also function as entitlement claiming devices in dialogic games played among producers and consumers of fiction. But entitlements to make moves in non-veridical games arise from sources rather different from the sources from which arise entitlements to make moves in non-veridical games.

By at least two different measures, merely objectual representations and fully objective representations are indistinguishable. First, there are no narrowly syntactic markers of referential success. The merely referentially fit and the fully referentially successful play indistinguishable syntactic roles in the language. Second, we play language games with a common dialogic structure with both the merely referentially fit and the fully referentially successful. In particular, we play entitlement commitment games with both the merely referentially fit and the fully referentially successful. The syntactic and dialogic similarity between the objectual and the objective can lead the inattentive to posit objects where there are none. One is liable to this mistake if one supposes that wherever we make rationally warranted moves with singular representations in some entitlement-commitment game, we are *ipso facto* getting at, or purporting to get at, how things are by some domain of objects. One is liable to think, for example, that in making rationally warranted moves in fictive entitlement-commitment games we are getting at how things are by a domain of *fictional objects* or that in playing mathematical entitlement-commitment games, we are getting at how things are by a domain of *mathematical objects*. Such mistakes are, I think, one source of a fairly pervasive skepticism about the prospects for a causal theory of reference. For anyone who is prepared to posit a domain of objects wherever there are entitlement-commitment games played with singular representations is liable to think that causal theories cannot explain the nature of our cognitive contact with the plethora of objects she acknowledges. Since we have no causal contact with fictional objects or with mathematical objects, it would seem to follow that the causal theory of reference cannot possibly be a correct general account of how the gap between the merely objectual and fully objective is bridged. The proper response to the line of thought is that there are no such objects, and so no burden on the causal theorist to explain either the peculiar nature of our epistemic 'contact' with such objects or our ability to refer to such objects. There are only non-veridical entitlement commitment games played with merely objectual singular representations. And though there is much work to be done in explaining what we are doing when we play such games and the source of such rational warrant as is enjoyed by moves in such games, the existence of such games causes no special problems for the causal theorist.

Once again, close attention to the syntax of the naming relation is the key to philosophical enlightenment. Such attention helps to dispel the illusory feel of objectivity surrounding our use of the merely referentially fit in non-veridical language games. For consider empty names more closely. Like names generally, empty names have the lexical-syntactic property that tokens of the same name again are guaranteed to co-refer. For names that fail to refer, this means that if any token of the name fails to refer, then every token of the name fails to refer. That is, in virtue of their lexical-syntactic property of being explicitly co-referential one with another, tokens of the same name stand or fall together with respect to referential success and failure in the sense that the referential success of any given token is the success of all and the referential failure of one is the failure of all. Consequently, even tokenings of an empty name can form chains of explicit co-reference. We might call such a chain a *chain of empty explicit co-reference*. The founding link in a chain of empty explicit co-reference will not have been produced in the course of successful reference to an actual existent. Rather, chains of empty explicit co-reference will typically be rooted in the making of fiction or myth or in failed attempts at reference to putatively existent object.

In the case of myth and fiction, for example, chains of empty explicit co-reference will be sustained by interlocking intentions to carry on a mythical or fictive practice. To token again a fictive or mythical name that others have tokened before is not to refer again, but by using the same fictional name again that others have used before, one may make a further move in a 'non-veridical' language game that others have played before.[7] By tokening 'Holmes' again, for example, I take part in what I call a shared imagining – the shared imagining that gives content to the Holmes stories. Indeed, the fact that my use of 'Holmes' is, and is intended to be, just a further episode in a certain chain of empty explicit co-reference is really all there is to the feeling that in imagining Holmes again, I imagine an *object* that others have imagined before and will imagine again. There is no Holmes to imagine. But by imagining *with* 'Holmes' in accordance with the rules that govern a certain non-veridical language game, I take part in a certain shared imagining.

Since empty names one and all refer to the same object, there is a sense in which all empty names might be said to be co-referential. But even for empty names we must distinguish co-incidental from explicit co-reference. As with names in general, the tokenings of a given empty name will form a chain of explicit co-reference – what we have called a chain of empty explicit co-reference. Moreover, as with names in general, two type distinct empty names will form disjoint chains of empty explicit co-reference. Consider, for example, 'Santa Claus' and 'Pegasus'. Tokenings of 'Santa Claus' are linked in a single chain of empty co-reference via a mechanism of co-reference that endows them all with a shared referential aim and fate. The explicit co-referentiality of the tokens of 'Santa Claus' makes it the case that the failure of 'Santa Claus' to refer is a failure shared by all of tokenings of that name, a failure they share in virtue of the fact that they aim to name together. 'Pegasus' too is constituted as the very name type that it is by a mechanism of co-reference, a mechanism of co-reference initiated in a founding act of myth-making, sustained for an historical period by intentions to continue the relevant mythical practice, and sustained to this day by intentions to co-refer that are no longer moored to ancient mythical practice. That mechanism of co-reference links tokenings of 'Pegasus' together in a chain of empty explicit co-reference such that the tokenings stand or fall together with respect to referential success and failure. But the 'Pegasus' chain of empty explicit co-reference is sustained by a mechanism of co-reference entirely independent of the mechanism of co-reference that sustains the 'Santa' chain of empty explicit co-reference. Hence the failure of 'Pegasus' to refer is a fact entirely independent of the failure of 'Santa Claus' to refer. So although 'Pegasus' and 'Santa' are in a trivial sense coincidentally co-referential, they are not explicitly co-referential.

I said above that the fact the tokens of 'Holmes' are explicitly co-referential one with another helps to explain how it is possible for cognizers to engage in certain shared imaginings without there having to be a fictional

---

[7]For further discussion of the distinction between veridical and non-veridical language games see Taylor (2003), especially Essay VI.

object Holmes to be the shared object of those shared imaginings. In a similar vein, I claim that the referential independence of 'Santa' and 'Pegasus' explains all there is to the feeling that the Santa Claus myth and the Pegasus myth have different subject matters. Just as we need not posit a fictional Holmes to be the common subject of all Holmes-imaginings, so we need not posit a mythical Santa and a mythical Pegasus to be the distinguishable subjects of Santa and Pegasus imaginings. The making of myth and fiction may indeed play a role in founding and sustaining chains of empty explicit co-reference, but they do not make mythical or fictional objects to exist.[8]

Sometimes, of course, empty names are tokened not in the making of fiction or myth, but in failed attempts at genuine reference. Here too the relevant name is constituted as the very name that it is by the existence of a chain of explicit co-reference that endows the tokenings of that name with a shared referential aim and fate. Even if there had been no planet causing perturbations in the orbit of Uranus, 'Neptune' would still have counted as a name. Contrary to Russell, we should not and would not feel any temptation to conclude on the basis of mere referential failure that 'Neptune' was not a name at all, but merely a definite description in disguise. Even referentially failed names have the property of aiming to name. Even tokens of such a name aim to name together. When a name (type) fails to refer, the name defining property of explicit co-referentiality guarantees that that failure will be a failure shared by all tokens of the name. So even empty names form chains of explicit co-reference. It is just that the links in chains of co-reference formed from the tokens of an empty name share referential failure rather than referential success. Thus in the case imagined, the existence of a mechanism of co-reference, rooted in a failed attempt to fix a reference for 'Neptune', would have endowed tokenings of 'Neptune' with a shared referential aim and fate.

There is much more to say about empty names and their linguistic behavior. For example, I have argued at length elsewhere that linguistic moves made with empty names are typically not fully propositional. Hence, there is nothing strictly literally said by a sentence containing an empty name. Nonetheless, I have argued, sentences containing empty names may pragmatically convey more or less determinate propositional contents. The pragmatic conveyances of the utterance of a sentence containing an empty name are species of what I call 'prepropositional' pragmatic externalities (Taylor, 2003). Such pragmatic externalities are generated via what I call one and a half stage pragmatics. Paradigmatically, one and half stage pragmatics happens where primary pragmatic processes 'misfire' or fail to come

---

[8]I argue for this claim further in Taylor (2003).

off. One and a half stage pragmatics presuppose a failed or 'misfired' attempt at constituting a strict, literal propositional content. Where primary processes fail, one and half stage processes may step in to fill the breach, by associating a non-literal content with the relevant utterance. Though such contents are not strict, literal contents, neither are they merely conversationally implicated by the relevant utterance – at least not if we suppose, as many do, that it takes the application of a secondary pragmatic processes to the propositional outputs of primary pragmatic processes to generate conversational implicatures. The proposition associated with an utterance by a one and half stage process is less tightly connected to the utterance than a strict literal content, but more tightly connected to it than a mere conversational implicature.

3.2 Acceptance and Substitution

Earlier in this essay, we examined some evidence that substitution of coincidentally co-referring names is insufficient, on its own, to make the preservation of subject matter manifest. Typically, whenever subject matter is preserved, but not manifestly so, an imputation of distinctness of subject matter is typically generated. This fact suggest that cooperative conversation is governed by a (defeasible) directive constraining discourse participants to make the preservation of subject matter manifest. Such a constraint predicts that despite the coincidental co-reference of 'Hesperus' and 'Phosphorous', they cannot, in general, be substituted one for the other in what we might call a dialectical significance preserving manner, where dialectical significance has to do with significance for the stage-wise evolution of a discourse, argument or conversation. To say that substitution of coincidental co-referents fails to preserve dialectical significance is not to say that such substitution fails to preserve truth value. Preservation of truth value is one thing, manifest preservation of subject matter is something entirely different.

Now in many contexts, substitution of coincidental co-referents can be directly licensed when an identity sign is used to make manifest the co-reference of two referentially independent designators. Propositional attitude contexts constitute, however an apparent exception to this generalization. In such contexts, even when referentially independent and coincidentally co-referential designators are linked via an explicit identity sign, substitution still may fail to preserve dialectical significance. For example, the inference from (30) and (31) to (32) below is not intuitively compelling, despite the fact that 'Hesperus' and 'Phosphorus' are linked via an explicit identity sign in (30):

(30) Smith believes that Hesperus is rising

(31) Hesperus is Phosphorus

(32) Smith believes that Phosphorus is rising.

Now philosophers of language have been widely convinced, partly on the basis of the felt invalidity of such inferences, that the semantic contribution of an embedded name to the truth conditions of the containing belief ascription cannot be *just* its referent. Embedding is widely supposed somehow to endow a name with a degree of what I call notional semantic significance in virtue of which an embedded name serves, by some means or other, to either directly or indirectly semantically specify, intimate, or designate the ascribee's notions, conceptions or modes of presentation of doxastically implicated objects.[9] But on my view the widely shared intuition that – to put it

---

[9]An exception is Bach (1997a, 1997b.) Bach and I agree in rejecting what he calls the 'specification assumption' – the assumption, roughly, that that clauses specify what I call notional contents. Bach's specification assumption is broader than my current target. Anyone who accepts that that clauses either semantically specify or pragmatically implicate notional contents accepts Bach's specification assumption. Hence, Salmon (1986) too counts as endorsing the specification assumption, since he holds that notional contents are pragmatically implicated rather than semantically specified. Despite rejecting the specification assumption, Bach maintains that ascriptions which differ only by the presence of co-referring names can differ in truth value. This is possible, he claims, because belief sentences are 'semantically incomplete'. As he puts it:

If substitution (of co-referring terms) makes no semantic difference, how can it affect the content of a belief report? How can substitution turn a true belief report into a false one? Part of the answer is that the sentences used to make the belief reports, though semantically equivalent, are also *semantically incomplete* (emphasis his). That is, they do not express complete propositions, and to that extent they are like such sentences as:

(a) Fred is ready

(b) Jerry has finished.

Though syntactically well-formed ... these sentences are semantically incomplete because of a missing argument .... However, lacking an argument is not the only way for a sentences to be semantically incomplete.... On the description view, belief sentences are semantically incomplete for different reasons. Like words, such as 'big' and 'short', a belief-predicate does not have a context-independent condition of satisfaction, so that a sentence containing it does not have a context-independent truth condition. A belief-predicate does not express, independently of context, a unique belief-property (Bach 1997a. 228).

I reject this last claim. In Taylor (2003), especially Essay XI, I argue that so-called semantic incompleteness is possible only where there are either suppressed or explicit parameters which demand, by their very nature, the contextual assignment of a value. I call the view there defended parametric minimalism. Bach and I agree, I think, that simple, unmodified belief sentences have no hidden or explicit argument place waiting to be filled by a contextually provided value. Here the two of us part company, I take it, with those who endorse the hidden indexical approach to belief sentences. Unlike Bach, however, I think it follows that therefore no pragmatic mechanism can make a belief sentence strictly literally say now one thing, now another, as a function of context. To reject this last inference is to reject the parametric minimalism defended in Taylor (2003) and Taylor (forthcoming-a). To accept this last inference is

neutrally – the acceptability of statements like (30) and (31) need not guarantee the acceptability of a statement like (32) has been widely misdiagnosed. Our intuitions of the badness of such inferences are standardly taken to be intuitions about truth-value dependence and independence.[10] I shall argue that such inferences really involve a kind of pragmatic infelicity, ultimately traceable to the influence of what below I call the default co-reference constraint on propositional attitude ascriptions.

I begin by introducing the notion of *the co-reference set* of a given term for a given agent at a given time. If a is an agent, and n is a name in a's lexicon at t, the co-reference set of n for a at t is the set of expressions in a's lexicon such that either: (a) t is explicitly co-referential with n or (b) if t is referentially independent of n, then t is in the co-reference set of n for a just in case a accepts the sentence $t = n$. When two referentially independent expressions m and n are such that a accepts $m = n$ at t, I will say that m and n are in-the-head-co-referential for a at t. In the head co-reference is distinct from real world co-reference. Expressions may be real world co-referential, without being in the head co-referential. Moreover, expressions may be in-the-head-co-referential, without being real world co-referential. Finally, it is important to stress that co-reference sets are defined agent by agent and moment by moment. In particular, two referring expressions may be in the head co-referential for a given agent at a given time, but not in the head co-referential for either the same agent or some distinct agent at a distinct time.

In the head co-reference is defined in terms of *acceptance of identity sentences*. Despite the intimate connection between acceptance and belief,

---

to accept parametric minimalism. This is not the place to settle the dispute between friend and foe of parametric minimalism. See Bach (1984) and Recanati (1993, 2001) for arguments against parametric minimalism. Recanati rejects minimalism altogether. Bach is a minimalist, but not a parametric minimalist.

[10]Soames (1985, 1987a, 1987b, 2001), Salmon (1986, 1989a, 1989b, 1995) and Braun (1998) are the most dogged exceptions. Soames and Salmon apparently believe that ordinary speakers themselves mistake what are really intuitions about pragmatic infelicity for intuitions about truth and falsity. Braun apparently holds that although speakers do have truth value intuitions those intuitions are mistaken. My aim here is to offer a re-diagnosis of our intuitions as intuitions about dialectical dependence/independence. To that extent, I agree with Soames and Salmon and disagree with Braun. On the other hand, although I do think that philosophers of language have by and large misdiagnosed our intuitions, I do not claim to know how 'the folk' understand those intuitions. Nor do I think it matters. I am trying to understand the intuitions themselves, and what drives them. I am not trying to explain the folk theory of those intuitions and feel no compulsion to respect that folk theory, whatever it is. The bedrock data before us is that the folk find some ascriptions acceptable in certain contexts, while finding others unacceptable. I am after a theory that explains such patterns of acceptance, not a theory which explains the folk explanation of those patterns of acceptance. Explaining the folk explanations might indeed be a very good thing to do. But it's not the same thing as explaining the bedrock data themselves.

acceptance, qua attitude toward a *sentence*, must be sharply distinguished from belief, qua toward the *proposition expressed by that very sentence*. To believe the proposition expressed by a sentence is not *ipso facto* to accept that sentence. One who has no knowledge of English and its sentences can believe the proposition expressed by the English sentence 'The cat is on the mat' even though she fails to accept that very sentence. Conversely, to accept a sentence is not *ipso facto* to believe the proposition expressed by that sentence. One can accept a sentence even if one does not know which proposition the sentence expresses. Now acceptance is itself a kind of belief. To accept a sentence S is to believe of S that it expresses some true proposition or other. But one can believe of a sentence that it expresses some true proposition or other, and thereby accept it, without *knowing which* proposition that sentence expresses. Suppose, for example, that Brown does not *know who* Smith and Jones are. Suppose further that Black utters the sentence 'Smith loves Jones'. Assume that Brown takes Black at her word. She thereby comes to believe of the sentence 'Smith loves Jones' that it expresses a truth, but she does not thereby come to believe that Smith loves Jones.

To be sure, if Brown merely recognizes some further grammatical and lexical facts about the sentence 'Smith loves Jones' and its constituents, then even if she does not know who Smith and Jones are, there may be further propositions, closely connected to the accepted sentence, that Brown does comes to believe in coming to accept the sentence 'Smith loves Jones'. For example, if she recognizes that 'Smith' and 'Jones' are names and knows the meaning of 'loves' then in coming to accept the sentence she thereby comes to believe the further and more articulated proposition that the referent of 'Smith' loves the referent of 'Jones'. But that, again, is still not the proposition expressed by 'Smith loves Jones'.[11] We might say that Black believes that Smith loves Jones *via* acceptance of the sentence 'Smith loves Jones' if she accepts 'Smith loves Jones' and knows which proposition it expresses. But we will not attempt to spell out at present just what it takes to know what proposition a sentence expresses. I take it to be a plausible (initial) hypothesis about the connection between belief and acceptance for creatures like us that if P is a proposition such that A (explicitly) believes that P, there is some sentence S such that A believes P via acceptance of S.[12]

Armed with the notion of a co-reference set, we can give an initial statement of the default co-reference constraint on (one-layer) belief ascriptions:

---

[11] It is rather, one form of what Perry (2001) calls reflexive content.

[12] Perry (1980) offers an account of the relationship between belief and acceptance very much in the spirit of the account offered here.

Default Co-Reference Constraint: If a sentence of the form

A believes that ....*n* ...

is dialectically permissible for a player *p* in a dialectical setting *D* at *t* and *m* is in the co-reference set of *n* for *A* at *t*, then a sentence of the form:

A believes that ...*m*...

is dialectically permissible for *p* in *D* at *t*.

S is dialectically permissible for a player in the dialectical setting *D* at *t*, roughly, if given the "common ground" of *D* at *t*, the production of *S* by *p* in *D* at *t* would violate no norms of cooperativeness, perspicuousness, coherence, relevance, or the like which jointly govern the players in *D* at *t*.[13] The co-reference constraint says, in effect, that (one-layer) belief ascriptions are defeasibly dialectically sensitive to facts about *ascribee* co-reference sets, rather than to facts about either *ascriber* co-reference sets or to facts about *real world* co-reference. The fact that belief ascriptions are defeasibly sensitive to *ascribee* co-reference sets explains why it is not in general dialectically permissible to move from (30) and (31) above to (32) above. When attitude ascriptions are sensitive to facts about ascribee co-reference sets, such ascriptions exhibit many of the hallmarks commonly associated with so-called *de dicto* ascriptions.

There are, however, dialectical settings in which the default sensitivity of (one layer) ascriptions to facts about ascribee co-reference sets is overridden in favor of sensitivity to facts about the co-reference sets which are elements of the common ground between speaker and hearer. In such dialectical settings, attitude ascriptions will exhibit many of the hallmarks of

---

[13]Following Grice, I distinguish *violating* norms of cooperativeness, perspicuousness, coherence, relevance from the *flouting* of such norms. Though one who flouts a norm may give the appearance of violating that norm, flouting a norm is not the same as either surreptitiously violating it or openly opting out of it. Flouting is also different from situations in which one must violate one or the other of two conflicting norms. Flouting a norm, according to Grice, is something that one does blatantly, with no intent to mislead, and where there is no apparent clash of conflicting norms. In so doing, one puts one's audience in the position of having to reconcile the open appearance of a violation with the assumption that one is, in fact, respecting the relevant norm. Conversational implicatures are generated, according to Grice, by the attempted reconciliation of what is explicitly said, in apparent violation of the norms of cooperativeness, with the assumption that the cooperative principle is in fact being observed. I am not offering an alternative analysis of how conversational implicatures are generated here. My point is merely to stress that semantically equivalent expressions need not be dialectically equivalent – perhaps because the utterance of one may, in a given context, generate a conversational implicature that an utterance of the other would not generate.

what are commonly called *de re* ascriptions. In such dialectical settings, whenever:

$$m = n$$

is part of the common ground of D at t and

A believes that ...m ....

is dialectically permissible in D at t, then:

A believes that ... n ...

is dialectically permissible in D at t.

For illustrative purposes, consider the following scenario. Daniel Taylor, formerly a practicing Christian, decides to convert to Islam. In the course of his conversion, he adopts 'Haazim Abdullah' as his legal name. Because he suspects that his devoutly Christian parents, Sam and Seretha, would be distressed by this turn of events, he informs them of neither his change of faith nor his change of name. He does, however, confide in his siblings, Robert and Diane, that he has changed his name, that he has converted to Islam and that Sam and Seretha are unaware of his conversion. It is mutually manifest to Robert and Diane that they, but not Sam and Seretha, accept the following identity:

(33) Haazim Abdullah = Daniel Taylor.

Some time goes by. Diane wishes to inform Robert that Seretha has still not figured out that Daniel, that is, Haazim, is no longer a practicing Christian. It is common ground between Diane and Robert that (a) (33) holds; (b) that Seretha does not accept (33); and (c) that she does not accept (33) because there is no name N in Seretha's lexicon such that 'Haazim Abdullah' belongs to the co-reference set of N for Seretha. In the imagined dialectical setting, the inference from (34) below to (35) seems perfectly acceptable:

(34) Seretha believes that Daniel is still a Christian
(35) Seretha believes that Haazim is still a Christian.

Because it is part of the common ground that 'Haazim Abdullah' belongs to the co-reference set of no name with which Seretha is competent, in the relevant dialectical setting, the inference from (34) to (35) generates no imputation that Seretha accepts (33). Because of what is common ground between Robert and Diane an imputation that might *otherwise* be generated is simply forestalled. Similarly, because of the common ground of the relevant dialectical setting, the inference from (34) to (35) generates no imputation to the effect that (36) below is true:

(36) Seretha accepts 'Haazim is still a Christian'.

If I am right about the potential of facts about common ground co-reference relations to forestall imputations of acceptance that might otherwise be generated, then there is a quite natural sense in which an occurrence of (35) in the sort of dialectical setting we have been imagining can be said to be dialectically governed by facts about common ground co-reference sets rather than by facts about ascribee co-reference sets.

Consider a dialectical setting in which the default sensitivity to ascribee co-reference sets is not overridden by any elements of the relevant common ground. Suppose that Seretha learns, by listening to the news on the radio, of the artistic achievements of one Haazim Abdullah, an Islamic poet of some renown. Suppose that she does so without also coming to accept (33). Indeed, suppose that Seretha would explicitly reject (33). And suppose that Robert and Diane mutually known that Seretha has learned of Haazim Abdullah's poetic achievements and that she has done so in a way that does not lead her to accept (33). Now consider the following ascriptions as they occur in a dialectical setting with a common ground of the sort just described:

(37) Seretha believes that Haazim is a very fine poet
(37') Seretha believes that Haazim is not a very fine poet
(38) Seretha believes that Daniel is not a very fine poet
(38') Seretha believes that Daniel is a very fine poet.

In such a dialectical setting, (37) and (38) can be simultaneously dialectically permissible, while both (37') and (38') are dialectically impermissible, despite the fact that it is common ground between Robert and Diane that Daniel Taylor is Haazim Abdullah. In such a dialectical setting, I claim, an occurrence of (37) would generate an imputation to the effect that Seretha accepts 'Haazim is a very fine poet' and an occurrence of (38) would generate an imputation that Seretha would accept 'Daniel is not a very fine poet'. Since Seretha does accept the relevant sentences, (37) and (38) are unproblematic. On the other hand, an occurrence of (37') would generate the unacceptable imputation that Seretha would accept 'Haazim is not a very fine poet'. And similarly for (38'). Hence neither (37') nor (38') is dialectically permissible. This is so because the relevant ascriptions are naturally interpreted as being dialectically governed by facts about ascribee co-reference sets rather than by facts about common ground co-reference sets.

The illustrative dialectical scenarios just considered do not tell the entire story about the pragmatics of attitude ascriptions. I have offered neither a deep explanation of just why the constraint holds nor a systematic account of which factors may serve, in a discourse context, to override the constraint. Nor will I attempt to do so here.[14] It is, however, worth noting that the defeasible co-reference constraint seems prima facie limited to singly-embedded belief ascriptions and not to ascriptions involving multiple embeddings. For example, the inference from (39) and (40) to (41) is not intuitively pragmatically compelling:

(39) John believes that Mary believes that Superman can fly
(40) John accepts 'Superman = Clark Kent'.

---

(41) John believes that Mary believes that Clark Kent can fly.

It is worth considering just why this is so.

We begin by considering some further data. Imagine a dialectical setting in which Smith intends by an utterance of (39) to inform Jones of John's beliefs about Mary's beliefs about the abilities of Superman. Suppose that Smith and Jones mutually accept the sentence 'Clark Kent = Superman' and that, moreover, it is common ground between them that John accepts it as well. Even Smith and Jones's mutual acceptance of 'Clark Kent = Superman' together with their mutual knowledge of John's acceptance of (40) seems intuitively insufficient to render (41) an acceptable way for Smith to report to Jones John's belief about Mary's belief about Superman. But notice that (41) feels more acceptable when (42) below is common ground between Smith and Jones:

(42) John believes that Mary accepts 'Clark Kent = Superman'.

This data suggests that the dialectical permissibility of the inner most clause of a doubly embedded ascription is (defeasibly) sensitive neither to facts about common ground co-reference sets nor to facts about the ascribee's co-reference sets, but to facts about the ascribee's *beliefs* about co-reference sets for what we might call the embedded ascribee.

Consider a scenario in which facts about co-reference sets for the embedded ascribee are common ground between the ascriber and the ad-

---

[14]See Taylor (2002), (2003) and Taylor (forthcoming a) for further discussion of attitude reports.

dressee. Suppose, for example, (43) below is, but (42) above is not part of the common ground between Smith and Jones:

(43) Mary accepts 'Clark Kent = Superman'.

Where (43) is common ground between Smith and Jones, the default co-reference constraint does seem to license a move from (44) as uttered by Smith to (45) as uttered by either Smith or Jones below:

(44) Mary believes that Superman can fly.
(45) Mary believes that Clark Kent can fly.

However, the standing of (43) as common ground between Smith and Jones still does not, it seems, render (41) permissible in light of (39) (and (40)). This fact lends additional weight to the hypothesis that it is facts about the ascribee's *beliefs* about the co-reference sets of the embedded ascriber that govern, perhaps defeasibly, the dialectical permissibility of the innermost clauses of an ascription containing a double embedding.

Our hypothetical nested co-reference constraint, as we might call it, entails that where $n = m$, discourse participants defeasibly lack entitlement to move from the utterance of an instance of the scheme (46) below to the utterance of an instance of the scheme (47) below merely on the basis of facts about co-reference sets for the embedded ascribee:

(46) A believes that S believes that $F(n)$
(47) A believes that S believes that $F(m)$.

Because the ascriber need have no direct access to whatever governing constraints were operative in the "original" discourse situation, if there was one or in a counterfactual discourse situation if no actual ascription has occurred, it is not at all surprising that something like the embedded co-reference constraint should hold. In ascribing to another a belief about another's beliefs, it is surely intuitively plausible that we should aim to be responsive, as it were, the words our ascribee would or did use to make her ascription to the embedded ascribee. If the ascribee is ignorant of facts about co-reference sets for the embedded ascribee, there will be many discourse situations in which the ascriber's ascriptions will be constrained to reflect the state of the ascribee's ignorance. There may also be discourse situations in which a certain indifference to the constraints to which the ascribe was or would have been subject is called for.

Notice that the dialectical permissibility of the outermost that clause of an ascription containing a double embedding is itself (defeasibly) governed by facts about ascribee co-reference sets. Suppose, for example, that Mary is sometimes called by the nickname 'Cookie' and that it is common ground between Smith and Jones that John accepts the sentence 'Mary is Cookie.' Imagine that Smith reports John's beliefs about Mary's beliefs to Jones via (39). In that case, (39) together with the relevant common ground seems sufficient to license:

(46) John believes that Cookie believes that Superman can fly.

If, in addition, (42) is part of the common ground between Jones and Smith, then (47) below will be acceptable as well:

(47) John believes that Cookie believes that Clark Kent can fly.

The provisional take-home lesson is that co-reference constraints, of one sort or another, govern even ascriptions containing multiple embeddings. The evidence we have so far considered suggest the hypothesis that for each level of embedding a new, but entirely predictable co-reference constraint is defeasibly operative. For a singly embedded ascription, the default co-reference constraint holds. For a doubly embedded ascription, the default co-reference constraint applies to the outermost that clause, while the embedded co-reference constraint applies to the innermost one. Though we lack the space to explore this hypothesis in greater detail at present, it seems evident that far from disconfirming the defeasible co-reference constraint for ascriptions involving a single level of embedding, evidence from cases involving double embeddings lend additional credence to that hypothesis. Indeed, the default co-reference constraint would seem to be the limiting case of an initially plausible, though perhaps unexpected general hypothesis for ascriptions containing n embeddings, for arbitrary n.

4   Conclusion

In this essay, I have addressed many phenomena that have long been hotly disputed among semanticists and philosophers of language. This phenomena include Frege's puzzle about the possibility of informative statements of identity, the behavior of empty names, and the failure of co-referring names to be substitutable within propositional attitude contexts. Though entire semantic programs have risen or fallen or their ability or lack thereof to such phenomena, one take home lesson of this essay is that many of the labors of generations of semanticists may well have been wasted. Semantics simply has fewer explanatory burdens to discharge than we have traditionally imagined. But to say that less of the work of explaining the mysteries and complexities of language in action falls to semantics and more to syntax and pragmatics is not a testament to the weakness of semantics, but of the richness of the resources that we have at our disposal. It is, I think, high time that philosophers of language exploit those resources to their fullest.

References

Bach, K. 1994. *Thought and Reference.* New York: Oxford University Press.

Bach, K. 1997a. What Belief Reports Don't Do. *The Maribor Papers in Naturalized Semantics*, ed. D. Jutronic. Maribor: Maribor University Press.

Bach, K. 1997b. Do Belief Reports Report Beliefs? *Pacific-Philosophical-Quarterly* 78 (3): 215-41.

Brandom, R. 1994. *Making It Explicit: Reasoning, Representing, and Discursive Commitment.* Cambridge, MA: Harvard University Press.

Braun, D. 1993. Empty Names. *Nous* 27 (4): 449-69.

Braun, D. 1998. Understanding Belief Reports. *Philosophical Review* 107 (4): 555-95.

Chomsky, N. 1981. *Lectures on Government and Binding.* Dordrecht: Foris Publications.

Chomsky, N. 1995. *Minimalism.* Cambridge, MA: MIT Press.

Fiengo R. and R. May 1998. Names and Expressions. *Journal of Philosophy* 95: 377-409.

Kripke, S. 1979. A Puzzle About Belief. *Meaning and Use*, ed. A. Margalit, 239-83. Dordrecht: Reidel.

Perry, J. 1980. Belief and Acceptance. *Midwest Studies in Philosophy* 5: 533-42.

Perry, J. 2001. *Reference and Reflexivity.* Stanford: CSLI Publications.

Recanati, F. 1993. *Direct Reference: From Language to Thought.* Oxford: Blackwell.

Recanati, F. 2001. What is Said. *Synthèse* 128: 75-91.

Reimer, M. 1995. A Defense of De Re Belief Reports. *Mind and Language* 10 (4): 446-63.

Richard, M. 1983. Direct Reference and Ascriptions of Belief. *Journal of Philosophical Logic* 12: 425-52.

Richard, M. 1990. *Propositional Attitudes: An Essay on Thoughts and how we Ascribe them.* Cambridge: Cambridge University Press.

Salmon, N. 1979. *Reference and Essence.* Princeton: Princeton University Press.

Salmon, N. 1986. *Frege's Puzzle.* Cambridge, MA: MIT Press.

Salmon, N. 1989a. Illogical Belief. *Philosophical Perspectives*: *Philosophy of Mind and Action Theory* 3: 243-85.

Salmon, N. 1989b. How to Become a Millian Heir. *Nous* 23: 211-20.

Salmon, N. 1995. Being of Two Minds: Belief with Doubt. *Nous* 29: 1-20.

Salmon, N. 1998. Nonexistence. *Nous* 32 (3): 277-319.

Salmon, N. and S. Soames 1988. *Propositions and Attitudes*. New York: Oxford University Press.

Soames, S. 1985. Lost Innocence. *Linguistics and Philosophy* 8: 59-71.

Soames, S. 1987a. Direct Reference, Propositional Attitudes, and Semantic Content. *Philosophical Topics* 15: 44-87.

Soames, S. 1987b. Substitutivity. *Essays in Honor of Richard Cartwright*, ed. J. Thompson, 99-132. Cambridge, MA: MIT Press.

Soames, S. 1989. Direct Reference and Propositional Attitudes. *Themes from Kaplan*, eds. J. Almog et al., 393-419. New York: Oxford University Press.

Soames, S. 2001. *Beyond Rigidity: The Unfinished Semantic Agenda of Naming and Necessity*. Oxford: Oxford University Press.

Taylor, K. 2002. De Re and De Dicto: Against the Conventional Wisdom. *Philosophical Perspectives: Language and Mind* 16: 225-65.

Taylor, K. 2003. *Reference and the Rational Mind*. Stanford: CSLI Publications.

Taylor, K. forthcoming a. *Referring to the World*. Oxford: Oxford University Press.

Taylor, K. forthcoming b. Misplaced Modification and the Illusion of Opacity. *Situating Semantics: Essays on the Philosophy of John Perry*, eds. M. O'Rourke and C. Washington. Cambridge, MA: MIT Press.

Name Index